بسم الله الرحمن الرحيم

Gibril Fouad Haddad

SUNNA NOTES

Studies in Ḥadīth and Doctrine

Volume II: The Excellent Innovation in the Qur'ān & Ḥadīth

with Ibn Rajab's

THE SUNNA OF THE CALIPHS

SUNNA NOTES
Studies in Hadith and Doctrine
Vol. 2: The Excellent Innovation in the Qur'ān & Ḥadīth
with Ibn Rajab's THE SUNNA OF THE CALIPHS

Reprint: Institute for Spiritual & Cultural Understanding, Fenton, M
USA
First edition: AQSA Publications, UK & WARDA Publications, Germar

Published in the US by Institute for Spiritual & Cultural Understanding 17195 Silver Parkway #401, Fenton, MI 48430 USA
Tel: (810) 593-1222
Email: info@sufilive.com
Web:
http://www.sufilive.com
Purchase online at: http://www.isn1.net

ISBN: 978-1-938058-79-0

Typesetting by Abd al-Hafidh Wentzel
Cover Calligraphy by Moncef Elh

Cataloging-in-Publication Data
A CIP catalogue record for this book is available from the British Library

بسم الله الرحمن الرحيم

قَالَ الإِمَامُ يَحْيَىٰ بْنُ يَحْيَىٰ اللَّيْثِيُّ الأَنْدَلُسِيُّ قَرَأْتُ عَلَىٰ مَالِكٍ عَنْ ابْنِ شِهَابٍ عَنْ عُرْوَةَ بْنِ الزُّبَيْرِ عَنْ عَبْدِ الرَّحْمَنِ بْنِ عَبْدٍ الْقَارِيِّ أَنَّهُ قَالَ:

خَرَجْتُ مَعَ عُمَرَ بْنِ الْخَطَّابِ فِي رَمَضَانَ إِلَى الْمَسْجِدِ فَإِذَا النَّاسُ أَوْزَاعٌ مُتَفَرِّقُونَ يُصَلِّي الرَّجُلُ لِنَفْسِهِ وَيُصَلِّي الرَّجُلُ فَيُصَلِّي بِصَلَاتِهِ الرَّهْطُ فَقَالَ عُمَرُ :« وَاللَّهِ إِنِّي لَأُرَانِي لَوْ جَمَعْتُ هَؤُلَاءِ عَلَى قَارِئٍ وَاحِدٍ لَكَانَ أَمْثَلَ» فَجَمَعَهُمْ عَلَى أُبَيِّ بْنِ كَعْبٍ قَالَ ثُمَّ خَرَجْتُ مَعَهُ لَيْلَةً أُخْرَى وَالنَّاسُ يُصَلُّونَ بِصَلَاةِ قَارِئِهِمْ فَقَالَ عُمَرُ :

« نِعْمَتِ الْبِدْعَةُ هَذِهِ »

قَوْلُهُ: قَالَ عُمَرُ: «نِعْمَ الْبِدْعَةُ» وَفِي بَعْضِ الرِّوَايَاتِ: «نِعْمَتِ الْبِدْعَةُ» بِزِيَادَةِ تَاءٍ: وَالْبِدْعَةُ أَصْلُهَا مَا أُحدِثَ عَلَى غَيْرِ مِثَالٍ سَابِقٍ؛ وَتُطْلَقُ فِي الشَّرْعِ فِي مُقَابِلِ السُّنَّةِ، فَتَكُونُ مَذْمُومَةً. وَالتَّحْقِيقُ أَنَّهَا إِنْ كَانَتْ مِمَّا يَنْدَرِجُ تَحْتَ مُسْتَحْسَنٍ فِي الشَّرْعِ، فَهِيَ حَسَنَةٌ. وَإِنْ كَانَتْ مِمَّا يَنْدَرِجُ تَحْتَ مُسْتَقْبَحٍ فِي الشَّرْعِ، فَهِيَ مُسْتَقْبَحَةٌ. وَإِلَّا، فَهِيَ مِنْ قِسْمِ الْمُبَاحِ، وَقَدْ تَنْقَسِمُ إِلَى الأَحْكَامِ الْخَمْسَةِ. **فتح الباري للحافظ ابن حجر**

CONTENTS

THE EXCELLENT INNOVATION IN THE QUR'ĀN & HADĪTH

Abbreviations 9

Introduction 11

Part One: The Meaning of Sunna and *Bid'a* & the New Sunnas of the *Salaf* in the Religion 17

The meaning of Sunna and *Ahl al-Sunna wal-Jamā'a* 19

"The Common Person's Imitation of the Learned One" from al-Bayhaqī's *al-Madkhal ilā al-Sunan al-Kubrā* 27

The Prophetic Recommendation of the Companions' Excellent New Sunnas 30

Companion-Reports on the Exemplariness of the Companions in the Religion 47

Successor-Reports on the Exemplariness of the Companions and Successors in the Religion 57

Ibn Rajab's Commentary on the Ḥadīth: "You Must Follow My Sunna and the Sunna of the Well-Guided Successors" 60

The Meaning of *Bid'a* 71

The Sunna Character of the Companions' Innovations 80

Companions' Innovations after the Time of the Prophet ﷺ or in His Absence 91

Sunna Innovations of the *Ṣaḥāba* in Worship 94

Sunna Innovations of the *Tabi'īn* in Worship 103

Sunna Innovations of the Later *Salaf* in Worship 109

The Misconstrued Ḥadīth "Every Innovation is Misguidance" 114

All-Inclusive Expressions Implying Exceptions 116
The Universal Understood in Terms of the Specific 118
The "Good New Sunna" and the "Innovation of Misguidance" 121
Al-Shāfi'ī's Definition of Innovation as Either "Good" or "Bad" 129
Division of *Bid'a* into Good and Bad among *Ahl al-Sunna* and Ẓāhirīs 132
Conclusion: The Prophet ﷺ Distinguished between Good *Bid'a* and Bad *Bid'a* 139
Part Two: Case Studies 141
Collective Supplication (*al-Du'ā'u Jamā'atan*) 143
Collective Loud Recitation of the Qur'ān 157
Partitions for Women in Mosques 160
The *Ḍuḥā* Prayer 166
Saying "*Sayyidinā* Muḥammad" in *Tashahhud* 180
Proofs for Visitation of the Graves by Women 184
The Ḥadīth: "Do not make my Grave an '*Īd*" 200
Rajab and Mid-Sha'bān Supererogatory Prayers 206
Epilogue – An Innovation of Misguidance: Unenlightened Feminism 214
Indexes 231
Index of Qur'ānic Verses 233
Index of Narrations 235
Bibliography 251

ABBREVIATIONS

ʿAbd al-Razzāq = his *Muṣannaf*

Abū Dāwūd = his *Sunan*

Abū Yaʿlā = his *Musnad*

Aḥmad = his *Musnad*

Al-Bazzār = his *Musnad*

Al-Bukhārī = his *Ṣaḥīḥ*

al-Dārimī = his *Musnad*, also known as the *Sunan*

Al-Ḥākim = his *Mustadrak ʿalā al-Ṣaḥīḥayn*

Al-Haythamī = his *Majmaʿ al-Zawāʾid*

Ibn Abī Shayba = his *Muṣannaf*

Ibn ʿAdī = his *Kāmil*

Ibn ʿAsākir = his *Tārīkh Dimashq*

Ibn Ḥibbān = his *Ṣaḥīḥ*

Ibn Khuzayma = his *Ṣaḥīḥ*

Ibn Mājah = his *Sunan*

Ibn Saʿd = his *Ṭabaqāt al-Kubrā*

al-Munāwī = his *Fayḍ al-Qadīr*

Mālik = his *Muwaṭṭaʾ*

Muslim = his *Ṣaḥīḥ*

Al-Nasāʾī = his minor *Sunan* known as *al-Mujtabā*

Al-Ṭayālisī = his *Musnad*

Al-Tirmidhī = his *Sunan*

Introduction

In the Name of Allah All-Beneficent Most Merciful

Glory belongs to Allah with a glorification that gives His favors their full right and matches His increase. O our Lord! To You belongs praise as is just and right for the majesty of Your Face and the magnificence of Your dominion. Glory to You, O our Lord! I cannot praise You enough, You are as You have praised Yourself. I bear witness that there is no god but Allah alone, without partner, and I bear witness that our liege-lord and Prophet Muḥammad is His servant and Messenger, His elect and most intimate friend, the best Prophet He has ever sent. Allah has sent him to the entire world as a bearer of glad tidings and a warner.

The Greatest *Mujtahid* Imām and *Mujaddid* from the House of the Holy Prophet ﷺ, Muḥammad ibn Idrīs al-Shāfiʿī ؓ, said:

> May Allah bless and give peace to our Prophet whenever his name is mentioned by those who mention him and whenever his name is unheeded by those who are heedless of him! May Allah bless him among the first and the last generation, with the most favorable, most abundant and purest blessing that He has bestowed upon any of His creatures! May He purify you and us through the invocation of blessings upon him more than He granted to any of his nation through their blessings and peace. May His peace, mercy, and blessings be upon Muḥammad! May Allah reward him on our behalf with the most abundant reward ever bestowed on any messenger sent on behalf of those to whom he was sent. For Allah has delivered

> us from falsehood through him and made us members of the best community ever established for people by following his Religion with which He was well-pleased, which He chose for us, and by virtue of which [Religion] He made pure His angels and those of His creatures He favored with it. Hence, no blessing – hidden or visible – has ever descended upon us through which we obtained spiritual or temporal gain or by which spiritual or temporal hurt was dispelled, but Muḥammad, upon him blessings and peace, was the cause of its dispatch, the leader to its benefit, and the guide to its right way, keeping [us] away from destruction and the sources of evil which oppose righteousness, warning [us] against whatever causes destruction, ever ready with advice for right guidance and warning [against evil]. May the blessings of Allah be upon him and his family as His blessings were upon Ibrāhīm and his family! You [Allah] are praiseworthy and glorious![1]

The most neglected name of the Religion of Islam today is probably *al-Ḥanīfiyyat al-Samḥa* – "The Natural, Easy Religion." The Last Prophet ﷺ described this *Ḥanīfiyyat al-Samḥa* as "the most beloved Religion of all to Allah" (*aḥabbu al-dīni ilā Allah*).[2] This natural and easy Religion brings nothing new but the same goodness proclaimed by the Prophets of old. {*Say: I am no new thing (bid'an) among the messengers of Allah nor know I what will be done with me or you. I do but follow that which is inspired in me, and I am but a plain warner*} (46:9).

Thus it is nothing new that Religion is ease (*yusr*), not puritanism; that it is good news (*bushr*), not fire and brimstone; and that it invites all with glad tidings and drives none away (*bashshirū wa-lā tunaffirū*).

[1] Adapted from Majed Khadduri's translation, *Al-Shāfi'ī's Risāla*, 2nd ed. (Cambridge: Islamic Texts Society, 1987, p. 63-64).

[2] Cited by al-Bukhārī *tarjimatan* and narrated from Ibn 'Abbās by Aḥmad with a fair chain cf. *Fatḥ*.

Yet certain groups among Muslims and non-Muslims alike work hard to construct a pseudo-Islam that appears to be more rigid than a straitjacket. They promote a racist, sexist, nationalist, tribalist, sectarian, judgmental, intolerant, culturally distorted, humorless, zealous, frightening cult – "an Islamic order reduced to a penal code, stripped of its humanism, aesthetics, intellectual quests, and spiritual devotion."[3] This nightmare religion is not about God and doing good but is obsessed with power and theological justifications for the discourse of power. It promises hell to most. In short, it is an immoral and wicked anti-religion.

One of the most common means used to create this anti-Islam is *taḥrīf* or the Orwellian manipulation of language to make the Qur'ān and ḥadīth mean the opposite of their actual meanings. As predicted by the Prophet ﷺ in his famous ḥadīth, the culprits are people "of our complexion and our [Arabic] language" standing at the gates of error, inviting ordinary Muslims to perdition.[4] They do this, not with foreign words and slogans, but with the words of the Book of Guidance and the ḥadīth of the Best of creation ﷺ.

In the field of the principles of jurisprudence (*uṣūl al-fiqh*), nowhere is this tampering with the truth felt more than in the redefinition of "Sunna" and "*bid'a*" in which the understanding of the pious *Salaf* such as Imām al-Shāfi'ī for these two terms is cast aside. Al-Shafi'ī ؓ had said: "***Bid'a* is of two kinds** (*al-bid'atu bid'atān*): **praiseworthy innovation** (*bid'atun maḥmūda*) **and blameworthy innovation** (*bid'atun madhmūma*)." This crystal-clear distinction has been abandoned and, in its place, later, controversial figures are invoked as "more representative of the *Salaf*" and a great historical hoax develops and grows like a snowball.

3 Eqbal Ahmad, *Dawn* Pakistan periodical (January-March 1999).
4 Narrated from Ḥudhayfa ibn al-Yamān by al-Bukhārī and Muslim.

Newfangled theories worm their way into the discourse on right and wrong. Those new theories say that (1) "absolutely everything new is a *bid'a*," (2) "every *bid'a* is without exception misguidance (*ḍalāla*)," and – the crowning conclusion and actual purpose of this hoax – (3) "there is no such thing as a good *bid'a*." Nothing could be further from the truth.

What is worse, entire generations of Muslims have been weaned on these perversions of the truth and go into the world mechanically parroting the words "Sunna" and "*bid'a*" without ever understanding them. Following a slew of uneducated and semi-educated Muslim Arabs, Africans and Central, South and Southeast Asians indoctrinated by the modernist "Salafi" movements in Egypt, North Africa and the Gulf, the choice victims for this campaign of disinformation have been English-speaking Muslims, especially new Muslims. These victims learn a few phrases then, coiffed with their new hat of condemnatory phrases like Torquemada's sergeants-at-arms, go out and blast away at other Muslims.[5]

The purpose of the following discussion is to do away once and for all with those misconceptions for the English-speaking reader and to present over 160 proofs for the Sunni understanding of Sunna and *bid'a* as it was – and continues to be – set forth in classical, moderate, mainstream Sunni terms according to the Sunni *Salaf* and *Khalaf* including the Four Schools of *Fiqh*.

The treatise is divided into two parts. The first part lists the textual and analogical proofs for the agreed upon, paradigmatic meaning of Sunna and *bid'a* in straightforward, untechnical language.

[5] Tomás de Torquemada (1420-1498 CE) was the first Grand Inquisitor of the Spanish Inquisition.

The conclusion shows that there are three divisions to the terminology of the Prophet ﷺ in matters of innovation. Namely, the Prophet ﷺ (a) generally condemned all innovations; (b) explicitly condemned bad innovations; and (c) explicitly praised good innovations. Therefore, the famous ḥadīth of general terminology, *kullu bidʿatin ḍalāla*, must be understood in the light of the ḥadīths of specific terminology in (b) and (c) and not in any other way.

The second part of this treatise consists in case studies covering some of what qualifies as good innovations or good new Sunnas in Islam. The epilogue warns against one of the more notorious innovations of our times.

The sinful pauper in hope of the forgiveness of his Lord, the author, Gibrīl Fouād Ḥaddād, was blessed and honored with a narrative link to the Master of all creatures ﷺ and to the best of centuries after his ﷺ for the narrations contained in this book, through over forty of the inheritors of the Prophet ﷺ who are protected with the light of both communal and special Friendship as well as the nobility of narration and ḥadīth science, among them the distinguished two descendants of the Messenger of the Lord of the two Wests ﷺ, the late Shaykh al-Islām fīl-Balad al-Ḥarām Shaykh Muḥammad ibn al-Sayyid ʿAlawī al-Mālikī al-Makkī and Shaykh Abū al-Hudā Muḥammad ibn al-Sayyid Ibrāhīm al-Yaʿqūbī al-Dimashqī.

May Allah Most High forgive the author's mistakes, make this work beneficial in the way of truth, and use it to remove misrepresentation in His Religion. *Wa-ṣallā Allahu ʿalā Sayyidinā Muḥammadin wa-ʿalā Ālihi wa-Ṣaḥbihi wa-sallam.*

Mount Qāsyūn, Damascus, Syria
Original draft completed Ṣafar al-Khayr 1423/April 2002
Final version completed Jumādā al-Awwal 1426/June 2005.

Part One

The Meaning of Sunna and *Bid'a*
&
The New Sunnas of the *Salaf* in the Religion

The Meaning of *Sunna* and *Ahl al-Sunna wal-Jamāʿa*

The Sunna in Islam is more rare and precious than Islam is rare and precious among the rest of the faiths. – Abū Bakr ibn ʿAyyāsh[6]

Sunna means the path that is trodden (al-ṭarīq al-maslūk), which entails holding fast to whatever the Prophet ﷺ and his rightly-guided successors held of doctrines, deeds, and sayings. This is the perfect and complete Sunna. That is why the Salaf of old refrained from applying the name of Sunna to anything that fell short of this.
– Ibn Rajab[7]

The Sunna is wisdom and wisdom is to place each thing in its right context. – Ismāʿīl al-Anṣārī[8]

The Arabic word "sunna" lexically means "road" or "practice." In the language of the Prophet ﷺ and the Companions it denotes the whole of licit practices followed in the Religion, particularly the pristine (*ḥanīf*) path of Prophets, whether pertaining to belief, religious and social practice, or ethics generally speaking.

In its technical sense, "sunna" has several meanings. In ḥadīth terminology it denotes any saying (*qawl*), action (*fiʿl*), spoken or tacit approval (*taqrīr*), or attribute (*ṣifa*), whether physical (*khilqiyya*) or moral (*khuluqiyya*) ascribed to (*uḍīfa ilā*) the Prophet ﷺ, whether before or after the beginning of his prophethood.[9] Thus the "sciences of the Sunna" (*ʿulūm al-Sunna*) refer to the biography of the Prophet ﷺ (*al-sīra*), the chronicle of his battles (*al-maghāzī*), his everyday sayings and acts or "ways" (*sunan*), his personal and moral qualities (*al-shamāʾil*), and the host of the ancillary ḥadīth sciences such as the circumstances of occurrence

[6] Narrated by al-Khaṭīb in *al-Jāmiʿ li-Akhlāq al-Rāwī* (2:172) and al-Lālikāʾī in his *Uṣūl* (1:65-66 §54).
[7] Ibn Rajab, *al-Jāmiʿ fīl-ʿUlūm wal-Ḥikam* (2:44).
[8] As quoted in ʿAwwāma, *Athar al-Ḥadīth* (p. 77).
[9] See al-Sibāʿī, *al-Sunna wa-Makānatuhā fīl-Tashrīʿ al-Islamī* (p. 47).

(*asbāb al-wurūd*), knowledge of the abrogating and abrogated ḥadīth, difficult words (*gharīb al-ḥadīth*), narrator criticism (*al-jarḥ wal-taʿdīl*), narrator biographies (*al-rijāl*), etc., as discussed in great detail in the authoritative books of al-Khaṭīb al-Baghdādī.

This meaning is used in contradistinction to the Qur'ān in expressions such as "Qur'ān and Sunna" and applies in the usage of ḥadīth scholars. Imām Aḥmad ﵀ said: "The Sunna in our definition consists in the reports transmitted from the Messenger of Allah ﷺ, and the Sunna is the commentary (*tafsīr*) of the Qur'ān and contains its directives (*dalā'il*)."[10]

The early Sunnī Masters such as Abū Ḥanīfa, al-Ḥumaydī, Ibn Abī ʿĀṣim, Abū Dāwūd, and Abū Naṣr al-Marwazī also used the term "the Sunna" in the narrow sense to refer to Sunnī Doctrine as opposed to the creeds of non-Sunnī sects.

In the terminology of *uṣūl al-fiqh* or principles of jurisprudence, "sunna" denotes a saying (*qawl*), action (*fiʿl*) or approval (*taqrīr*) related from (*nuqila ʿan*) the Prophet ﷺ or issuing (*ṣadara*) from him other than the Qur'ān.

In the terminology of *fiqh* or jurisprudence, "sunna" denotes whatever is firmly established (*thabata*) as called for (*maṭlūb*) in the Religion on the basis of a legal proof (*dalīl sharʿī*) but without being obligatory, the continued abandonment of which constitutes disregard (*istikhfāf*) of the Religion and sin, and incurs blame (*lawm, ʿitāb, taḍlīl*) or also punishment (*ʿuqūba*)[11] according to some jurists. However, some jurists made a distinction between what they called "Emphasized Sunna" (*sunna mu'akkada*) or "Sunna of Guidance" (*sunnat al-hudā*), such as what the Prophet ﷺ ordered or emphasized in word or in deed,

[10] Narrated from ʿAbdūs ibn Mālik al-ʿAṭṭār by al-Lālikā'ī in *Sharḥ Uṣūl* (1:156).
[11] See al-Lacknawī, *Tuḥfat al-Akhyār*, chapter entitled "The Legal Status of the Emphasized Sunna and of its Abandonment" (*Ḥukm al-Sunnat al-Mu'akkada wa-Tarkihā*) (p. 87-92).

and other types of Sunna considered less binding in their legal status, such as what they called "Non-Emphasized Sunna" (*sunna ghayr mu'akkada*) or "Sunna of Habit" (*sunnat al-ʿāda*).

The above jurisprudential meanings of Sunna are used in contradistinction to the other four of the five legal categories for human actions – *farḍ* ("obligatory"), *sunna*, *mubāḥ* ("indifferent"), *makrūh* ("offensive"), *ḥarām* ("prohibited") – and applies in the usage of jurists from the second Hijri century. **However, the jurists have stressed that the basis for all acts of worship categorized as *sunna* is "obligatoriness" not mere "permissiveness"** (*al-aṣlu fīl-sunna al-wujūb lā al-ibāḥa*).[12] Sunna is thus defined as the strongest of several near-synonymous categories:

"praiseworthy" (*mandūb*);
"desirable" (*mustaḥabb*);
"voluntary" (*taṭawwuʿ*);
"refinement" (*adab*);
"obedience" (*ṭāʿa*);
"supererogatory" (*nafl*);
"drawing near" (*qurba*);
"recommended" (*rāghība, murghab fīh*);
"excellent" (*ḥasan*);
"excellence" (*iḥsān*);
"meritorious" (*faḍīla*); and
"best" (*afḍal*).

[12] This illustrates the potential danger of expressions such as "Such-and-such is merely a Sunna." Our teacher Shaykh Nūr al-Dīn ʿItr said: "Many a questioner, after hearing a *fatwā*, asks the Shaykh one more question: 'Is this Sunna or *wājib*?', then breathes a sigh of relief when he hears that it is Sunna. But – do you not love the Prophet ﷺ? Do you not want to get closer to him?"

Al-Dhahabī relates from Isḥāq ibn Rāhūyah the saying: "If al-Thawrī, al-Awzā'ī, and Mālik concur on a given matter, that matter is a Sunna." Al-Dhahabī comments:

> Rather, **the Sunna is whatever the Prophet ﷺ made Sunna and the rightly-guided Caliphs after him**. As for Consensus (*ijmā'*), it is whatever the Ulema of the Community both early and late have unanimously agreed upon, through either assumed (*ẓannī*) or tacit (*sukūtī*) agreement. Whoever deviates from such consensus among the Successors or their successors, it is tolerated for him alone. As for those who deviate from the three above-named Imāms, then such is not named a deviation from Consensus, nor from the Sunna. All that Isḥāq meant was that if they concur on a given matter then it is most probably correct, **just as we say, today, that it is nearly impossible to find the truth outside of what the Four Imāms of scholarly endeavor agreed upon**. We say this at the same time that we admit that their agreement on a given matter does not dictate the Consensus of the Community, but we refrain from asserting, in relation to a matter upon which they all agreed, that the correct position is otherwise.[13]

In the largest sense, "Sunna" does denote the true knowledge and practice of the Religion and is antonymous with "innovation" (*bid'a*), as in the expression "People of the Sunna" or Sunnīs (*Ahl al-Sunna*). Al-Junayd said: "The way to Allah is closed except to those who follow the traces of the Prophet ﷺ and adhere to his Sunna. Allah ﷻ said, {*Verily in the Messenger of Allah you have a good example for him who looks unto Allah and the last Day, and remembers Allah much*} (33:21)."[14]

[13] Al-Dhahabī, *Siyar A'lām al-Nubalā'* (1997 ed. 7:92).

[14] Narrated by Abū Nu'aym in the *Ḥilya* (10:257), al-Khaṭīb in *al-Faqīh wal-Mutafaqqih* (1:150= Dammām ed. 1:389), al-Sulamī in *Ṭabaqāt al-Ṣūfiyya* (p. 159), al-Qushayrī in *al-Risāla* (1:117), Ibn al-Jawzī in *Talbīs Iblīs* (p. 19) and *Ṣifat al-Ṣafwa* (2:418), and al-Suyūṭī in *Miftāḥ al-Janna* (p. 148 §333, p. 155 §357).

The Term *Ahl Al-Sunna wal-Jamāʿa*

The literal translation of the term *Ahl al-Sunna wal-Jamāʿa* is "the people of the Prophetic Way and the Congregation of the Muslims." The term denotes the people who follow the Prophetic Sunna and adhere to the largest mass of the Muslims beginning with the congregation of the Companions of the Prophet ﷺ. Its antonym is *Ahl al-Bidʿa wal-Ḍalāla* which means the people of innovation and misguidance, *i.e.* non-Sunni Muslims.

Muḥammad ibn Sīrīn (d. 110) said: "We used to accept as true what we heard, then lies spread and we began to say: Name your transmitters. If they belonged to *Ahl al-Sunna,* their ḥadīth would be accepted while *Ahl al-Bidaʿ* were identified and their ḥadīth was rejected."[15] Confirming this is al-Ḥasan al-Baṣrī's (d. 110) reaction to someone who requested his *isnād*: "O man! I neither lie nor was ever called a liar!"[16] Sufyān al-Thawrī (d. 161) said: "When certain narrators used lies, we used history against them,"[17] and Ibn al-Mubārak (d. 181) declared: "The *isnād* is an integral part of the Religion, otherwise anyone can say anything."[18] All this is based on the saying of the Companions and Successors: **"Truly, this knowledge is our Religion, therefore let each of you look carefully from whom he takes his Religion."**[19]

[15] Narrated by Muslim in the introduction to his *Ṣaḥīḥ* and by al-Tirmidhī in his *Sunan* and *ʿIlal.*

[16] Narrated by al-Mizzī in *Tahdhīb al-Kamāl* (1:259).

[17] Cited by al-Sakhāwī in *al-Iʿlān wal-Tawbīkh* (p. 9).

[18] Narrated by Muslim, introduction to his *Ṣaḥīḥ* and al-Khaṭīb, *Tārīkh* (6:166). Ibn al-Subkī in *Ṭabaqāt al-Shāfiʿiyya al-Kubrā* (1:314) mentions this and other similar statements of the *Salaf*: "The *isnād* is the believer's weapon" (Sufyān al-Thawrī); "Religion does not disappear except with the disappearance of the *isnād*" (al-Awzāʿī); "Every religion has its knights, and the knights of this Religion are the bearers of *isnāds*" (Yazīd ibn Zurayʿ); "Pursuing the highest *isnād* [*i.e.* the shortest chain with the least narrator-links] is part of the Religion" (Aḥmad ibn Ḥanbal).

[19] Narrated *mawqūf* from Abū Hurayra by al-Khaṭīb in *al-Jāmiʿ li-Akhlāq al-Rāwī* (1991 ed. 1:195 §137, §140) and Ibn ʿAbd al-Barr in *al-Tamhīd* (1:45); from Anas by Ibn ʿAbd al-Barr in *al-Tamhīd* (1:45-46) and al-Mizzī in his *Tahdhīb* (26:438);

The Prophet ﷺ said: "My Community shall divide into seventy-three sects, all of them in the Fire except one: [Those that follow] that which I and my Companions follow."[20] Another version states: "My Community shall divide into seventy-three sects, all of them in the Fire except one: the Congregation (*jamā'a*)."[21]

In the same sense, the Prophet ﷺ also said: "My Companions are trustees for my Community"[22] and "Mankind makes up one portion (*ḥayyiz*) and I and my Companions make up one portion [counter-balancing it]." The complete narration states:

maqṭū' from Ibn Sīrīn by Muslim in the introduction to his *Ṣaḥīḥ*, al-Tirmidhī at the very end of the *Shamā'il*, al-Dārimī in the introduction to his *Sunan*, Khaythama in his *Juz'* (p. 167), Ibn Abī Shayba (5:334 §26636), Ibn Sa'd (7:194), Ibn Shāhīn in *al-Ma'rifa wal-Tārīkh* (3:154), al-Jūzjānī in *Aḥwāl al-Rijāl* (p. 36, 211), al-Rāmahurmuzī in *al-Muḥaddith al-Fāṣil* (p. 414), Ibn 'Adī (4:174), Ibn 'Asākir (28:298), al-Mizzī in his *Tahdhīb* (25:352), al-Sim'ānī in *Adab al-Imlā' wal-Istimlā'* (p. 55), Ibn 'Abd al-Barr in *al-Tamhīd* (1:46), al-Bājī in *al-Ta'dīl wal-Tajrīḥ* (2:677), al-Khaṭīb in *al-Faqīh wal-Mutafaqqih* (2:378 §1133-1134), and al-Dhahabī in *Mu'jam al-Muḥaddithīn* (p. 228) and the *Siyar* (Risāla ed. 4:611); also from Ibn Sīrīn and al-Ḍaḥḥāk by Ibn Abī Ḥātim in *al-Jarḥ wal-Ta'dīl* (2:15) and al-Khaṭīb in the *Kifāya* (p. 121), and from Zā'ida ibn Qudāma by al-Rāmahurmuzī in *al-Muḥaddith al-Fāṣil*. Also narrated *marfū'* from Anas by Ibn 'Adī (1:155, 236), al-Khaṭīb in *al-Jāmi' li-Akhlāq al-Rāwī* (1991 ed. 1:194 §136, §139), Tammām in his *Fawā'id* (1:135 §312), and al-Jurjānī in *Tārīkh Jurjān* (p. 473), and Abū Hurayra by al-Sajzī in *al-Ibāna* and others, both with weak chains cf. Ibn al-Jawzī in *al-'Ilal al-Mutanāhiya* (1:131), al-Sakhāwī in *Fatḥ al-Mughīth* (1:327= Sunna ed. 2:59), and Ibn Rajab in *Sharḥ 'Ilal al-Tirmidhī* ('Itr ed. 1:61=1:362). The latter adds it is also narrated as a saying of Zayd ibn Aslam, al-Ḥasan al-Baṣrī, and Ibrāhīm al-Nakha'ī by Ibn Ḥibbān in *al-Majrūḥīn* (1:15-16). This great precept is also narrated as a saying of al-Awzā'ī by Ibn 'Asākir (6:361) and Mālik by al-Khaṭīb in the *Kifāya* (p. 159), Ibn 'Asākir (55:361 and 352), Ibn 'Abd al-Barr, *Tamhīd* (1:47, 1:67), and al-Nawawī, *Tibyān*, last third of the chapter on the etiquette of the teacher cf. al-Dhahabī, *Siyar* (Risāla ed. 5:342).

[20] See note 65.

[21] See § 45.

[22] See note 67.

"When the verse {*When comes the Help of Allah, and Victory*} (110:1) was revealed, the Messenger of Allah ﷺ recited it until he finished it and said: 'Mankind makes up one portion and I and my Companions make up one portion.' And he said: 'There is no longer emigration (*hijra*) after victory but there remains *jihād* and intention (*niyya*) [for emigration].'"[23]

Any doubt that the majority is meant in the word *jamāʿa* is dispelled by the narrations elucidating *jamāʿa* to mean the largest mass or *al-sawād al-aʿẓam*. The basic sense of this massive majority is that forwarded by the Ulema first and last, beginning with the *Ṣaḥāba*.

To the claim that *Ahl al-Sunna* is a contested term that no more clearly defines an actual community than does the term "Muslim", the reply is that both are clear definers but with different emphases. A Muslim should feel at home in any Muslim home on the face of the globe, perhaps more so than in that of his own non-Muslim relatives. As for the defining sense of *Ahl al-Sunna*, it depends on the doctrinal or juridical aspect being emphasized. Imām Abū Ḥanīfa said: "Sunna and *Jamāʿa* are defined by giving preference to the Two Shaykhs [Abū Bakr and ʿUmar as Caliphs], love of the Two Sons-in-Law [ʿUthmān and ʿAlī], and [the permissibility of] wiping over leather socks [in ablution]."[24] Of course, Abū Ḥanīfa considered that belief in Divine foreordained destiny (*qadar*), the vision of Allah in the hereafter, the intercession of the Prophet ﷺ, the uncreatedness of the Qur'ān, etc. were also an inseparable part of Sunni doctrine.

[23] See note 76.
[24] Narrated by Ibn ʿAbd al-Barr in *al-Intiqā'* through several chains.

Another defining aspect of the term *Ahl al-Sunna* for the near totality of Sunni Muslims is the fact of belonging to one of the Four Schools. Al-Qāḍī Yūsuf al-Nabhānī said:

> Know that to follow one of those Four Schools which the *Umma* of Muḥammad ﷺ has unanimously agreed upon accepting and following since their founders until now and for as long as Allah wishes, has exactly the same status as following the Book and the Sunna. For these Schools are explanations for the Book and the Sunna. Hence, when the expression *Ahl al-Sunna wal-Jamāʿa* is used in absolute terms – since one thousand years ago until the present day – what is understood is those Four Schools. Therefore, whoever leaves their compass (*dāʾiratihā*) is not counted among *Ahl al-Sunna wal-Jamāʿa*. Nor does anyone leave it other than the people of vain lusts and innovations in every century until now.[25]

[25] Al-Nabhānī, *Arbaʿūna Ḥadīthan fī Madḥ al-Sunna wa-Dhamm al-Bidʿa* (p. 68).

Al-Bayhaqī's Chapter Entitled "The Common Person's Imitation of the Learned One" (*Taqlīd al-ʿĀmmī lil-ʿĀlim*) in *Al-Madkhal ilā al-Sunan al-Kubrā*[26]

Allah Most Glorious said: {*Ask the people of the remembrance if you know not*} (21:7) and {*Obey Allah, obey the Prophet, and those of you who have authority...*} (4:59).

Ibn ʿAbbās said concerning this verse: "It means the people of *Fiqh* and Religion as well as those that obey Allah and teach others the meanings of their Religion, commanding good and forbidding evil. Allah has made it obligatory to obey them."[27]

Abū Hurayra explained the same verse to mean "those who are in command" (*al-umarā'*). Wakīʿ said: "It means those that were in command of the expeditionary forces (*al-sarāyā*) the Prophet ﷺ was sending."

Mujāhid and Jābir said: "[It means] those of you who possess understanding of the Law (*ulī al-fiqh*)." Ibn ʿAqīl added: "and righteousness" (*wal-khayr*). Al-Ḥasan and ʿAṭā' both said it means the people of *fiqh* and *ʿilm*.[28]

[26] Al-Bayhaqī, *al-Madkhal ilā al-Sunan al-Kubrā* (1:237-247). The chains of transmission cited by al-Bayhaqī have been abridged.

[27] Narrated by al-Ḥākim (1:123) cf. al-Suyūṭī in *al-Durr al-Manthūr* (2:176) and Ibn Kathīr in his *Tafsīr* (2:303).

[28] Narrated as a saying of Jābir by al-Ḥākim (1:122-123 *ṣaḥīḥ*) cf. Ibn Abī Shayba (6:418); ʿAṭā' by al-Dārimī, *Muqaddima* of his *Sunan*, al-Ṭabarī, *Tafsīr* (5:94), Ibn ʿAbd al-Barr, *Jāmiʿ Bayān al-ʿIlm* (2:28-29); Mujāhid by al-Ṭabarī in his *Tafsīr* (5:94) and Abū Khaytama in *al-ʿIlm* (p. 124 §62); al-Ḥasan and Mujāhid in ʿAbd al-Razzāq's *Tafsīr* (1:166); Abū al-ʿĀliya in Ibn Abī Shayba; Abū Hurayra (cf. Ibn Abī Shayba 6:418), Wakīʿ, and Mujāhid by al-Aʿmash, *Nuskhat Wakīʿ* (§19-20) and al-Ṭabarī, *Tafsīr* (5:93-94). The latter also narrates from Ibn ʿAbbās and Maymūn ibn Mahrān that it means the military commanders while he narrated from al-Aʿmash that he said: "Those who possess *fiqh* and *ʿilm*." The former is the position of al-Shāfiʿī in *al-Umm* and *Aḥkām al-Qur'ān* as well as al-Bukhārī and that of the *Jumhūr* according to al-ʿIrāqī in *Ṭarḥ al-Tathrīb* while the latter is "the position of most of the *Tābiʿīn* and Mālik" per Ibn al-ʿArabī in *Aḥkām al-Qur'ān*.

Mujāhid said: "[It means] those who possess *fiqh* and *ʿilm*, {*and if you have a dispute concerning any matter, refer it to Allah...*} that is, the Book of Allah, {*and the Messenger*} (4:59), that is, to the Sunna of the Messenger of Allah ﷺ." Then he [Mujāhid] recited {*if they had referred it to the Messenger and such of them as are in authority, those among them who are able to think out the matter would have known it*} (4:83). It is also narrated that he said "{*And those of you who have authority*} means those who possess understanding of the Religion and intelligence (*ulī al-fiqhi fil-dīni wal-ʿaql*)."[29]

Al-Ḥasan said, "It means those who possess *fiqh*, *ʿilm*, discernment (*raʾī*), and merit (*faḍl*)."[30]

Abū Wāʾil related that ʿAbd Allah ibn Masʿūd said:

> Today a man came to me asking about something and I had no idea what to answer him. He said, "Consider men who are responsible and energetic and who go out with our commanders on military campaigns but then they make demands of us over things beyond our count!" I replied, "I swear by Allah that I do not know what to answer you other than that we used to be with the Messenger of Allah ﷺ and he may have not demanded anything of us as a command more than once until we did it." Truly, each of you shall always be in a good state as long as he fears Allah Almighty. If someone has misgivings about something, let him ask a man who shall heal him [of his misgivings] although you might hardly find him! I swear by Allah beside Whom there is none, I remember the past of this world but as a cool spring of which the purest part (*ṣafw*) has been drunk and only the turbid part remains.[31]

Al-Zaylaʿī in *Tabyīn al-Ḥaqāʾiq* and Ibn Nujaym in *al-Baḥr al-Rāʾiq* prefer the latter as the most correct position. See also al-Jaṣṣāṣ, *Aḥkām al-Qurʾān* and al-Māwardī, *al-Aḥkām al-Sulṭāniyya*.

[29] Al-Ṭabarī and Khaythama, *op. cit.*

[30] Al-Ṭabarī, *op. cit.*

[31] The Prophet ﷺ also compared the age of the world to a little rain water on a

Al-Bukhārī narrated it in the *Ṣaḥīḥ* from ʿUthmān ibn Abī Shayba. Another version states that he said: "Truly, each of you shall always be in a good state as long as he fears Allah Almighty. If something nags his conscience he can come to a man of knowledge and ask him so that he can heal him. Oh, by Allah! Most surely, you will hardly find him!"

Saʿīd ibn Wahb narrated that ʿAbd Allah ibn Masʿūd said, "The people shall always be in a good state as long as they take their knowledge from their elders, their trusted ones, and their people of knowledge. When they start taking it from their boys and their reprobates, they shall be destroyed."[32]

mountain plateau of which the *ṣafw* had already been drunk and from which only the *kadar* or dregs remained. Narrated from Ibn Masʿūd by al-Ḥākim (4:320 *isnād ṣaḥīḥ*, al-Dhahabī concurring) as well as *mawqūf* by al-Bukhārī. Al-Suyūṭī declared it sound in *al-Jāmiʿ al-Ṣaghīr* (§1710). Ibn al-Athīr defines *ṣafw* and *ṣafwa* in *al-Nihāya* as "the best of any matter, its quintessence and purest part."

32 Narrated by Abū ʿUbayd and Yaʿqūb ibn Shayba as cited by Ibn Ḥajar in the *Fatḥ* (13:291), Ibn al-Mubārak in *al-Zuhd* (p. 281), Maʿmar ibn Rāshid with a sound chain in his *Jāmiʿ* (in ʿAbd al-Razzāq's *Muṣannaf* 11:246), al-Ṭabarānī in *al-Kabīr* (9:114 §8589-8592) and *al-Awsaṭ* through narrators that were declared trustworthy according to al-Haythamī (1:135), al-Khaṭīb chainless in *al-Faqīh wal-Mutafaqqih* (2:79), Ibn ʿAbd al-Barr in *Jāmiʿ Bayān al-ʿIlm* (1:158, 2:159), and Abū Khaythama in *al-ʿIlm* (§155).

The Prophetic Recommendation of the Companions' Excellent New Sunnas

There is Consensus in the *Umma* that the act or saying of a Companion can never be called a *bid'a*. There is also agreement among the Ulema that in the absence of an explicit stipulation to the contrary, the act or saying of a Companion is a proof in the Religion. This holds especially true for the Rightly-Guided Caliphs due to their specific approbation by the Prophet ﷺ. The Sunna status of what the Rightly-Guided Caliphs innovated is established by the ḥadīths of the Prophet ﷺ to that effect such as the following:

Follow My Rightly-Guided Caliphs

1. "You must follow my Sunna and the Sunna of the rightly-guided, upright successors!"[33]

[33] Narrated from al-'Irbāḍ ibn Sāriya by al-Tirmidhī (*ḥasan ṣaḥīḥ*) with four chains, Abū Dāwūd [this is his wording], Ibn Mājah with two chains, Aḥmad – he declared it *ṣaḥīḥ* according to Ibn Rajab – with four chains (Arna'ūṭ ed. 28:367-377 §17142-17147 *ṣaḥīḥ*=Zayn ed. 13:278-280 §17077-17080 *ṣaḥīḥ*), al-Dārimī, Ibn Ḥibbān (1:178-179 §5 *ṣaḥīḥ*), al-Ḥākim with five chains (1:95-97=1990 ed. 1:174-177) – declaring it *ṣaḥīḥ* while al-Dhahabī confirmed it – and in *al-Madkhal ilā al-Ṣaḥīḥ* (p. 80-81), al-Ājurrī with four chains in *al-Sharī'a* (p. 54-55 §79-82=p. 46 *ṣaḥīḥ*), Ibn Abī 'Āṣim in *al-Sunna* (p. 29 §54 *ṣaḥīḥ*), al-Ṭaḥāwī in *Mushkil al-Āthār* (2:69=3:221-224 §1185-1187 *ṣaḥīḥ*), Muḥammad ibn Naṣr al-Marwazī with four chains in *al-Sunna* (p. 26-27 §69-72 *ṣaḥīḥ*), al-Ḥārith ibn Abī Usāma in his *Musnad* (1:197-198), al-Rūyānī in his *Musnad* (1:439), Abū Nu'aym who cited it "among the *ṣaḥīḥ* narrations of the people of Shām" in *Ḥilyat al-Awliyā'* (1985 ed. 5:220-221, 10:115), al-Ṭabarānī with several chains in *Musnad al-Shāmiyyīn* (1:254, 1:402, 1:446, 2:197, 2:298) and *al-Kabīr* (18:245-257), al-Bayhaqī in *al-Sunan al-Kubrā* (10:114), *al-Madkhal* (p. 115-116), *al-I'tiqād* (p. 229), and *Shu'ab al-Īmān* (6:67), al-Baghawī who declared it *ḥasan* in *Sharḥ al-Sunna* (1:205 §102 *isnād ṣaḥīḥ*), Ibn al-Athīr in *Jāmi' al-Uṣūl* (1:187, 1:279), Ibn 'Asākir in *al-Arba'īn al-Buldāniyya* (p. 121), Ibn 'Abd al-Barr in *al-Tamhīd* (21:278-279) and *Jāmi' Bayān al-'Ilm* (2:924 §1758) where he declared it *ṣaḥīḥ*, and others.

Al-Baghawī said: "In this ḥadīth there is a proof that if a single one of the Rightly-Guided Caliphs says something while other Companions contravene him, his position takes precedence. This is the position of al-Shāfiʿī in the Old School."[34] This is also the *fatwā* of Imām Aḥmad according to Ibn Rajab:

> The Ulema differed about the consensus of the Four Caliphs: Does it constitute Consensus or merely a final proof *(ḥujja)*, and does this apply if other Companions differ with them or only when not? Two opinions are related from Imām Aḥmad concerning this. Abū Khāzim al-Ḥanafī in the time of al-Muʿtaḍid ruled for the inheritor-status of maternal relatives, paying no heed to whoever differed with the [Four] Caliphs, and this ruling of his was enforced far and wide. What if one of the Four Caliphs holds a certain position [in *ijtihād*] in which none of the other three contradicts him, but others of the Companions do? Does the Caliph's position have precedence over the other Companions? There are also two kinds of responses from the Ulema pertaining to this. What was textually stipulated by Aḥmad is that the Caliph's position takes precedence over that of the other Companions. Thus did al-Khaṭṭābī and others relate it. The sayings of most of the *Salaf* confirm this position, particularly with regard to ʿUmar.[35] [Ibn Rajab then adduces several reports illustrating ʿUmar's preeminence in rulings.][36]

[34] Al-Baghawī, *Sharḥ al-Sunna* (1:207) cf. al-Nawawī, *Mā Tamassu ilayhi al-Ḥāja* (p. 85). On al-Shāfiʿī's "Old" and "New School" see our *Four Imāms and Their Schools*.

[35] Ibn Rajab, *Jāmiʿ al-ʿUlūm wal-Ḥikam* (2:46).

[36] Cf. below, reports 10-13 and the chapter entitled "Ibn Rajab's Commentary on the Ḥadīth: "You must follow my Sunna and the Sunna of the Well-Guided Successors."

Al-Shawkānī said:

> The *jumhūr* consider that the consensus of the Four Caliphs is not a final proof *(ḥujja)* because they are but part of the *Umma*, while some of the Ulema consider that it is a final proof in light of the reports to that effect such as the sayings of the Prophet ﷺ: "You must follow my Sunna and the Sunna of the rightly-guided, upright successors after me" and: "Take for your leaders the two that come after me, Abū Bakr and ʿUmar" – two authentic, sound ḥadīths – and other similar evidence. It was replied that the two ḥadīths contain proof that they are suitable exemplars *(ahlun lil-iqtidā'i bihim)* but not that their position is necessarily a final proof over that of others. For the *mujtahid* is religiously enjoined to search for a proof until what he considers the truth becomes apparent to him. Thus, if such [ḥadīths] meant the final evidentiary nature *(ḥujjiyya)* of the position of the Caliphs or of one of them then the ḥadīth "I am happy that my Community have whatever Ibn Umm ʿAbd [=Ibn Masʿūd] is happy that they have" would suggest the final evidentiary nature of the position of Ibn Masʿūd and so would the ḥadīth "Abū ʿUbayda ibn al-Jarrāḥ is the trustee of this Community,"[37] and they are both sound.[38]

Follow Abū Bakr and ʿUmar

2. "Take for your leaders the two that come after me, Abū Bakr and ʿUmar, and whatever Ibn Masʿūd narrates to you, believe it!"[39]

[37] Narrated from Anas by al-Bukhārī and Muslim.

[38] Al-Shawkānī, *Irshād al-Fuḥūl* (2000 ed. 1:393-394=1992 ed. p. 151-152=1979 ed. p. 78). On the ḥadīth of Ibn Masʿūd see below (§ 28). In other words, the Companions have a unique paradigmatic (*qidwa*) status in any case.

[39] Narrated from Ḥudhayfa by al-Tirmidhī (*ḥasan*) and Aḥmad (Arna'ūṭ ed. 38:418-419 §23419 *ḥasan*) cf. notes 127 and following.

Abū Nuʿaym said: "This ḥadīth is among the signs of Prophethood since he foretold that his successor would be Abū Bakr and the latter's successor would be ʿUmar, and it was just as he said."[40]

Ibn Rajab said: "The Messenger of Allah ﷺ therefore explicitly stipulated *(naṣṣa)* toward the end of his life those who should be followed as leaders after him."[41]

3. "If the people obey Abū Bakr and ʿUmar they will follow the right direction!" He ﷺ said it three times.[42]

4. To the woman who said: "Messenger of Allah! What if I come back but do not find you?" – as if she meant death – the Prophet ﷺ replied: "Then go to Abū Bakr!"[43]

5. Anas ؓ said: "The delegation of Banū al-Muṣṭaliq instructed me to ask the Messenger of Allah ﷺ, 'If we come next year and do not find you, to whom should we remit our [obligatory] *ṣadaqāt*?' I conveyed to him the question and he replied: 'Remit them to Abū Bakr!' I told them his answer but they said, 'What if we do not find Abū Bakr?' I conveyed to him the question and he replied: 'Remit them to ʿUmar!' They asked again, 'What if we do not find ʿUmar?' He said, 'Tell them, remit them to ʿUthmān – and may you perish the day ʿUthmān is killed!'"[44]

---

[40] Abū Nuʿaym, *Dalāʾil al-Nubuwwa* (1989 ed. p. 130).

[41] Ibn Rajab, *Jāmiʿ al-ʿUlūm wal-Ḥikam* (2:45).

[42] Narrated from Abū Qatāda by Muslim, Aḥmad, Abū ʿAwāna in his *Musnad* (2:259), al-Bayhaqī in *al-Iʿtiqād* (p. 340) and *al-Madkhal* (p. 122), al-Firyābī and Abū Nuʿaym each in their *Dalāʾil al-Nubuwwa*, and the Jahmī ḥadīth Master ʿAlī ibn al-Jaʿd (d. 230) in his *Musnad* (p. 450) – al-Dhahabī calls him "al-Imām al-Ḥāfiẓ al-Ḥujja" in the *Siyar* (9:165 §1690)!

[43] Narrated from Jubayr ibn Muṭʿim by al-Bukhārī, Muslim, al-Tirmidhī, and Aḥmad.

[44] Narrated from Anas by Abū Nuʿaym, *Ḥilya* (1985 ed. 8:358), Ibn ʿAsākir (39:177), and Nuʿaym in the *Fitan* (1:107-108 §260, 1:125 §295) cf. *Kanz* (§36333). This ḥadīth is also among the proofs of Prophethood.

6. When Mu'āwiya asked Abū Bakrah to narrate to him something from the Prophet ﷺ he related that a man said: "Messenger of Allah! I saw in my dream as if a balance came down from the heaven in which you were weighed against Abū Bakr and outweighed him, then Abū Bakr was weighed against 'Umar and outweighed him, then 'Umar was weighed against 'Uthmān and outweighed him, then the balance was raised up." The Prophet ﷺ was grieved by this and said: "Successorship of prophethood *(khilāfa nubuwwa)*! Then Allah ﷻ will give kingship to whomever He will."[45]

7. The narration of the balance is confirmed by the ḥadīth of the Prophet ﷺ: "In a dream I saw myself drawing water from a well. Abū Bakr came and drew a large bucket *(dhanūb)* or two, but there was some weakness in his efforts – and Allah forgives him. Then 'Umar ibn al-Khaṭṭāb came and the bucket turned into a huge pail *(gharab)* in his hands. I never saw anyone do such accomplished work *(yafrī fariyyah)* as he did until all the people drank to satiation and watered their camels that knelt down there."[46]

In a similar version the Prophet ﷺ said: "Last night as [I dreamed] I was hoisting up [water from a well] I saw a flock of

[45] Narrated from Abū Bakrah by Aḥmad with three chains, Abū Dāwūd, al-Ṭayālisī (§866), Ibn Abī Shayba (11:60-61, 12:18-19), Ibn Abī 'Āṣim in *al-Sunna* (§1131-1136), al-Bazzār (§3652), al-Ṭaḥāwī in *Sharh Mushkil al-Āthār* (§3348), al-Bayhaqī, *Dalā'il al-Nubuwwa* (6:342) and *al-I'tiqād* (p. 364), and – without the last statement of the Prophet ﷺ – al-Tirmidhī who said: *ḥasan ṣaḥīḥ*; also from Safīna by Abū Dāwūd (*ḥasan*) and al-Bazzār with a fair chain as indicated by al-Haythamī. Al-Ḥākim (3:71) narrates the latter with a chain similar to al-Tirmidhī's grading it *ṣaḥīḥ*, and al-Dhahabī concurred. It is confirmed by the identical dream of the Prophet ﷺ himself as narrated from Jābir and Ibn 'Umar by Aḥmad (al-Arna'ūṭ 23:124 §14821 and 9:338 §5469) and others. It is strange that al-Arna'ūṭ declares Abū Bakrah's narration only *ḥasan* (34:94-97 §20445).

[46] Narrated from 'Abd Allah ibn 'Umar and Abū Hurayra by al-Bukhārī, Muslim, al-Tirmidhī, and Aḥmad.

black sheep and dirt-white sheep. Abū Bakr came and hoisted a bucket or two. I saw some weakness in his hoisting and Allah forgives him. Then ʿUmar came and the bucket changed into a pail! The drinking-basin became full and quenched the thirst of all that came to it. I never saw any strong master of his people *(ʿabqariyyan)* hoisting water better than ʿUmar! I interpreted the black [sheep] to refer to the Arabs and the dirt-white [sheep] to refer to the non-Arabs."[47] In another narration the interpretation of the hoisting dream is given by Abū Bakr.[48]

Al-Shāfiʿī glossed the word "weakness" as referring to the short duration of Abū Bakr's caliphate and the fact that his turning to the *Ridda* wars delayed him from the conquests and expansions achieved by ʿUmar during the latter's much longer tenure.[49]

8. Khalaf ibn Khalīfa said: "I saw ʿUmar ibn ʿAbd al-ʿAzīz addressing the people when he was caliph, and he said in his sermon: ʿLo! Truly what the Messenger of Allah ﷺ and his Two Companions instituted is a duty of the Religion. We put it into practice and we deem it conclusive.'"[50]

[47] Narrated from Abū al-Ṭufayl ʿĀmir ibn Wāthila through ʿAlī ibn Zayd ibn Judʿān (cf. n. 108) by Aḥmad, Abū Yaʿlā (2:198 §904), Ibn Abī ʿĀṣim in *al-Āḥād wal-Mathānī* (2:200-201 §951), al-Bazzār (7:211 §2785), al-Ṭabarānī "with a fair chain" per Ibn Ḥajar in the *Fatḥ* (7:39 and 12:414) and al-Haythamī (5:180, 7:183, 9:71-72) cf. also al-Muḥibb al-Ṭabarī, *al-Ryāḍ al-Naḍira* (1:350), also with a strong *mursal* chain from al-Ḥasan al-Baṣrī by Aḥmad in *Faḍā'il al-Ṣaḥāba* (1:163 §150).
[48] Narrated from ʿAbd al-Raḥmān ibn Abī Laylā, [1] from Abū Ayyūb al-Anṣārī by al-Ḥākim (4:395=1990 ed. 4:437) and [2] from Abū Bakr himself but al-Dāraquṭnī in his *ʿIlal* (1:289) avers that this narration is more probably *mursal* from Ibn Abī Laylā cf. Ibn Abī Shayba (6:176 §30479). Narrated *mursal* from the *Tābiʿī* Abū Maysara ʿAmr ibn Shuraḥbīl al-Hamdānī by al-Muḥibb al-Ṭabarī in *al-Ryāḍ al-Naḍira* (2:64 §478) cf. al-Suyūṭī, *Khaṣā'iṣ* (2:192) and something similar *mursal* from Qatāda by Maʿmar ibn Rāshid in his *Majmaʿ* (ʿAbd al-Razzāq 11:66).
[49] In *Fatḥ al-Bārī* (7:32). Similar to this is Ibn Rajab's commentary on the same narration. (see below, p. 69-70)
[50] Narrated by Abū Nuʿaym in the *Ḥilya* (5:298).

9. Imām al-Shāfiʿī said: "Allah said, {*And whatsoever the Messenger gives you, take it, and whatsoever he forbids, abstain from it*} (59:7). Sufyān [ibn ʿUyayna] narrated to us from Zāʾida, from ʿAbd al-Mālik ibn ʿUmayr, from Mawlā Ribʿī, from Ḥudhayfa that the Messenger of Allah said: 'Take for your leaders the two that come after me – Abū Bakr and ʿUmar.' This is the Book and the Sunna."[51]

Trust ʿUmar

10. The Prophet also said: "Allah has engraved truth on the tongue of ʿUmar and his heart."[52] Ibn Rajab said that the caliph ʿUmar ibn ʿAbd al-ʿAzīz used to follow ʿUmar's rulings, adducing this Prophetic ḥadīth as his proof. There are two more strong Prophetic confirmations of ʿUmar's exemplariness:

11. The Prophet said: "In the nations long before you were people who were communicated to (*muḥaddathūn*) [by the angels] although they were not prophets. If there is anyone of them in my Community, truly it is ʿUmar ibn al-Khaṭṭāb."[53]

12. He also said: "Had there been a Prophet after me, verily it would have been ʿUmar."[54]

---

[51] In Abū Nuʿaym, *Ḥilya* (1985 ed. 9:109) and al-Dhahabī, *Siyar* (8:417) and *Tadhkirat al-Ḥuffāẓ* (2:755).

[52] Narrated from Ibn ʿUmar by al-Tirmidhī (*ḥasan ṣaḥīḥ gharīb*), Aḥmad, and Ibn Ḥibbān with a fair chain according to al-Arnaʾūṭ (15:318 §6895); from Abū Dharr by Aḥmad, Abū Dāwūd, and al-Ḥākim; from Abū Hurayra by Aḥmad, Ibn Ḥibbān with a sound chain according to al-Arnaʾūṭ (15:312-313 §6889), Abū Yaʿlā, al-Ḥākim, Ibn Abī Shayba (12:21), Ibn Abī ʿĀṣim in *al-Sunna* (§1250), and al-Bazzār (§2501) with a sound chain as indicated by al-Haythamī (9:66); and from Bilāl and Muʿāwiya by al-Ṭabarānī in *al-Kabīr*. See al-Baghawī in *Sharḥ al-Sunna* (14:85), Ibn Abī ʿĀṣim in *al-Sunna* (p. 567 §1247-1250), Ibn Saʿd (21:99), and Ibn al-Athīr in *Jāmiʿ al-Uṣūl* (9:444).

[53] Narrated from Abū Hurayra and ʿĀʾisha by al-Bukhārī and Muslim, the latter without the words "although they were not Prophets."

[54] Narrated from ʿUqba ibn ʿĀmir by Aḥmad and al-Tirmidhī who graded it

13. ʿAlī said: "Truly ʿUmar followed the straightest way (*kāna rashīd al-amr*)."⁵⁵

ʿUthmān and ʿAlī Included

The Rightly-Guided Caliphs whom the Prophet ﷺ ordered people to take as their leaders are not only Abū Bakr and ʿUmar – which he named explicitly – but also ʿUthmān and ʿAlī ؓ as implied in the following sound narrations from the Prophet ﷺ:

14. "Successorship (*al-khilāfa*) after me shall last for thirty years. After that, there will be kingship."⁵⁶ As stated by Ibn Rajab, Imām

---

ḥasan, and by al-Ḥākim (3:85) who graded it *ṣaḥīḥ* as confirmed by al-Dhahabī. Also narrated from ʿIṣma ibn Mālik by al-Ṭabarānī with a weak chain in al-Kabīr (17:298), as stated by al-Haythamī (9:68) and al-Munāwī.

⁵⁵ The complete narration states that the people of Najrān came to ʿAlī saying: "O Commander of the Believers, the edict is now in your right hand and your intercession is upon your tongue: ʿUmar expelled us from our lands, so return us to them." He replied: "Woe to you! Truly ʿUmar was following the right way." Narrated from Sālim by Ibn Abī Shayba (6:357, 7:426), al-Khaṭīb in *Tārīkh Baghdād* (6:185), and – with slight differences – al-Bayhaqī in *al-Sunan al-Kubrā* (10:120), Ibn Qudāma in *al-Mughnī* (10:104), al-Shawkānī in *Nayl al-Awṭār* (8:216), and ʿAbd Allah ibn Aḥmad in *Faḍāʾil al-Ṣaḥāba* (1:366) and *al-Sunna* cf. Ibn Ḥajar, *Talkhīṣ al-Ḥabīr* (4:125) and al-Fākihī in *Akhbār Makka* (5:108) from Ibn Jaʿla.

⁵⁶ A sound ḥadīth narrated from Safīna by al-Tirmidhī (*ḥasan*) with a fair chain according to Shaykh ʿAbd Allah al-Talīdī who declared it *ṣaḥīḥ* because of its corroborative and witness-chains in *Tahdhīb al-Khaṣāʾiṣ* (p. 293 §375); also narrated by al-Nasāʾī, Abū Dāwūd, Aḥmad with two chains; al-Ḥākim; Ibn Ḥibbān with two fair chains as stated by al-Arnaʾūṭ (15:34 §6657, 15:392 §6943); al-Ṭayālisī (p. 151, 479); and al-Ṭabarānī in *al-Kabīr* with several chains. This narration is among the "Proofs of Prophethood" (*dalāʾil al-nubuwwa*) as the sum of the first five caliphates is exactly thirty years: two years and three months for Abū Bakr, ten and a half years for ʿUmar, twelve years for ʿUthmān, four years and nine months for ʿAlī, and six months for al-Ḥasan as narrated from Safīna by al-Suyūṭī in *Tahdhīb al-Khaṣāʾiṣ* (p. 293 §375) and *Tārīkh al-Khulafāʾ* (p. 22, 198-199). Al-Dhahabī cites the saying by Muʿāwiya: "I am the first of the kings" (*anā awwalu al-mulūk*) in the *Siyar* (3:157). Ibn al-ʿArabī weakened the ḥadīth in *al-ʿAwāṣim* (p. 201) to pre-empt the claim that the thirty-year span includes al-Ḥasan's successorship after ʿAlī, whereas al-Ḥasan, after ʿAlī's murder, pledged fealty (*bayʿa*)

Aḥmad declared this narration sound and adduced it as a proof for the caliphate of the four Imāms.[57]

15. "There shall be Prophethood among you then there shall be successorship on the pattern of Prophethood."[58] Ibn Rajab adduced this narration as another proof for following the Sunna of the Rightly-Guided Caliphs.

In other reports, the Prophet ﷺ names ʿUthmān and ʿAlī ؓ explicitly:

to Muʿāwiya in the year 41 as stated by al-Suyūṭī in *Tārīkh al-Khulafā'* (p. 199). Al-Ḥasan's pledge was foretold by the Prophet ﷺ in his ḥadīth from the pulpit with al-Ḥasan by his side: "Verily, this son of mine – al-Ḥasan – is a leader among men (*sayyid*), and Allah may put him in a position to reconcile two great factions of the Muslims." Narrated by al-Bukhārī from Abū Bakrah with four chains, al-Tirmidhī (*ḥasan ṣaḥīḥ*), al-Nasā'ī, Abū Dāwūd, and Aḥmad with four chains. Ibn al-ʿArabī (*op.cit.* p. 210) further rejects the authenticity of the thirty-year ḥadīth on the basis of Allah's praise of kingship and its synonymity with prophethood in the verse {*And Allah gave him* [*Dāwūd* ؑ] *the kingdom and wisdom*} (2:251). Another proof adduced against the authenticity of the thirty-year ḥadīth is the much stronger ḥadīth: "Verily, this matter shall not be terminated until there come to pass among them twelve Caliphs, all of them from Quraysh." Narrated from Jābir ibn Samura by al-Bukhārī and Muslim. However, none of these three proofs actually contradicts the thirty-year ḥadīth as pointed out by al-Nawawī in *Sharḥ Ṣaḥīḥ Muslim* (1972 ed. 12:201) and al-Munāwī (cf. al-Mubārakfūrī, *Tuḥfat al-Aḥwadhī* 6:396 and al-ʿAẓīm Ābādī, *ʿAwn al-Maʿbūd* 11:245). The twelve caliphs according to al-Suyūṭī in *Tārīkh al-Khulafā'* (p. 24) are the Four Rightly-Guided Caliphs, then Muʿāwiya after al-Ḥasan's pledge to him, then his son Yazīd, then ʿAbd al-Mālik ibn Marwān, then the latter's four sons al-Walīd, Sulaymān, Yazīd, and Hishām, then al-Walīd ibn Yazīd ibn ʿAbd al-Mālik. Al-ʿAẓīm Ābādī (12:253) recommends in this chapter Shāh Walī Allah al-Dihlawī's two books *Izālat al-Khafā' ʿan Khilāfat al-Khulafā'* and *Qurrat al-ʿAynayn fī Tafḍīl al-Shaykhayn*.

[57] In ʿAbd Allah ibn Aḥmad ibn Ḥanbal, *al-Sunna* (p. 235-236 §1276-1277) and Ibn Ḥajar, *Fatḥ al-Bārī* (1959 ed. 7:58 §3494). This is attributed to Safīna himself by al-Qurṭubī, *Tafsīr* (12:298) and al-ʿAẓīm Ābādī in *ʿAwn al-Maʿbūd* (12:260).

[58] See note 139.

16. Murra ibn Kaʻb ❦ said: "I heard the Messenger of Allah ﷺ mention a trial, at which time a man cloaked in his garment passed by. He said: 'This man, at that time, shall follow right guidance.' I went to see him and it was ʻUthmān."[59]

17. When the Prophet ﷺ sent ʻAlī to Yemen the latter said: "Messenger of Allah! You are sending me to people who are older than me so that I judge between them!" The Prophet ﷺ said: "Go, for verily Allah shall empower your tongue and guide your heart." ʻAlī said: "After that I never felt doubt as to what judgment I should pass between two parties."[60]

18. The Prophet ﷺ said: "The most compassionate of my Community towards my Community is Abū Bakr; the staunchest in the Religion of Allah is ʻUmar; the most truthful in his modesty is ʻUthmān, and the best in judgment is ʻAlī."[61] ʻUmar is related to say: "'Alī is the best in judgment among us and Ubay is the most proficient in the Qurʼānic readings."[62]

Ibn Masʻūd said: "We used to say that the best in judgment among the people of Madīna was ʻAlī."[63] Al-Nawawī excluded Abū Bakr and ʻUmar from the meaning of the Prophet's ﷺ statement: "the best in judgment is ʻAlī," and said the phrase did not necessitate precedence in knowledge nor in absolute merit.[64]

---

[59] Narrated from Kaʻb ibn Murra al-Bahzī by al-Tirmidhī (*ḥasan ṣaḥīḥ*), Ibn Mājah with a weak chain, Aḥmad with several fair chains, *Musnad* and *Faḍāʼil al-Ṣaḥāba* (1:450), al-Ḥākim (1990 ed. 3:109, 4:479 *ṣaḥīḥ*), Ibn Abī Shayba (6:360 §32025-32026, 7:442 §37090) with three chains, al-Ṭabarānī in *al-Kabīr* (19:161-162 §359, §362, 20:315 §750), and Nuʻaym ibn Ḥammād in *al-Fitan* (1:174 §461).
[60] Narrated by Aḥmad with two sound chains. One version lacks ʻAlī's final words.
[61] Part of a longer ḥadīth narrated with two *ṣaḥīḥ* chains from Anas by Ibn Mājah.
[62] Narrated from Ibn ʻAbbās by Aḥmad, al-Bukhārī, Ibn Saʻd (2:339), Ibn ʻAbd al-Barr in *al-Istīʻāb* (3:39-41), Ibn ʻAsākir (42:404), and Abū Nuʻaym in the *Ḥilya*.
[63] Narrated by al-Ḥākim (3:135), Ibn Saʻd (2:338), and Ibn ʻAsākir (42:404).
[64] Al-Nawawī, *Fatāwā* (p. 264).

Follow my Companions

On the basis of all the above, following the Companions in learning the Prophet's ﷺ Sunna, especially the Four Rightly-Guided Caliphs, is an obligation upon Muslims. This obligation is spelled out in further Prophetic ḥadīths and many Companion-reports, among them the following:

19. "My Community shall divide into seventy-three sects – all of them in the Hellfire except one group: [Those that follow] that which I and my Companions follow."[65]

20. "I recommend to you my Companions, then those that come after them, then those that come after them. Afterwards, falsehood will spread."[66]

21. "My Companions are trustees for my Community."[67] The complete ḥadīth states: "The stars are trustees for the heaven, and when the stars wane, the heaven is brought what was promised [*i.e.* of the corruption of the world and the coming of the Day of Judgment]; and I am a trustee for my Companions, so when I go, my Companions will be brought what was promised them [*i.e.* of *fitna* and division]; and my Companions are trustees for my

[65] A sound narration from ʿAbd Allah ibn ʿAmr by al-Tirmidhī (*ḥasan gharīb*), Muḥammad ibn Naṣr al-Marwazī in *al-Sunna* (p. 23), Ibn ʿAsākir, Abū Nuʿaym in *Maʿrifat al-Ṣaḥāba*, al-Ṭabarānī in *al-Saghīr*, and al-Ḥākim (1:129=1990 ed. 1:218), with chains containing ʿAbd al-Raḥmān ibn Zyād al-Ifrīqī, who was declared weak by some but fair in his narrations by others, and from Anas by al-Ṭabarānī in *al-Awsaṭ*. Al-Lālikāʾī declared this ḥadīth *ṣaḥīḥ* in his *Sharḥ Uṣūl Iʿtiqād Ahl al-Sunna* (1:100) and it was included – with its variant versions – by al-Kattānī in his *Naẓm al-Mutanāthir* (p. 45-47) and Ibn al-Athīr in *Jāmiʿ al-Uṣūl* (10:408). Abū Manṣūr al-Baghdādī's entire *Farq bayn al-Firāq* is an elucidation of this one ḥadīth.

[66] Narrated from ʿUmar by al-Tirmidhī who graded it *ḥasan ṣaḥīḥ gharīb*, Aḥmad with a sound chain, and Ibn Mājah, as part of a longer ḥadīth. See al-Tirmidhī's *al-ʿIlal al-Kabīr* (p. 323 §596) and al-Dāraquṭnī's *ʿIlal* (2:65-68).

[67] Narrated from Abū Mūsā al-Ashʿarī by Muslim and Aḥmad as part of a longer ḥadīth.

Community, so when they go my Community will be brought what was promised to you [*i.e.* following *hawā* and vying for *dunyā*]." In the foregoing narration the Prophet ﷺ compares himself and his Companions ♣ to the stars. This comparison is quite unique in the ḥadīth and, together with the verse {*and by the stars they find a way*} (16:16), shows the truth of the narration whereby the Prophet ﷺ is related to say:

22. "My Companions are like the stars; whoever among them you use for guidance, you will be rightly guided."[68]

[68] Narrated from [1] Ibn 'Umar by 'Abd ibn Ḥumayd in his *Musnad* (*Muntakhab* Kuwait ed. 2:28=Cairo ed. p. 250), Ibn 'Abd al-Barr in *Jāmi' Bayān al-'Ilm* (2:924 §1759), and Ibn 'Adī in *al-Kāmil* (2:785-786), all with very weak chains through the forger Ḥamza ibn Abī Ḥamza al-Ju'fī al-Jazīrī cf. al-Suyūṭī in *Manāhil al-Ṣafā* (p. 193 §1027), Ibn 'Adī in *al-Kāmil*, and *Talkhīṣ al-Ḥabīr* (4:190); [2] Jābir by al-Dāraquṭnī in *Faḍā'il al-Ṣaḥāba* and *al-Mu'talif wal-Mukhtalif* (4:1778), Ibn 'Abd al-Barr in *Jāmi' Bayān al-'Ilm* (2:925 §1760=2:110-111 *ḍa'īf*), and Ibn Ḥazm in *al-Iḥkām* (6:244 *mawḍū'*) with a weak chain because of Sallām ibn al-Ḥārith although this is the best chain in this chapter and al-Bayhaqī declares it strong in *al-I'tiqād* (p. 319); Ibn Ḥazm narrates it through Sallām ibn Sulaymān (ibn Sawwār) who is also weak; [2a] Jābir by al-Dāraquṭnī in *Gharā'ib Mālik* through an unknown from Imām Mālik cf. *Talkhīṣ al-Ḥabīr*; [3] Abū Hurayra by al-Quḍā'ī in *Musnad al-Shihāb* (2:275 §1346) with a very weak chain because of Ja'far ibn 'Abd al-Wāḥid al-Hāshimī who was declared a liar as stated by Ibn Ḥajar; [4] 'Umar (a ḥadīth *qudsī*) by al-Bayhaqī in *al-Madkhal* (p. 162=1:145-146 §151), al-Khaṭīb in *al-Kifāya* (p. 48=p. 66=p. 95), al-Bazzār who graded it *ḍa'īf munkar* as quoted by Ibn 'Abd al-Barr in *Jāmi' Bayān al-'Ilm* (2:924), Niẓām al-Mulk (408-485) in *Majlisān min Amālī Niẓām al-Mulk* (p. 52), al-Sijzī in *al-Ibāna*, and Ibn 'Asākir, all with a very weak chain because of 'Abd al-Raḥīm ibn Zayd al-'Ammī who is discarded cf. Ibn al-Jawzī, *'Ilal* (1:282), al-Dhahabī, *Mīzān* (*bāṭil*), al-Suyūṭī, *Jāmi' Ṣaghīr* (§4603 *ḍa'īf*), al-Ṣan'ānī, *Tawḍīḥ al-Afkār* (p. 264), al-Munāwī, *Fayḍ al-Qadīr* (4:76 *bāṭil*), and al-Ghumārī, *al-Mughīr* (p. 56 *mawḍū'*); [5] Ibn 'Abbās *munqaṭi'* by al-Khaṭīb in *al-Kifāya* (p. 48=p. 65-66=p. 95), al-Bayhaqī in *al-Madkhal* (p. 163-164=1:147-148), and Ibn 'Asākir cf. al-Suyūṭī, *Miftāḥ al-Janna* (p. 45=p. 93-94 §180), all with a very weak chain because of Juwaybir ibn Sa'īd al-Azdī (cf. *Taqrīb*) in addition to its being broken between al-Ḍaḥḥāk and Ibn 'Abbās; [6] Anas through al-Bazzār cf. Ibn Ḥajar in *Talkhīṣ al-Ḥabīr* (4:191 *isnād wāhin*) and *al-Maṭālib al-'Āliya* (4:146 *isnād ḍa'īf*). [7] Jawwāb ibn 'Ubayd Allah the *Tābi'ī mursal* by al-Bayhaqī in *al-Madkhal* (p. 163=1:148

§153) through Juwaybir. Qāḍī ʿIyāḍ attributes it positively to the Prophet ﷺ in *al-Shifā'* (p. 535 §1302). Al-Bajawī said in his commentary of the *Shifā'* (2:613): "The ḥadīth Master al-ʿIrāqī said: The author (ʿIyāḍ) should not have cited it as if it were definitely a ḥadīth of the Prophet." Al-Ḥalabī said: "The author should not have cited it as if it were definitely a ḥadīth of the Prophet ﷺ due to what is known about it among the scholars of this science, and he has done the same thing several times before." Al-Qārī replies in his *Sharḥ al-Shifā'* (2:91): "It is possible that he [ʿIyāḍ] had established a chain for it, or that he considered the multiplicity of its chains to raise its grade from *ḍaʿīf* to that of *ḥasan*, due to his good opinion of it, not to mention the fact that even the weak ḥadīth may be put into practice for meritorious acts (*faḍā'il al-aʿmāl*), and Allah knows best." See also Ibn al-Athīr, *Jāmiʿ al-Uṣūl* (8:556-557). Al-Bayhaqī in *al-Madkhal* concludes, "Its *matn* is well-known and its chains are weak, not one of them being sound" but he declares one of its chains strong and adduces it in *al-Iʿtiqād* (p. 319), confirming its meaning while Ibn Ḥajar supports him in *Talkhīṣ al-Ḥabīr* (4:191). Cf. al-Mubārakfūrī, *Tuḥfat al-Aḥwadhī* (10:156). Al-Ḥakīm al-Tirmidhī in *Nawādir al-Uṣūl* (3:62) considers its meaning true. Ibn ʿAbd al-Barr rejects al-Bazzār's grading of *munkar* and also tends to strengthen it cf. Ibn Ḥajar in his *Takhrīj Aḥādīth Mukhtaṣar Ibn al-Ḥājib* (*i.e.* Ibn al-Ḥājib's abridgment of his own *Muntahā al-Sūl wal-Amal fī ʿIlmay al-Uṣūli wal-Jadal*) as cited in al-Ṣanʿānī's *Tawḍīḥ al-Afkār* (p. 264). Al-Ṣāghānī declared it fair (*ḥasan*) as stated by Ḥasan al-Ṭībī and al-Sayyid's respective commentaries on the *Mishkāt*. Shaykh ʿAbd al-Fattāḥ Abū Ghudda in his commentary on al-Qārī's *Fatḥ Bāb al-ʿInāya* (1:13) and his *Maṣnūʿ fī Maʿrifat al-Ḥadīth al-Mawḍūʿ* (p. 273) rejects the grading of *mawḍūʿ* and equally rejects al-Lacknawī's grading of *ṣaḥīḥ* – in his marginalia on the latter's *Tuḥfat al-Akhyār* entitled *Nukhbat al-Anẓār* (p. 53) and the introduction to his *al-Āthār al-Marfūʿa fīl-Akhbār al-Mawḍūʿa* – for which the latter cited al-Shaʿrānī's phrase in the *Mīzān al-Kubrā*: "Even if the authenticity of this ḥadīth is questioned among the Scholars of ḥadīth, nevertheless it is sound among the people of spiritual unveiling (*kashf*)." See also the Tamīm brothers' marginalia on al-Qārī's supercommentary *Sharḥ Sharḥ Nukhbat al-Fikar* (p. 557). The "Salafī" Saʿīd Maʿshāsha in his tract *al-Muqallidūn wal-A'immat al-Arbaʿa* (Beirut: al-Maktab al-Islamī and Dār Ibn Ḥazm, 1999) (p. 102) said, "this ḥadīth is forged (*mawḍūʿ*) as Ibn Ḥazm said in *Uṣūl al-Aḥkām* (§810), al-Shawkānī in *al-Qawl al-Mufīd* (p. 30), and al-Albānī in *al-Silsila al-Ḍaʿīfa* (§58) and a number of the scholars." This statement is a flat untruth as al-Shawkānī adduces this narration in *Irshād al-Fuḥūl* (1:337, 1:394) and all he said in *al-Qawl al-Mufīd fī Adillat al-Ijtihād wal-Taqlīd* on page 9 of its original 1347/1929 edition is: "This ḥadīth was narrated through different routes from Jābir and Ibn ʿUmar, and the Imāms of narrator-criticism have explicitly said that none of them are sound (*lā yaṣiḥḥu minhā shay'*) and that this ḥadīth is not firmly established as a Prophetic narration. [...] In sum, this ḥadīth forms no proof." This

23. 'Umar referred to this paradigmatic guidance of the Companions when he defined them as "Those whom people look at and take (knowledge) from" at the time he disapproved of the difference of opinion between Ubay ibn Ka'b and 'Abd Allah ibn Mas'ūd.[69] Imām Aḥmad confirmed this understanding in his definition: **"The Religion is nothing but imitation itself"** *(al-dīn innamā huwa al-taqlīd)* and he continued, **"This imitation is for the Companions of the Messenger of Allah ﷺ."**[70] To al-Ṣayrafī who was asking him whether it is permissible to examine the variant positions of the Companions "in order to know which is correct so that we may follow it" Aḥmad replied: "It is not permissible to examine [the differences] among the Companions of the Messenger of Allah ﷺ!" Al-Ṣayrafī said: "Then what do we do?" He replied: **"You imitate whomever of them you like!"** *(tuqallidu ayyahum aḥbabt).*[71] This is an explicit stipulation *(naṣṣ)* from Imām Aḥmad that by *taqlīd* he means *taqlīd*, not "following the proof" or *"ittibā'"* or some such invented distinctions aimed at diluting or nullifying the meaning of *taqlīd*. Abū Bakr ؓ said to a desert Arab who had objected to the allotment for him agreed upon by the Muslims: "If the Emigrants are satisfied, you are but followers!"[72] – using the word "followers" *(taba'ūn)* to mean "without any prerogative to consider, question, or discuss."

---

is the same opinion as those we have quoted from the majority of the scholars, but it is a far cry from saying the ḥadīth is forged. Furthermore, it is untrue that "a number of the scholars" have declared it forged, as the only scholar who did so was Ibn Ḥazm, imitated in our time by various semi-Ulema. One of the ironies of Ma'shāsha's book is that he attacks *taqlīd* on every page, yet relies blindly on Albānī for ḥadīth authentication, without any reference to the ḥadīth Masters!

[69] Narrated by Ibn 'Abd al-Barr in *Jāmi' Bayān al-'Ilm* (Miṣr: Dār al-Ṭibā'at al-Munīriyya 2:84).

[70] Narrated from Abū Muḥammad al-Barbahārī by Ibn Abī Ya'lā in *Ṭabaqāt al-Ḥanābila* (1:29).

[71] Narrated by Ibn 'Abd al-Barr in *Jāmi' Bayān al-'Ilm* (2:909 §1705).

[72] Narrated by al-Muḥibb al-Ṭabarī in *al-Riyāḍ al-Naḍira* (2:235-236).

Similar to this is the word of Allah ﷻ: {*When those who were followed (uttubiʿū) disown those who followed (ittabaʿū)*}(2:166), which uses follow *(ittibāʿ)* for the most basic blind imitation. Similarly, Aḥmad said to al-Maymūnī: "Abū al-Ḥasan! Never speak over any matter in which you do not have an Imām [to imitate]."[73] Al-Ḥakīm al-Tirmidhī said in *Nawādir al-Uṣūl*: "Not everyone that met him ﷺ and followed him or saw him once is meant by this ḥadīth ['My Companions are like the stars'], but only those that studiously kept his company morning and evening, received his conveyance of the Revelation, took from him the Law that became the path of the Umma, and looked to him for the ethics of Islam and to his noble traits. Those became, after him, the **Imāms and proofs in which resides right guidance and in whose path is found right emulation and in them is safety and right belief.**"[74]

24. "The simile of the people of learning *(al-ʿulamā')* on the earth is as the stars in the sky by which one is guided in the darkness of the land and the sea. When the stars are clouded over, the guides are about to be lost."[75]

[73] Narrated by Ibn al-Jawzī in *Manāqib Aḥmad* (p. 178).
[74] Al-Ḥakīm al-Tirmidhī, *Nawādir al-Uṣūl* (*Aṣl* 222).
[75] Narrated from Anas by Aḥmad (al-Arna'ūṭ ed. 20:52 §12600=al-Zayn ed. 10:508 §12537=3:157 §12606) with a very weak chain according to al-Arna'ūṭ because of Rishdīn ibn Saʿd who is weak, Abū Ḥafṣ – the narrator from Anas – who is unknown, and ʿAbd Allah ibn al-Walīd who is "soft" (*layyin*), although al-Zayn declared it fair with his usual laxity as did al-Suyūṭī in *al-Jāmiʿ al-Ṣaghīr* cf. al-Haytamī (1:121). Also narrated by al-Khaṭīb in *al-Faqīh wal-Mutafaqqih* (2:70=2:138 §763), al-Rāmahurmuzī in *al-Amthāl* (p. 51) – both with the same chain – and Aḥmad in *al-Zuhd*, *mawqūf* from Abū al-Dardā'. Also narrated *mursal* from al-Ḥasan al-Baṣrī by al-Bayhaqī in *al-Madkhal* (p. 274).

25. "Mankind makes up one portion *(ḥayyiz)* and I and my Companions make up one portion [counter-balancing it]."[76]

26. As the Companions passed by someone's remains they commended that person, whereupon the Prophet ﷺ said: "It is guaranteed. It is guaranteed. It is guaranteed (*wajabat*)." Then they passed by another and condemned him. The Prophet ﷺ said: "It is guaranteed. It is guaranteed. It is guaranteed." ʿUmar said: "My father and mother be your ransom! We passed by someone's remains and commended that person, whereupon you said: 'It is guaranteed. It is guaranteed. It is guaranteed.' Then we passed by another and condemned him, whereupon you said: 'It is guaranteed. It is guaranteed. It is guaranteed.'" The Messenger of Allah ﷺ said: "Whoever you commend, Paradise is guaranteed for him, and whoever you condemn, the Fire is guaranteed for him. **You are the witnesses of Allah on earth. You are the witnesses of Allah on earth. You are the witnesses of Allah on earth!**"[77]

Follow Ibn Masʿūd and ʿAmmār ibn Yāsir

27. The Prophet ﷺ said, after the injunction to follow the leadership of Abū Bakr and ʿUmar : "Hold fast to the covenant of Ibn Umm ʿAbd [= Ibn Masʿūd] and follow ʿAmmār's guidance."[78]

[76] Narrated from Abū Saʿīd al-Khudrī, Rāfiʿ ibn Khadīj, and Zayd ibn Thābit by Aḥmad and al-Ṭabarānī in *al-Kabīr* (3:341 §4444), the former with a chain of sound narrators according to al-Haythamī (5:250, 10:17), "a sound chain" according to al-Zayn in the *Musnad* (10:72 §11110, 16:43 §21521) and al-Ḥākim (2:258, al-Dhahabī concurred) while al-Arna'ūṭ declares Aḥmad's chain broken (*munqaṭiʿ*) but the ḥadīth itself *ṣaḥīḥ li-ghayrih* in his edition of the *Musnad* (17:258 §11167); also by Ibn Abī Shayba (14:498-499), al-Ṭayālisī (§2205), al-Quḍāʿī in *Musnad al-Shihāb* (§845), and al-Bayhaqī in *Dalā'il al-Nubuwwa* (5:109-110). See the complete wording above, section entitled, "The Term *Ahl al-Sunna wal-Jamāʿa*."

[77] Narrated from Anas by al-Bukhārī, Muslim, al-Tirmidhī, al-Nasā'ī, and Aḥmad.

[78] See notes 127-134.

28. "I am happy that my Community *(raḍītu li-ummatī)* have whatever Ibn Umm ʿAbd [=Ibn Masʿūd] is happy that they have and I detest for them whatever he detests for them."[79]

29. "Ibn Masʿūd instituted a Sunna for you, so follow that Sunna" *(inna Ibna Mas ʿūdin sanna lakum sunnatan fastannū bihā).*[80] The meaning of *sanna* here and in the following ḥadīth is to start an act without precedent, as shown below. These three narrations are among the shining Prophetic supports for the rule spelled out by Ibn Masʿūd ﷺ that "whatever the Muslims consider right is right in the sight of Allah, and whatever they consider bad is bad in the sight of Allah." Ḥudhayfa said that Ibn Masʿūd most resembled the Prophet ﷺ while Abū Mūsā observed that Ibn Masʿūd and his mother were part of the household (*ahl al-bayt*) of the Prophet ﷺ.[81]

Follow Muʿādh ibn Jabal

30. "Muʿādh [ibn Jabal] instituted a Sunna for you, so follow it exactly" *(inna Muʿādhan sanna lakum sunnatan fakadhālika fafʿalū).*[82]

[79] Narrated from Ibn Masʿūd by al-Bazzār (5:354 §1986) and al-Ṭabarānī in *al-Kabīr* (9:80) – cf. *al-Awsaṭ* (7:69-70) – with a chain of trustworthy narrators cf. al-Haythamī (9:290), Aḥmad in *Faḍā'il al-Ṣaḥāba* (2:838-840), al-Ḥākim (1990 ed. 3:359 *isnād ṣaḥīḥ ʿalā sharṭ al-shaykhayn*), and al-Bayhaqī in *al-Madkhal* (p. 138), *ṣaḥīḥ* per al-Suyūṭī in *al-Jāmiʿ al-Ṣaghīr* (§4458) and al-Shawkānī cf. above (§1), but possibly *mursal* from al-Qāsim ibn ʿAbd al-Raḥmān ibn ʿAbd Allah ibn Masʿūd cf. al-Dāraquṭnī, *al-ʿIlal* (5:201 §820). Cited by Ibn Ḥibbān in his *Thiqāt* (2:60) and al-Munāwī (4:33). See also al-Kawtharī's *Fiqh Ahl al-ʿIrāq* (p. 94).

[80] Narrated by ʿAbd al-Razzāq (2:229). The sunna in question consists in following the imām in the third *rakʿa* of his *witr* prayer, even if the follower would have normally ended his prayer after two *rakʿas.*

[81] Both reports in al-Bukhārī and Muslim.

[82] Narrated by Abū Dāwūd with a sound chain according to Ibn Daqīq al-ʿĪd in *al-Imām* as stated in *ʿAwn al-Maʿbūd* (2:131-132), and al-Bayhaqī in *al-Sunan* (3:93 §4922). The sunna in question consists in joining the group prayer at whatever point the latecomer finds the imām has reached, making up what he missed only after the imām ends it.

Companion-Reports on the Exemplariness of the Companions in the Religion

31. In al-Bukhārī and Muslim from ʿĀ'isha ﵂, Abū Bakr ﵁ said: "I do not leave out anything which the Prophet ﷺ did but I do it. Were I to leave a single command of his, I fear I would deviate."

32. ʿUmar ﵁ said: "The *Sunan* have been instituted for you, the obligations have been imposed upon you, and you have been left upon the crystal-clear path lest you cause people to incline right and left."[83] The expression "lest you cause people to incline right and left" shows ʿUmar's awareness of the status of the Companions as objects of imitation in the Religion on the part of the larger public.

33. ʿUmar also wrote to Shurayḥ instructing him: "Pass judgment according to what is in the Book of Allah. If [basis for judgment is] not in the Book of Allah, then according to what is in the Sunna of the Messenger of Allah. If [basis for judgment is] not in the Sunna of the Messenger of Allah, then according to what the righteous (*al-ṣāliḥūn*) have judged. If it is not in the Book of Allah, nor in the Sunna of the Messenger of Allah ﷺ, nor did the righteous pass judgment concerning it, then you may forward a judgment and, if you like, you may postpone it. I believe postponing it will be best for you. *Wal-salāmu ʿalaykum.*"[84]

34. When ʿAlī ﵁ was asked to define who "the Rightly-Guided successors" were, he wept and said: "Abū Bakr and ʿUmar ﵄ the two leaders of rightful guidance and the two Shaykhs of Islam, the two men of Quraysh, the two who are followed after the

[83] Ibn Abī Zayd, *al-Jāmiʿ fil-Sunan* (1990 ed. p. 151 §21).
[84] Narrated from al-Shaʿbī by al-Nasā'ī in the *Sunan* and *al-Sunan al-Kubrā* (3:468 §5909). Al-Maqdisī included it among the *ṣaḥīḥ* in his *Mukhtāra* (1:238-239).

Messenger of Allah ﷺ! Whoever follows these two gains respect; whoever lives up to the legacy of these two is guided to a straight path; whoever sticks with these two is from the party of Allah, {*and the party of Allah – these are the successful*}."⁸⁵

35. ʿAlī also said: "The best of this Community after its Prophet are Abū Bakr and ʿUmar. As for myself, I am only an ordinary man among the Muslims."⁸⁶ In one version he said, "I saw the Messenger of Allah ﷺ with these two eyes of mine – or else let them be struck blind! – and heard him with these two ears of mine – or else let them be struck deaf! – say: 'None was ever born in all Islam [other than Prophets] purer nor better than Abū Bakr then ʿUmar!'"⁸⁷ Ibn ʿAsākir said that the more correct version is that these are the words of ʿAlī.

36. ʿAlī ؓ in a certain matter was asked for his source and replied: "It was an opinion I consider true (*innamā huwa raʾyun raʾaytuhu*), therefore, whoever wishes, let him follow it, and whoever wishes, let him leave it."⁸⁸

37. ʿAlī also said: "I am not a Prophet nor do I receive revelation! But I put into practice the Book of Allah and the Sunna of His

---

⁸⁵ Muḥibb al-Dīn al-Ṭabarī, *al-Riyāḍ al-Naḍira* (1:379 §276); al-Zamakhsharī, *Mukhtaṣar al-Muwāfaqa* folio 23; al-Sakhāwī, *al-Jawāhir wal-Durar*, Introduction.

⁸⁶ This is a mass-narrated (*mutawātir*) saying of ʿAlī according to al-Dhahabī, spoken from the pulpit in Kūfa and narrated from Muḥammad ibn al-Ḥanafiyya by al-Bukhārī in his *Ṣaḥīḥ* and Abū Dāwūd with a sound chain; Wahb al-Suwāʾī, ʿAlqama ibn Qays, Shurayḥ, and ʿAbd Khayr by Aḥmad in his *Musnad*, each through several chains; from ʿAbd Allah ibn Salama by Ibn Mājah with a fair chain; and from Shurayḥ by Ibn Shādhān, al-Khaṭīb, Ibn Abī Shayba, al-Lālikāʾī, Ibn Mandah, Ibn ʿAsākir, and others. See also *Kashf al-Khafāʾ* under the ḥadīth: "I am the city of knowledge and ʿAlī is its gate."

⁸⁷ Narrated from al-Aṣbagh ibn Nabāta and al-Shaʿbī by Ibn ʿAsākir (44:196) cf. *Kanz* (§32685, §36732).

⁸⁸ Narrated in al-Ṭabarānī's *Awsaṭ* (1:180, 2:69). Cf. ʿUmar ibn ʿAbd al-ʿAzīz further below.

Prophet ﷺ as much as I can. Therefore, as long as I order you to obey Allah, you must obey me whether you like it or not!"[89]

38. Ibn Masʿūd ؓ was approached by a group who put to him a difficult question which he refused to answer at first. They said, "You are the last of the Companions of the Prophet ﷺ here, if we do not ask you then who can we ask?" After a month he said, "This is the most difficult question that was ever put to me. I shall exert my own personal opinion concerning it (*sa'aqūlu fīhā bi-juhdi ra'yī*). If I am right then it is from Allah, and if I am wrong then it is from me and from Satan, and Allah and the Prophet ﷺ are innocent of it."[90]

39. Ibn Masʿūd similarly said: "Pass judgment according to what is in the Book of Allah. If [basis for judgment is] not in the Book of Allah, then according to what is in the Sunna of the Messenger of Allah. If [basis for judgment is] not in the Sunna of the Messenger of Allah, then according to what the righteous (*al-ṣāliḥūn*) have judged. <And if something comes up that is not in the Book of Allah, nor did the Prophet ﷺ pass judgment concerning it, nor did the righteous pass judgment concerning it, then let one exert his own reasoning (*faliyajtahid ra'yahu*).>[91] Let no one say: 'I am afraid, I am afraid [to judge]!' The lawful is clear and the unlawful is clear, and between the two are doubtful matters. Therefore, leave what seems dubious to you for what does not seem dubious to you."[92]

[89] Narrated by Muslim and Aḥmad.

[90] Narrated by Aḥmad, al-Nasā'ī, Ibn Ḥibbān with a sound chain by Muslim's criterion, al-Ḥākim (*ṣaḥīḥ*, al-Dhahabī concurring), Ibn Abī Shayba, and others.

[91] Bracketed segment missing from al-Dārimī's version.

[92] Narrated from Ḥurayth ibn Zuhayr by al-Nasā'ī both in the *Sunan* and *al-Sunan al-Kubrā* (3:469 §5911), al-Dārimī, al-Ṭabarānī in *al-Kabīr* (9:187), al-Bayhaqī in *al-Sunan al-Kubrā* (10:115 §20115), and Ibn Abī Shayba with a sound chain according to Ibn Ḥajar in *Fatḥ al-Bārī* (1959 ed. 13:288). The Prophetic ḥadīth "The lawful is clear and the unlawful is clear..." is narrated from al-

40. Another version states that Ibn Mas'ūd said: "If a case comes before you which you cannot defer, judge it according to what is in the Book of Allah. If you are unable to, then judge it according to the Sunna of the Prophet of Allah ﷺ. If you are unable, then judge it according to the judgment passed by the righteous. If you are unable, then motion tacitly to defer it and leave no stone unturned [to pass judgment]. If you are unable, then run away from it and do not be ashamed."[93]

41. 'Ubayd Allah ibn Abī Yazīd said: "Whenever Ibn 'Abbās was asked about something, if it was in the Qur'ān or the Sunna he would quote them and, if not, he would exert his judgment (*ijtahada ra'yah*)."[94]

42. The above six reports confirm and are confirmed by the ḥadīth of the Prophet ﷺ to Mu'ādh ؓ when he sent the latter to the city of al-Janad in Yemen as a judge: "When the Messenger of Allah ﷺ sent me to Yemen he said: 'How will you pass judgment if a judgment is asked of you?' I replied: 'I shall pass judgment on the basis of the book of Allah.' He said: 'What if it is not in the

Nu'mān ibn Bashīr in the Six Books. The Prophetic ḥadīth "Leave what seems dubious to you for what does not seem dubious to you" is narrated from al-Ḥasan ibn 'Alī by al-Tirmidhī (*ḥasan ṣaḥīḥ*), al-Nasā'ī, Aḥmad, al-Dārimī, al-Ṭabarānī in *al-Kabīr* (3:75-77 §2708-2711), 'Abd al-Razzāq (3:117-118 §4984), al-Ṭayālisī (p. 163 §1178), Abū Nu'aym in *Akhbār Aṣbahān* (1:45) and the *Ḥilya* (8:264), al-Bayhaqī in *al-Sunan al-Kubrā* (5:335), Ibn Ḥibbān (2:498 §722 *ṣaḥīḥ* according to al-Arna'ūṭ), al-Baghawī in *Sharḥ al-Sunna* (7:16-17 §2032), al-Ḥākim (2:13, 4:99, *ṣaḥīḥ* according to al-Dhahabī). Also narrated from Anas by Aḥmad; Wābiṣa ibn Ma'bad by al-Ṭabarānī in *al-Kabīr*; and Ibn 'Umar by al-Ṭabarānī in *al-Saghīr* (1:102), Abū al-Shaykh in *al-Amthāl* (§40), Abū Nu'aym in *Akhbār Aṣbahān* (2:243) and the *Ḥilya* (6:352), al-Khaṭīb in *Tārīkh Baghdād* (2:220, 2:387, 6:386), and al-Quḍā'ī in *Musnad al-Shihāb* (§645).

[93] Narrayted from al-Qāsim ibn 'Abd al-Raḥmān by 'Abd al-Razzāq (8:301) and al-Ṭabarānī in *al-Kabīr* (9:187).

[94] Narrated from Sufyān ibn 'Uyayna by Ibn Sa'd (2:366) and al-Balādhirī's *Ansāb al-Ashrāf* (3:32) cf. al-Dhahabī, *Tārīkh al-Islam* (Years 61-80 p. 159).

book of Allah?' I replied: 'Then on the basis of the Sunna of the Messenger of Allah ﷺ.' He said: 'What if it is not in the Sunna of the Messenger of Allah?' I replied: 'Then I shall strive on my own and leave no stone unturned.' Whereupon the Prophet ﷺ slapped my chest and said: 'Praise to Allah ﷻ Who has graced the messenger of the Messenger of Allah with what pleases the Messenger of Allah.'"[95]

[95] This ḥadīth is not established from the perspective of *isnād* but nevertheless considered authentic and relied upon by the generality of the *Umma* and the massive majority of the Ulema. Narrated by Abū Dāwūd, al-Tirmidhī who said that a link of its chain was missing, Aḥmad, al-Dārimī, Ibn Abī Shayba (4:543, 6:13), al-Ṭayālisī (p. 76), ʿAbd ibn Ḥumayd in his *Musnad* (p. 72), al-Ṭabarānī in *al-Kabīr* (20:170), Ibn Saʿd (2:347-348, 3:584), al-Khaṭīb in his *Tārīkh* (13:77) and *al-Faqīh wal-Mutafaqqih* (1:188-189), al-Bayhaqī in *al-Sunan al-Kubrā* (10:114), *Maʿrifat al-Sunan* (1:173-174 §291) and *al-Madkhal* (p. 207), Ibn ʿAbd al-Barr in *Jāmiʿ Bayān al-ʿIlm* (2:844-846 §1592- 1594=2:56), al-Baghawī in *Sharḥ al-Sunna* (10:116), Ibn ʿAsākir, al-Qāḍī Wakīʿ in *Akhbār al-Quḍāt* (1:98), Ibn ʿAdī (2:613), and others. Al-Bukhārī in *al-Tārīkh al-Kabīr* (2:277) stated that it has no sound chain, as did ʿAbd al-Ḥaqq al-Ishbīlī, Ibn Ḥazm in *al-Iḥkām* (7:417=6:36), and Ibn al-Jawzī in *al- ʿIlal al-Mutanāhiya* (2:758-759 §1264) who conceded its meaning was true. However, because it is unanimously considered authentic by the jurists, it is considered *ṣaḥīḥ* as a ḥadīth as indicated by al-Khaṭīb, Abū Bakr al-Rāzī in *Aḥkām al-Qurʾān* (3:179), Ibn al-ʿArabī in *ʿĀriḍat al-Aḥwadhī*, Ibn Kathīr in his *Tafsīr* (1:4), Ibn al-Qayyim in *Iʿlām al-Muwaqqiʿīn* (1:202-203), Ibn Ḥajar in *Talkhīṣ al-Ḥabīr* (4:182-183 §2076), al-Tahānawī in *Muqaddimat Iʿlāʾ al-Sunan* (2/2:57-58), al-Arnaʾūṭ in al-Ṭaḥāwī's *Sharḥ Mushkil al-Āthār* (9:213-214 §3584), al-Zayn in *Musnad Aḥmad* (16:164 §21906), and Abū Ghudda in his edition of al-Lacknawī's *al-Ajwibat al-Fāḍila* (p. 228-238). Other similarly weak-chained ḥadīths that are accepted by scholars as authentic: "No harm should be done nor reciprocated," "Seawater is pure and purifying" and "The killer's extended family is responsible for the indemnity." Concerning these, Ibn al-Qayyim said: "Even if these ḥadīths are not firmly authenticated in their chains of transmission (*ghayr thābit*), since virtually all scholars have related them, the ḥadīths' authenticity, which they accept, eliminates their need to verify the channels of transmission." (Cf. *Reliance of the Traveller* p. 954-957.)] See also al-Ghumārī's *al-Ibtihāj* (p. 210-211, 244). Al-Kawtharī in his *Maqālāt* (p. 155) said: "The jurists of the *Tābiʿīn* and their successors received this ḥadīth with approval and put its principle into practice generation after generation." Al-Albānī alone graded it "rejected" in his *Silsila Ḍaʿīfa* and in his notes on al-Qāsimī's *al-Masḥ ʿalā al-Jawrabayn* (p. 38)

43. Ibn Mas'ūd said: "Allah ﷻ looked into the hearts of creatures and found the heart of Muḥammad ﷺ to be the best heart of all creatures. So He chose Him for Himself and sent him with His Message. Then he looked into the hearts of creatures after the heart of Muḥammad ﷺ and found the hearts of Muḥammad's Companions to be the best hearts of all creatures. So He made them the ministers of His Prophet and those who would fight in defense of His Religion. Therefore, whatever the Muslims consider right is right in the sight of Allah, and whatever they consider bad is bad in the sight of Allah."[96]

44. Ibn Mas'ūd and Ibn 'Umar ؓ also said: "Whoever wishes to follow the Sunna, let him follow the Sunna of those that died – the Companions of Muḥammad ﷺ! They were the purest of heart in all this Community, the deepest in knowledge, the least pretentious, the straightest in guidance, the most excellent in state! They were a people whom Allah ﷻ chose for His Prophet's ﷺ company and the establishment of His Religion. Therefore be aware of their superiority and follow them in their views, and hold fast to whatever you are able to hold from their manners and their lives! Verily they were on the straight path."[97]

derided the jurists for considering it authentic! Al-Qurṭubī related in his *Tafsīr* (7:191): "One of the knowers of Allah said: A certain group that has not yet come up in our time but shall show up at the end of time, will curse the scholars and insult the jurists." On Mu'ādh ؓ see the excellent biographical notice by Abū Ghudda in his marginalia on al-Qarāfī's *al-Iḥkām* (p. 47-50).

[96] A sound *mawqūf* report from Ibn Mas'ūd narrated by Aḥmad (1:379 §3599 =Shākir ed. 3:505 §3600 *isnād ṣaḥīḥ*=al-Arna'ūṭ ed. 6:84 §3600 *isnād ḥasan*), also al-Bazzār in his *Zawā'id* (§130), al-Ṭabarānī in *al-Kabīr* (§8582, 8593) with chains of trustworthy narrators cf. al-Haythamī (1:177-178); also al-Khaṭīb, *al-Faqīh wal-Mutafaqqih* (1:167=1:422 §445) and al-Bayhaqī in *al-I'tiqād* (p. 208).

[97] Narrated from Ibn Mas'ūd by Ibn 'Abd al-Barr in *Jāmi' Bayān al-'Ilm* (2:947 §1810) and from Ibn 'Umar by Abū Nu'aym in the *Ḥilya* (1:305-306). Ibn Abī Zayd cites it from Ibn Mas'ūd in *al-Jāmi' fil-Sunan* (1982 ed. p. 118-119=1990 ed. p. 151 §20).

45. The Prophet ﷺ already spelled out the principle stated by Ibn Mas'ūd in the above statement when he ﷺ said: "My Community shall never concur on error. Therefore, when you see disagreement, you must stay with the largest mass."[98] Another version states: "Allah shall not make my [or: this] Community ever concur on error. The Hand of Allah is with the *Jamā'a*."[99] Another version continues: "Whoever dissents from them departs to Hell."[100]

The Prophet ﷺ also said: "The Hand of Allah is with the *Jamā'a*."[101] Al-Ṭabarī defined the *Jamā'a* as "the largest mass."[102] Another version continues: "Follow the largest mass, for verily whoever dissents from them departs to Hell."[103]

[98] Narrated from Anas by Ibn Mājah, 'Abd ibn Ḥumayd in his *Musnad* (p. 367 §1220), and al-Lālikā'ī in his *Sharḥ Uṣūl al-I'tiqād* (1:105 §153), all with very weak chains cf. al-Būṣīrī in the *Miṣbāḥ* (4:169) but the ḥadīth is declared sound by al-Ṣuyūṭī in *al-Jāmi' al-Ṣaghīr* due to the multiplicity of its chains.
[99] Narrated from Ibn 'Abbās by al-Bayhaqī in *al-Asmā' wal-Ṣifāt* (al-Ḥāshidī ed. 2:136 §702 *isnād ṣaḥīḥ*).
[100] Narrated from Ibn 'Umar by al-Tirmidhī *(gharīb)* with a weak chain.
[101] Narrated from Ibn 'Abbās by al-Tirmidhī *(gharīb)* with a chain of trustworthy narrators.
[102] Cf. *Fatḥ al-Bārī*, ḥadīth of Ḥudhayfa: "People used to ask the Messenger of Allah ﷺ about the good, but I wished to ask him about the evil..." and al-Mubārakfūrī, *Tuḥfat al-Aḥwadhī*, ḥadīth "The Hand of Allah is with the *Jamā'a*."
[103] Narrated from Ibn 'Abbās by al-Ḥākim and al-Ṭabarī, and from Ibn 'Umar by Abū Nu'aym in the *Ḥilya* (3:37), al-Ḥākim with three chains (1:115-116=1990 ed. 1:199-201), al-Lālikā'ī in his *Sharḥ Uṣūl* (1:106), al-Dānī in *al-Sunan al-Wārida fīl-Fitan* (3:748), al-Ḥakīm al-Tirmidhī in *Nawādir al-Uṣūl* (*Aṣl* 88), and al-Daylamī in *Musnad al-Firdaws* (5:258). The late Shaykh 'Abd al-Fattāḥ Abū Ghudda wrote in his appendix to Ibn 'Abd al-Barr's *al-Intiqā'* (p. 348-349): "It happened that the self-important claimant to scholarship, al-Albānī, commented on al-Tibrīzī's *Mishkāt al-Maṣābīḥ* (1:26)... at the ḥadīth §147: From Ibn 'Umar: He said: The Messenger of Allah ﷺ said: 'Follow the largest mass *(al-sawād al-a'ẓam)* for whoever deviates, deviates into the Fire.' ... Al-Albānī then said: '... I did not find it in any of the known books of the Sunna, not even the 'Dictation' monographs *(al-Amālī)* nor the 'Benefits' *(al-Fawā'id)*, nor the rest of the monographs that I looked up, all totalling hundreds of books;' – this is what he said! – 'nor did al-Suyūṭī mention it in *al-Jāmi' al-Kabīr*.' Now this is a sweeping, categorical denial as you can see, whereas the said ḥadīth was cited by al-Sakhāwī in *al-Maqāṣid al-Ḥasana*

The Prophet ﷺ also said, "The Israelites divided into seventy-one sects, seventy of which are in the Fire; the Christians into seventy-two sects, seventy-one of which are in the Fire; and this Community shall separate into seventy-three sects, all of them in the Fire except one which will enter Paradise." We said: "Describe it for us." He said: "The *Sawād al-A'ẓam*."[104]

Abū Umāma is also related to say, "You must stick with the largest mass." When asked to define it, he said, "This verse in Sūrat al-Nūr: {*Say: Obey Allah and obey the Messenger. But if you turn away, then it is for him to do only that wherewith he has been charged, and for you to do only that wherewith you have been charged. If you obey him, you will go aright. But the Messenger has no other charge than to convey (the message), plainly*} (24:54)."[105] The *Sawād al-A'ẓam* means "a massive gathering of human beings" as ascertained by the narration that during his Ascension the Prophet ﷺ passed by Prophets followed by their nations and he passed by Prophets followed by their groups and he passed by Prophets followed by no one until he saw a tremendous throng

(p. 406) and the *muḥaddith* al-'Ajlūnī in *Kashf al-Khafā* (2:350)... [quoting] Abū Nu'aym in the *Ḥilya*, al-Ḥākim in his *Mustadrak*, al-Lālika'ī in *al-Sunna*, Ibn Mandah, and al-Ḍiyā' [al-Maqdisī] in *al-Mukhtāra*.... The ḥadīth is found in all those books which are in everyone's hands, yet al-Albānī rejected it by saying: 'I did not find it in any of the known books of the Sunna, not even the *Amālī* nor the *Fawā'id*, nor the rest of the monographs that I looked up, all totalling hundreds of books'!! But to reject a hadith in part or in whole or any word in it is not something the likes of us can do for we are weak in memory and rely on books. It is imperative, in this noble Science, to possess a strong, vast, and swift memory in addition to the attributes that I have mentioned [elsewhere] before, together with discretion and prudence, soberness, and consistency in using terms of rejection with utmost precaution. And Allah Most High knows best."

[104]Narrated from Abū Umāma by al-Ṭabarānī in *al-Kabīr* and *Awsaṭ* with trustworthy narrators cf. al-Haythamī (7:258-259), Ibn Abī Shayba (7:554), Ibn Abī 'Āṣim in *al-Sunna* (1:34), Abū Naṣr al-Marwazī in *al-Sunna* (p. 22 §55), and al-Bayhaqī in *al-Sunan* (8:188).

[105]Narrated by Aḥmad, al-Bazzār, and al-Ṭabarānī with trustworthy narrators cf. al-Haythamī.

(sawād ʿaẓīm) and said: "Who are these?" The answer came: "These are Mūsā and his nation, but raise your head and look up," whereupon the Prophet ﷺ said: "[I saw] a tremendous throng *(sawād ʿaẓīm)* that had blocked up the entire firmament from this side and that!" And it was said: "These are your Nation..."[106]

46. Ḥudhayfa ibn al-Yamān ؓ said: "Only three types of persons give *fatwās* to people: A man who is either an Imām or a governor, and a man who can tell the abrogating verses of the Qur'ān from the abrogated." They asked: "Who is such a man?" He said: "ʿUmar ibn al-Khaṭṭāb. Other than those three types, there are only overreaching fools."[107]

47. ʿImrān ibn Ḥuṣayn ؓ: "The Qur'ān was revealed and the Messenger of Allah instituted the *Sunan*; so follow us [Companions] or, by Allah! if you do not, you shall go astray."[108]

48. A man asked ʿAbd Allah ibn ʿUmar: "Abū ʿAbd al-Raḥmān, we find the prayer of fear (*ṣalāt al-khawf*) and the prayer of residence (*ṣalāt al-ḥaḍar*) in the Qur'ān, but we do not find the prayer of travel (*ṣalāt al-safar*)!" Ibn ʿUmar replied: "Dear cousin: Allah ﷻ sent forth Muḥammad ﷺ and we knew nothing. We only do whatever we saw him do."[109]

[106]Narrated from Ibn ʿAbbās by al-Tirmidhī *(ḥasan ṣaḥīḥ).*

[107]Narrated from Muḥammad ibn Sīrīn by al-Dārimī with a chain of sound narrators.

[108]Narrated by Aḥmad with a fair-to-weak chain because of ʿAlī ibn Zayd ibn Judʿān cf. al-Būṣirī in *Miṣbāḥ al-Zujāja* (2:95) although al-Tirmidhī considers him "truthful" (*ṣadūq*), he is retained by Ibn Khuzayma and by Muslim as an auxiliary narrator (*maqrūn*), Ibn Ḥajar grades his chain fair in the *Fatḥ* (7:39), al-Haythamī (7:183, 4:310, 9:71-72) grades him "trustworthy with a poor memory" (*thiqa sayyiʾ al-ḥafẓ*) and his narrations "fair," al-Dhahabī in his marginalia on al-Ḥākim (3:190=1990 ed. 3:210) grades his chain passable (*ṣāliḥ*), and Ibn Kathīr in *al-Bidāya* (6:137-138) grades him as meeting the authenticity criteria of the *Sunan*. Cf. also al-Suyūṭī, *Khaṣāʾiṣ* (2:257).

[109]A sound narration from Ibn Shihāb by Mālik, al-Nasāʾī, Ibn Mājah, and Aḥmad.

49. Similarly Jābir ibn ʿAbd Allah ﷺ said: "The Messenger of Allah ﷺ was among us while the Qur'ān was being revealed to him and he knew its explanation. Whatever he put into practice, we put into practice."[110]

[110] Narrated from Muḥammad al-Bāqir as part of a long ḥadīth by Muslim, Abū Dāwūd, and Aḥmad.

Successor-Reports on the Exemplariness of the Companions and Successors in the Religion

50. Ibrāhīm al-Nakha'ī ﷺ said: "If the Companions made ablution to the wrists I swear I would do the same, even as I read the verse of ablution as stating {*to the elbows*} (5:6)."[111]

51. 'Umar ibn 'Abd al-'Azīz ﷺ said in a certain matter in which he had changed his mind after some time: "It was an opinion which I considered true (*innamā huwa ra'yun ra'aytuhu*), therefore, whoever wishes, let him follow it, and whoever wishes, let him leave it."[112]

52. Muḥammad ibn Sīrīn ﷺ, when asked about certain beverages, would say: "An Imām of right guidance forbade them – 'Umar ibn 'Abd al-'Azīz, Allah be well-pleased with him and grant him mercy!"[113]

53. Mālik ﷺ related that 'Umar ibn 'Abd al-'Azīz said:

> The Messenger of Allah ﷺ and those in authority after him instituted ways (*sanna sunanan*). To hold to these ways is to hold fast to the Book of Allah and to achieve strength in order to establish the Religion of Allah. It is not for anyone to substitute or modify or probe any of those ways. Whoever is guided by them is well-guided. Whoever seeks them to gain victory shall achieve victory. Whoever leaves them and follows the path of other than the Muslims, Allah ﷻ shall abandon him to what he has taken upon himself, He shall make him burn in Hellfire. A hapless journey's end!" [A reference to the verse {*And whosoever opposes the Messenger after the guidance (of Allah) has been*

[111]Ibrāhīm al-Nakha'ī as cited by Ibn Abī Zayd al-Qayrawānī in *al-Jāmi' fil-Sunan* (p. 150 §18).
[112]In Ibn Abī Shayba (5:487) and from 'Alī in al-Ṭabarānī's *Awsaṭ* (1:180, 2:69).
[113]Narrated from Ibn 'Awn by Abū Nu'aym in the *Ḥilya* (5:258).

manifested unto him, and follows other than the believers' way, We appoint for him that unto which he himself has turned, and expose him unto hell – a hapless journey's end!} (4:115).][114]

54. When the Companions were mentioned, al-Ḥasan al-Baṣrī ﵁ said: "They were the purest of heart in all this Community, the deepest in knowledge, the least in affectation! They were a people whom Allah ﷻ chose for His Prophet's ﷺ company. Therefore imitate their manners and their ways, for truly they were – by the Lord of the Kaʿba! – on the straight path."[115]

55. When Ibn Mahdī took care of Sufyān al-Thawrī in his last days, he asked him about the permissibility of leaving the congregational prayer for that reason. Sufyān said: "Serving a Muslim in need for one hour is better than congregational prayer." Ibn Mahdī said: "From whom did you hear this?" Sufyān replied: "ʿĀṣim ibn ʿUbayd Allah narrated to me from ʿAbd Allah ibn ʿĀmir ibn Rabīʿa, from his father [the Companion ʿĀmir ibn Rabīʿa al-ʿAnzī]: 'I would prefer serving one man among the Muslims who is in need for a single day, to sixty years of congregational prayers in which I never missed the opening *takbīra*!'"[116] Al-Shāfiʿī said: "I never saw a man who follows the Sunna more rigorously or in whose body I would love to be more than Sufyān al-Thawrī."[117]

[114]Narrated from Muṭarrif by Abū Nuʿaym in *Ḥilyat al-Awliyā* (1985 ed. 6:324), al-Dhahabī in the *Siyar* (Risāla ed. 8:98-99), Ibn al-Qayyim in his commentary on Abū Dāwūd's *Sunan* (in ʿAẓīm Ābādī's *ʿAwn al-Maʿbūd* 13:45), and al-Suyūṭī in *al-Durr al-Manthūr* (1:393).
[115]Narrated by Ibn ʿAbd al-Barr in *Jāmiʿ Bayān al-ʿIlm* (2:946 §1807).
[116]Narrated by al-Dhahabī in the *Siyar* (7:189-190).
[117]Narrated by Abū Nuʿaym in the *Ḥilya* (7:6) and al-Dhahabī in the *Siyar* (7:192).

56. Abū Ḥātim al-Rāzī narrated in his *Manāqib al-Shāfiʿī* from Ḥarmala that Imām al-Shāfiʿī said: "The Caliphs (*al-khulafāʾ*) are five: Abū Bakr, ʿUmar, ʿUthmān, ʿAlī, and ʿUmar ibn ʿAbd al-ʿAzīz," meaning, the Rightly-Guided Caliphs. In his *Dīwān* al-Shāfiʿī named them "leaders of their people, by whose guidance one obtains guidance."

57. Ibn Wahb narrated that Imām Mālik said: "A ruling is one of two kinds (*al-ḥukmu ḥukmān*): a ruling brought by the Book of Allah and a ruling stipulated by the Sunna." Mālik also said: "And the opinion of a *mujtahid* for it may be that he shall be granted success." He also mentioned the pretender and disparaged him.[118]

[118]Narrated from Ibn Wahb by Ibn ʿAbd al-Barr in *al-Tamhīd* (4:266).

Ibn Rajab's Commentary on the Ḥadīth: "You Must Follow My Sunna and the Sunna of the Well-Guided Successors"[119]

Al-ʿIrbāḍ ibn Sāriya[120] ﷺ said:

> The Messenger of Allah ﷺ prayed among us that day then turned to face us and admonished us intensely so that the eyes wept and the hearts trembled. A man said: "Messenger of Allah! This resembles the admonishment of one who bids farewell, therefore what solemn promise do you require of us?" He replied: "I exhort you to beware of Allah ﷻ! I exhort you to hear and obey even if your leader is a black Ethiopian. Lo! Whoever of you lives shall live to see great divisions. **You must follow my Sunna and the Sunna of the rightly-guided, upright successors after me.** Hold on to it firmly, bite upon it with your very jaws! Beware of newfangled matters. Every newfangled matter is an innovation, and every innovation is misguidance."[121]

Concerning the saying of the Prophet ﷺ: "Lo! Whoever of you lives shall live to see great divisions. You must follow my Sunna and the Sunna of the rightly-guided, upright successors after me. Hold on to it firmly, bite upon it with your very jaws!" By saying this he ﷺ gave information about what would befall his Community after him in the way of abundant divergences both in the foundations of the Religion and its branches, in deeds, sayings,

[119] Ibn Rajab, *Jāmiʿ al-ʿUlūm wal-Ḥikam* (2:43-48).

[120] One of "those who wept much" (*al-bakkāʾun*) as stated by Ibn Abī ʿĀṣim in *al-Sunna* (p. 29 §54). It was concerning him that the following verse was revealed: {*Nor unto those whom, when they came to you asking that you should mount them, you did tell: I cannot find whereon to mount you. They turned back with eyes flowing with tears, for sorrow that they could not find the means to spend*} (9:92) as stated in al-Ājurrī's *al-Sharīʿa* (p. 55). He was one of "the People of the Shelter" (*Ahl al-Ṣuffa*) as listed by Abū Nuʿaym in *Ḥilyat al-Awliyāʾ* (1:398-400, 2:390-392) and al-Sakhāwī in *al-Fatāwā al-Ḥadīthiyya* (p. 300-301).

[121] See note 33.

and doctrines. This is in agreement with what was narrated from him pertaining to the division of his Community into seventy-odd sects, all of them in the Fire but one – that which remains on his path and that of his Companions.[122] Similarly, in this ḥadīth he has ordered that when divisions and divergences take place, we must hold fast to his Sunna and the Sunna of the well-guided successors after him.

"Sunna" means the path that is trodden (*al-ṭarīq al-maslūk*), which entails holding fast to whatever he and his Rightly-Guided successors held of doctrines, deeds, and sayings. This is the perfect and complete Sunna. That is why the *Salaf* of old refrained from applying the name "Sunna" to anything that fell short of this. This meaning has been related from al-Ḥasan [al-Baṣrī], al-Awzāʿī, and al-Fuḍayl ibn ʿIyāḍ. Many of the later Ulema apply the name "Sunna" specifically to what pertains to doctrine.[123] For the Sunna is the root of the Religion and whoever contravenes it is in great peril.

In the mention of the phrase ["You must follow..."] after his order to hear and obey those in command, is a sign that no obedience is due to those in command in other than obeying Allah ﷻ, just as it is authentically related from him ﷺ that he said: "Obedience is only in good matters."[124] It is also related in the *Musnad* from Anas that Muʿādh ibn Jabal said: "Messenger of Allah, what do you say if there are over us rulers who do not follow your Sunna (*lā yastannūna bisunnatik*), nor abide by your commands? What do you order [us] with respect to them?" The Messenger of Allah ﷺ said: "No obedience is due to whoever does not obey Allah."[125] Ibn Mājah narrated from Ibn Masʿūd ﷺ

[122]See § 19.

[123]Cf. above, page 20.

[124]See note 286.

[125]Narrated by Aḥmad and Abū Yaʿlā (7:102) with a chain containing ʿAmr ibn Zunayb who is unknown according to al-Haythamī (5:225). Al-Ḍiyā' al-Maqdisī

that the Messenger of Allah ﷺ said: "After me your affairs will be ruled by men who shall extinguish the Sunna with innovation and practice innovation. They shall delay the prayer from its time." Ibn Mas'ūd said: "Messenger of Allah, if I see them what should I do?" He replied: "No obedience is due to whoever does not obey Allah"[126]

The sequence of the Prophet's ﷺ order to follow his Sunna and the Sunna of the well-guided Successors, coming after his order to hear and obey governors generally, is a proof that **the Sunna of the Rightly-Guided Successors must be followed just as his own Sunna must be followed**, contrary to the case of other governors.

Aḥmad and al-Tirmidhī narrate from Ḥudhayfa ؓ:

> We were sitting with the Prophet ﷺ when he said: "Truly I know not the remaining extent of my stay among you. So take for your leaders the two that come after me, <gesturing toward>[127] Abū Bakr[128] and 'Umar,[129] follow 'Ammār's[130] guidance,[131] and

declared its chain fair (ḥasan) in *al-Aḥādīth al-Mukhtāra* (6:319) while al-Munāwī (6:432) claimed that Ibn Ḥajar said: "Its chain is strong" but the truth is Ibn Ḥajar was referring to a different chain (see *Fatḥ al-Bārī*, 1959 ed. 13:123). This ḥadīth is confirmed by the next one.

[126] Narrated by Ibn Mājah and Aḥmad with three chains, one of them sound, as well as al-Ṭabarānī in *al-Kabīr*. Also narrated from 'Ubāda ibn al-Ṣāmit as part of a longer ḥadīth by Aḥmad, al-Ṭabarānī, and al-Ḥākim.

[127] In some sound narrations, while other sound narrations omit the Prophet's ﷺ gesture and name Abū Bakr and 'Umar within his direct speech.

[128] This Prophetic stipulation for Abū Bakr's succession is confirmed by the sound ḥadīth whereby a woman came to the Prophet ﷺ asking for something, whereupon he told her to come back at some other time, so she asked: "Messenger of Allah! What if I come back but do not find you?" by which she meant death. The Prophet ﷺ replied: "Then go to Abū Bakr." Narrated from Jubayr ibn Muṭ'im by al-Bukhārī and Muslim. Al-Shāfi'ī said: "In this is a proof for Abū Bakr's successorship." Cf. note 43 above.

[129] Narrated to this point from Ḥudhayfa ibn al-Yamān by al-Tirmidhī with a chain containing the Shī'ī Salīm al-Murādī who is most probably trustworthy [al-Arna'ūṭ, *Ṣaḥīḥ Ibn Ḥibbān* (15:328 n. 2)] although weak according to some [al-

whatever Ibn Mas'ūd narrates to you, believe it."[132]

Mizzī, *Tahdhīb al-Kamāl* (10:161); al-'Uqaylī, *al-Ḍu'afā'* (2:150)], Ibn Mājah, Ibn Abī Shayba (6:350), Ibn Abī 'Āṣim in *al-Sunna* (p. 531-532 §1148-1149, *ṣaḥīḥ*), Aḥmad with two chains in *Faḍā'il al-Ṣaḥāba* (1:332) and - without the first sentence - from Ḥudhayfa by al-Tirmidhī (*ḥasan*, confirmed by al-Dhahabī in the *Siyar* 1-2:512 with regard to the chain), Aḥmad (Arna'ūṭ ed. 38:280-282 §23245 *ḥasan*=al-Zayn ed. 16:566-567 §23138) and with three chains in *Faḍā'il al-Ṣaḥāba* (1:238, 1:359, 1:426), al-Ṭaḥāwī with six sound chains according to al-Arna'ūṭ in *Sharḥ Mushkil al-Āthār* (3:257-259 §1227-1232), al-Bayhaqī in *al-Sunan al-Kubrā* (5:212 §9826, 8:153 §16353), Ibn Balbān in *Tuḥfat al-Ṣiddīq* (p. 63-64), al-Khalīlī who declared it sound in *al-Irshād* (1:378, 2:664-665), and Ibn 'Abd al-Barr in *al-Tamhīd* (22:126); also from Ibn Mas'ūd by al-Tirmidhī (*ḥasan*) through five chains and Aḥmad in *Faḍā'il al-Ṣaḥāba* (1:238); and from Ibn 'Umar with an erroneous chain as stated by Ibn Ḥajar in *Lisān al-Mīzān* (1:188) and *Talkhīṣ al-Ḥabīr* (4:190), cf. Ibn Kathīr, *Tuḥfa* (p. 165).

[130]'Ammār ibn Yāsir ibn 'Āmir Abū al-Yaqẓān al-'Anasī, one of the Foremost and First (*al-sābiqūn al-awwalūn*) among the Emigrants, one of seven who first made public their Islam, he and his father used to be tortured by the pagans of Makka, whereupon the Prophet ﷺ would pass them by and say: "Bear patiently, Family of Yāsir, your tryst is in Paradise!" He emigrated to Madīna and fought in all the battles, then later at al-Yamāma. 'Alī ؓ and Khālid ibn Walīd ؓ respectively narrated from the Prophet ﷺ that the latter said: "'Ammār is filled with belief to his marrow" and "Whoever fights 'Ammār, Allah ﷻ fights him; and whoever angers 'Ammār, Allah ﷻ is angry with him!" The reports have reached the rank of mass transmission (*tawātur*) that the Prophet ﷺ foretold his death at the hands of "the rebellious faction" (*al-firqat al-bāghiya*). He was killed in the year 87 at the battle of Ṣiffīn on 'Alī's side, at the age of 93. See Ibn Ḥajar, *al-Iṣāba* (4:575).

[131]Narrated to this point from Ḥudhayfa by Ibn Abī Shayba (7:433) but with the wording, "Hold fast to 'Ammār's covenant" (*wa-tamassakū bi-'ahdi 'Ammār*).

[132]A fair narration from Ḥudhayfa by al-Tirmidhī (*ḥasan*), Aḥmad in the *Musnad* (Arna'ūṭ ed. 38:309-311 §23275 cf. 38:418-419 §23419 *ḥasan*=al-Zayn ed. 16:576 §23169, 16:620 §23312) as well as in *Faḍā'il al-Ṣaḥāba* (§479), Ibn Ḥibbān with a fair chain as stated by al-Arna'ūṭ (15:327-328 §6902), Ibn Sa'd with the same chain (2:334), al-Khallāl in *al-Sunna* (1:275), al-Ḥākim (3:75=1990 ed. 3:79), al-Khaṭīb in *Tārīkh Baghdād* (4:346, 12:20), and al-Haythamī in *Mawārid al-Ẓam'ān* (p. 538). Some narrations such as Ibn Ḥibbān's and al-Haythamī's have the wording "accept it" (*fa-qbalūh*) instead of "believe it" (*fa-ṣaddiqūh*) while some have the [weak] wording "and hold fast to 'Ammār's covenant." Also narrated from Ibn Mas'ūd by al-Tirmidhī (*ḥasan gharīb*) with a weak chain because of Yaḥyā ibn Salama ibn Kuhayl as stated by Ibn Kathīr in *Tuḥfat al-Ṭālib* (p. 164-165).

Another narration states: "Hold fast to Ibn Umm ʿAbd's [= Ibn Masʿūd's] covenant[133] and follow ʿAmmār's guidance."[134]

[133] ʿAlī ﷺ narrates that the Messenger of Allah ﷺ summoned Ibn Masʿūd one day. He [came and] climbed a tree to get something for him [to eat]. His companions looked at ʿAbd Allah's leg and laughed at the slenderness (*ḥumūsha*) of his legs, whereupon the Messenger of Allah ﷺ said: "Why are you laughing? I swear that the foot of ʿAbd Allah shall weigh more heavily than Uḥud in the Balance on the Day of Judgment." Narrated by al-Ḥākim (§5385) who declared it *ṣaḥīḥ* and al-Dhahabī concurred. Also narrated from Qarra ibn Iyās al-Muzanī in the following wording: Ibn Masʿūd climbed a tree and they started laughing at the slenderness of his legs, whereupon the Prophet ﷺ said: "I swear that they shall be heavier in the Balance than Mount Uḥud." Narrated by Aḥmad (§920), Abū Yaʿlā (§539), al-Ṭabarānī in *al-Kabīr* (§38516), Ibn Saʿd (3:109), Abū Nuʿaym in *Ḥilyat al-Awliyā* (1:127), and al-Ḥākim. Al-Haythamī indicated that its chain was sound (§15561).

[134] Narrated from Ḥudhayfa by al-Tirmidhī (*ḥasan gharīb*), Aḥmad (Arna'ūṭ ed. 38:399 §23386 *isnād layyin*=al-Zayn ed. 16:611 §23279 *isnād ṣaḥīḥ*) and in *Faḍā'il al-Ṣaḥāba* (1:187), al-Khaṭīb in *Tārīkh Baghdād* (14:366 and 7:402 – the latter with a chain containing Abū Farwa who is weak. Also narrated – without the first sentence – by al-Ṭaḥāwī with several sound and fair chains according to al-Arna'ūṭ in *Sharḥ Mushkil al-Āthār* (3:256-257 §1224-1226, 3:259 §1233), Ibn Abī Shayba (12:11), al-Ḥākim (3:75-76=1990 ed. 3:79-80) with three sound chains as stated by him and al-Dhahabī, al-Bayhaqī in *al-Sunan al-Kubrā* (8:153 §16352), *al-Madkhal* (p. 122), and *al-Iʿtiqād* (p. 340-341), and al-Ṭabarānī in *al-Awsaṭ* with a weak chain as indicated by al-Haythamī (§15606). Also narrated from Ibn Masʿūd by Tammām al-Rāzī in *al-Fawā'id* (2:276) and al-Ṭabarānī in *al-Kabīr* (9:72), and from Anas by al-Ṭabarānī as stated by al-ʿAjlūnī in *Kashf al-Khafā* (1:181). Al-Ṭabarānī in *Musnad al-Shāmiyyīn* (2:57) and al-Qaṣṣār as stated by al-Ṭabarī in *al-Riyāḍ al-Naḍira* (1:348) also narrate from Abū al-Dardā' the following wording: "take for your leaders the two that come after me: Abū Bakr and ʿUmar, for truly they are Allah's rope extended, and whoever holds fast to them {*has grasped a firm handhold which will never break*}" (2:156) with chains containing unknown narrators as stated by al-Haythamī (9:53). This ḥadīth was declared weak by two ḥadīth Masters only: Ibn Ḥazm in *al-Iḥkām* (6:242-243) and al-Bazzār. Their ruling was refuted by Ibn Ḥajar in *Talkhīṣ al-Ḥabīr* (4:190) where he declared that the chains of the ḥadīth are good and firmly established as authentic. Note that Ibn Ḥazm had no knowledge of al-Tirmidhī's and Ibn Mājah's *Sunan*.

The Messenger of Allah ﷺ therefore explicitly stipulated (*naṣṣa*) toward the end of his life those who should be followed as leaders after him.[135] The Rightly-Guided Caliphs whom he ordered people to take as their leaders were Abū Bakr, ʿUmar, ʿUthmān, and ʿAlī ☬, for it was related in the ḥadīth of Safīna[136] from the Prophet ﷺ: "Successorship (*al-khilāfa*) after me shall last for thirty years. After that, there will be kingship."[137] Imām Aḥmad declared this narration sound and adduced it as a proof for the caliphate of the four Imāms.[138] Many of the Imāms also stipulated that ʿUmar ibn ʿAbd al-ʿAzīz is also a Rightly-Guided successor.

Another proof [for following the Sunna of the rightly-guided successors] is what Imām Aḥmad related from Ḥudhayfa's ☬ narration from the Prophet ﷺ who said: "There will be Prophethood among you for as long as Allah wishes. Then He will lift it up when He wishes. Then there will be caliphate after the pattern (*minhāj*) of Prophethood for as long as Allah wishes. Then He will lift it up when He wishes. Then there will be a trying kingship (*mulkan ʿāḍḍan*) for as long as Allah wishes it to be. Then He will lift it up when He wishes. Then there will be a tyrannical kingship (*mulkan jabriyyatan*) for as long as Allah wishes it to be.

---

[135] Abū Nuʿaym said in *Dalāʾil al-Nubuwwa* (1989 ed. p. 130): "This ḥadīth is among the signs of Prophethood whereby he foretold that his successor would be Abū Bakr and the latter's successor would be ʿUmar, and it was just as he said."

[136] Safīna ☬ (d. 71) is the Prophet's ﷺ freedman whose name was Mahrān. One day, when the Prophet ﷺ saw him carrying all his comrades' belongings, the Prophet ﷺ said to him: "Today you are none other than a ship (*safīna*)" (*mā kunta al-yawma illā safīna*). Narrated from Safīna by Aḥmad with a fair chain and others. Al-Mizzī in *Tahdhīb al-Kamāl* (7:388) and al-Dhahabī in the *Siyar* (4:324) narrate that when he alighted on a desert island after a shipwreck and saw a lion he said: "Lion! I am Safīna, the freedman of the Messenger of Allah ﷺ," whereupon the lion showed him the way and muttered something. Safīna said: "I believe he meant *salām*." The same happened to the *Tābiʿī* Ṣila ibn Ashyam.

[137] See note 56.

[138] See note 57.

Then He will lift it up when He wishes. Then there will be successorship on the pattern of Prophethood."[139]

A man came to see ʿUmar ibn ʿAbd al-ʿAzīz when the latter was made caliph and related to him the above report. ʿUmar was pleased to hear it.

Muḥammad ibn Sīrīn, when asked about certain beverages, would say: "An Imām of right guidance forbade it – ʿUmar ibn ʿAbd al-ʿAzīz, may Allah be well-pleased with him and grant him mercy."[140]

The Ulema differed about the consensus of the Four Caliphs: Does it constitute Consensus or merely a major proof (*ḥujja*), and does this apply if other Companions differ with them or only when not? Two opinions are related from Imām Aḥmad concerning this. Abū Khāzim al-Ḥanafī in the time of al-Muʿtaḍid ruled for the inheritor-status of maternal relatives, paying no heed to whoever differed with the [Four] Caliphs, and this ruling of his was enforced far and wide.

[139]A sound-chained ḥadīth narrated from Ḥudhayfa ibn al-Yamān by Aḥmad (al-Zayn ed. 14:163 §18319 *isnād ṣaḥīḥ*=al-Arna'ūṭ 30:355-357 §18406 *isnād ḥasan*), al-Bazzār (7:223-224 §2796), al-Ṭabarānī in part in *al-Awsaṭ* (§6577) cf. al-Haythamī (5:188-189): "Narrated by Aḥmad, al-Bazzār with a more complete wording, and al-Ṭabarānī partly, in *al-Awsaṭ*. The narrators in its chain are trustworthy"; al-Ṭayālisī in his *Musnad* (p. 58-59 §438), and al-Dāraquṭnī in *al-Afrād* (2:127). Cited by Ibn Rajab in *Jāmiʿ al-ʿUlūm wal-Ḥikam* (Arna'ūṭ ed. 2:122 *ḥasan*). Also narrated from Abu ʿUbayda by al-Ṭabarānī in *al-Kabīr* (1:157) with the wording "There will be kingship and tyranny" after the mention of the first caliphate. Al-Baʿlī in *al-Arbaʿūn min Riyāḍ al-Janna min Āthār Ahl al-Sunna* cites it (§20) and declares it sound. The narration is similar to the ḥadīth: "Successorship of Prophethood" as indicated by Ibn Ḥajar who said in *Fatḥ al-Bārī* (1959 ed. 12:392 §6600): "By 'successorship after me,' he meant successorship of Prophethood; as for Muʿāwiya and those who followed him, most of them were after the pattern of kings, even if they are still called 'successors' (*khulafā'*), and Allah knows best." The ḥadīth he cites goes as follows: The Prophet ﷺ asked: "Did any of you see anything in his dream?" etc. (see § 6 above).

[140]Narrated from Ibn ʿAwn by Abū Nuʿaym in the *Ḥilya* (5:258).

What if one of the Four Caliphs holds a certain position [in *ijtihād*] in which none of the other three contradicts him, but others of the Companions do: does the caliph's position have precedence over the other Companions? There are also two kinds of responses from the Ulema pertaining to this. What was textually stipulated by Aḥmad is that the Caliph's position takes precedence over that of the other Companions. Thus did al-Khaṭṭābī and others relate it.

The sayings of most of the *Salaf* confirm this position, particularly with regard to 'Umar ibn al-Khaṭṭāb ☙. For it was narrated fom the Prophet ﷺ through different chains that he said: "Allah has engraved truth on the tongue of 'Umar and his heart."[141] 'Umar ibn 'Abd al-'Azīz used to follow 'Umar's rulings, adducing this Prophetic ḥadīth as his proof.

Mālik said that 'Umar ibn 'Abd al-'Azīz said:

> The Messenger of Allah ﷺ and those in authority after him instituted ways (*sanna sunanan*). To hold to these ways is to hold fast to the Book of Allah and to achieve strength in order to establish the Religion of Allah. It is not for anyone to substitute nor modify nor probe any of those ways. Whoever is guided by them is well-guided. Whoever seeks them to gain victory shall achieve victory. Whoever leaves them and follows the path of other than the Muslims, Allah ﷻ shall abandon him to what he has taken upon himself and He shall make him burn in Hellfire. A hapless journey's end! [A reference to the verse {*And whosoever opposes the messenger after the guidance (of Allah) has been manifested unto him, and follows other than the believers' way, We appoint for him that unto which he himself has turned, and expose him unto hell – a hapless journey's end!*} (4:115).][142]

[141] See note 52.
[142] See note 114.

ʿAbd Allah ibn al-Ḥakam narrated from Mālik that he said: "I like ʿUmar [ibn ʿAbd al-ʿAzīz]'s resolve in this matter." In fact, ʿAbd al-Raḥmān ibn Mahdī narrated these words directly from Mālik, not from ʿUmar. Khalaf ibn Khalīfa said: "I saw ʿUmar ibn ʿAbd al-ʿAzīz addressing the people when he was caliph, and he said in his sermon: 'Lo! Truly what the Messenger of Allah ﷺ and his Two Companions instituted is a duty of the Religion. We put it into practice and we deem it conclusive.'"[143]

Abū Nuʿaym narrated from ʿArzab al-Kindī that the Messenger of Allah ﷺ said: "New matters shall arise after me, so endeavor to stick to (*ijtahidū ilā an talzamū*) whatever ʿUmar innovates (*mā aḥdatha ʿUmar*)."[144] ʿAlī ؓ used to follow ʿUmar's judgments and rulings, saying: "Truly ʿUmar was a wise leader (*kāna rashīd al-amr*)!"[145] Similarly, al-Ashʿath narrated from al-Shaʿbī that he said: "If the people differ about something, see what ʿUmar's judgment was in the matter. For ʿUmar did not pass a judgment in something without precedent except that he first consulted with others."[146] Mujāhid said: "If people differed about something, see what ʿUmar's judgment was in the matter." Ayyūb narrated from al-Shaʿbī that he said: "See what Muḥammad's ﷺ Community agreed upon, for Allah ﷻ would not make it concur on misguidance. If they differed, then see what ʿUmar ibn al-Khaṭṭāb did and follow it."[147]

[143]Narrated by Abū Nuʿaym in the *Ḥilya* (5:298).
[144]Narrated by Ibn Mandah in *Maʿrifat al-Ṣaḥāba* with a chain containing two unknown narrators as stated by Ibn Ḥajar in *al-Iṣāba* (4:483), including ʿAzrab Sinān, over whose Companion-status there is disagreement.
[145]See note 55.
[146]Narrated by Abū Nuʿaym in the *Ḥilya* (4:320).
[147]Narrated by Aḥmad in *al-ʿIlal* (2:258).

'Ikrima was asked about the status of the slave who gives birth to her master's son. He replied: "She is manumitted at the time her master dies." They asked him: "Based on what proof?" He said: "The Qur'ān." They asked: "Where in the Qur'ān?" He replied: "{*Obey Allah, and obey the messenger and those of you who are in authority*} (4:59), and 'Umar ؓ is among those in authority."[148] Wakī' said: "If 'Umar and 'Alī concur on something: that is authority." And it was narrated from Ibn Mas'ūd that he used to swear: "Truly the straight path is that upon which 'Umar was firmly established until he entered Paradise."

At any rate, whatever 'Umar gathered the Companions upon in agreement and whatever they concurred upon in his time: there is no doubt that that is the truth. [...] [Concerning] the ḥadīth of the Prophet ﷺ:

> In a dream I saw myself drawing water from a well. Abū Bakr came and drew a large bucket (*dhanūb*) or two, but there was some weakness in his efforts – and Allah forgives him. Then 'Umar ibn al-Khaṭṭāb came and the bucket turned into a huge pail in his hands. I never saw anyone do such accomplished work as he did until all the people drank to satiation and watered their camels that knelt down there. (Another version states:) I never saw a greater leader (*'abqarī*) among the people drawing water the way Ibn al-Khaṭṭāb drew water! (Another version states:) Until the trough was bursting with water.[149]

This is an indication that 'Umar ؓ did not die before he disposed of all matters in their proper order and all affairs were settled. This is explained by the length of his tenure and the undivided attention he gave to all events, while Abū Bakr's ؓ

---

[148]Narrated by Sa'īd ibn Manṣūr in his *Musnad* as stated by al-Suyūṭī in *al-Durr al-Manthūr* (1:316).
[149]See notes 46-47.

tenure was short and he was occupied with the conquests of new territories and the provision of troops, so he could not devote his attention to all events.[150] Perhaps, in the latter's tenure, he was not aware of everything that took place nor was every matter reported to him the way it was reported to ʿUmar. Thus did ʿUmar strive in directing people to the truth and point to them the right path to follow. May Allah be well-pleased with them!

[150] Cf. Imām al-Shāfiʿī above (§ 7 page 34-35) on the meaning of "some weakness."

The Meaning of *Bid'a*

***The first innovation** (bid'a) **that took place after the Messenger of Allah ﷺ was satiety** (al-shab').* – 'Ā'isha ؓ[151]

The lexical meaning of *bid'a* in the Arabic language is "novelty" while its technical meaning in Islam is a novelty begun after the time of the *Tābi'īn* in contravention of the Qur'ān and Sunna as defined variously by the authorities:

Al-Jurjānī: "Whatever contrivance (*fi'latun*) contradicts the Sunna, and it is named *bid'a* because whoever supports it innovated it without basis from an Imām. It consists in a novel matter which the Companions and Successors did not follow and which is unsupported by a legal proof."[152]

Imām Abū Shāma and Imām al-Suyūṭī: "Everything invented without precedent basis" (*kullu mukhtara'in min ghayri aṣlin sabaq*);[153]

Imām al-Lacknawī: "All that did not exist in the first three centuries and for which there is no basis among the Four Foundations of Islam" *i.e.*, Qur'ān, Sunna, *Ijmā'*, and *Qiyās*.[154]

Imām Ibn Ḥajar al-Haytamī: "*Bid'a* in terms of the Law is everything innovated in contravention of the Lawgiver's command and the latter's specific and general proof."[155]

Ibn al-Jawzī: "*Bid'a* in legal convention is whatever is blameworthy for contravening the foundations of the Law."[156]

[151] In al-Ṣan'ānī, *Subul al-Salām* (4:179).
[152] Al-Jurjānī, *Ta'rīfāt* (p. 62).
[153] Abū Shāma, *al-Bā'ith 'alā Inkār al-Bida' wal-Ḥawādith* (Ryadh 1990 ed. p. 13-14), al-Suyūṭī, *Tanwīr al-Ḥawālik* (1:137).
[154] Al-Lacknawī, *Iqāmat al-Ḥujja* (p. 12).
[155] Al-Haytamī, *al-Tabyīn fī Sharḥ al-Arba'īn* (p. 32).
[156] Ibn al-Jawzī, *Gharīb al-Ḥadīth* (1:61).

Qāḍī Abū Bakr Ibn al-ʿArabī: "Only the *bidʿa* that contradicts the Sunna is blameworthy."[157]

All of this elucidates Imām al-Shāfiʿīs luminous subdivision of *bidʿa* into two types, which we examine below. Thus, **it is not enough for something to be novel to be a *bidʿa***, contrary to the misunderstanding of those who use that term most vocally nowadays.

Some of the best works on the precise definition of *bidʿa* are:

[1] Imām ʿAbd al-Ḥayy al-Lacknawī's *Tuḥfat al-Akhyār* and

[2] the first part of his *Iqāmat al-Ḥujja* – both with a commentary by Shaykh ʿAbd al-Fattāḥ Abū Ghudda;

[3] Al-Sayyid ʿAbd Allah Maḥfūẓ al-Ḥaddād's masterpiece *al-Sunna wal-Bidʿa*;

[4] The most concise, most practical textbook on the topic to date, *Kalimatun ʿIlmiyyatun Hādiyatun fil-Bidʿati wa-Aḥkāmihā* by our beloved teacher Shaykh Wahbī Sulaymān Ghāwjī al-Albānī;

[5] Dr. ʿIzzat ʿAṭiyya's *al-Bidʿa: Taḥdīduhā wa-Mawqif al-Islāmi minhā*;

[6] Al-Sayyid ʿAbd Allah ibn al-Ṣiddīq al-Ghumārī's *Itqān al-Ṣunʿa fī Taḥqīq Maʿnā al-Bidʿa* ("Precise Handiwork in Ascertaining the Meaning of Innovation");

[7] Shaykh ʿĪsā al-Ḥimyarī's two works, *Ḍawʾ al-Shamʿa fī Taḥqīq Maʿnā al-Bidʿa* ("The Candlelight in Verifying the Meaning of *Bidʿa*") and

[8] *al-Bidʿatu al-Ḥasanatu Aṣlun min Uṣūl al-Tashrīʿ* ("The Excellent Innovation Is One of the Sources of Islamic Legislation");

157 Ibn al-ʿArabī, *ʿĀriḍat al-Aḥwadhī* (10:147).

[9] The fourth part of Sayyid Muḥammad ibn 'Alawī's book *Manhaj al-Salaf*;

[10] Chapter 15 of al-Sayyid Abūl-Ḥasanayn 'Abd Allah al-Hāshimī's *al-Salafiyya al-Mu'āṣira* and

[11] His *al-Ittibā' wal-Ibtidā'*.[158]

Shaykh Muḥammad Sa'īd Ramaḍān al-Būṭī said:

> There is no doubt that innovation (*bid'a*) is absolutely prohibited and that it is misguidance. [...] However, what is innovation? Innovation is "**every matter that was innovated and injected into the Religion while it is not part of it** (*al-bid'atu kullu amrin ustuḥditha wa-uqḥima fil-dīni wa-huwa laysa minh*)." As much as the expressions of the Ulema differ in explaining *bid'a* and defining it, none of those various expressions differs from this comprehensive meaning: "every matter that was innovated," that is, it did not exist beforehand; "and injected into the Religion while it is not part of it." In this [specific] way, an innovation cannot be other than an innovation of misguidance.
>
> An example for this [innovation of misguidance] is if a person should invent a prayer other than the five prayers which Allah Most High has made Law. Another example would be those invented additions pertaining to funerals, such as the supplications that are raised out loud at the forefront of funerals,[159] the *adhān* that was innovated upon lowering the deceased into

[158] Cf. the excerpts from the latter cited in *al-Nūr al-Lāmi' fī Ma'thūr al-Mawlid al-Nabawī al-Jāmi'* (p. 67-73) by the contemporary Moroccan Shaykh Mūḥtāyin al-Ḥājj 'Abd Allah al-Fārisī.

[159] A Damascene practice that consists in blaring the name of the deceased over a microphone and asking people to pray for the deceased from the front car of a slow procession toward the mosque or the cemetery in contravention of the Sunna – which explicitly states the procession should be swift and silent – and in imitation of Christians.

his grave, and those invented states during *dhikr* such as jumping [up and down] and what the jurists call "dancing and swaying from side to side" (*al-raqṣ wal-tamāyul*)[160] and the like.

[160]Dr. al-Būṭī's position contradicts the *fatwā* of his own School as stated by Imām al-Haytamī in his *Fatāwā Ḥadīthiyya* (p. 298): "It is permissible to stand and dance during gatherings of remembrance [of Allah] and audition (*samā'*) according to a group of great scholars, among them Shaykh al-Islām Ibn 'Abd al-Salām." Hence, it is correct to say that the Jurists of Shām, Egypt, the Maghreb, and the rest of the Muslim world no more concede to al-Būṭī this misrepresentation of the *ḥaḍra* as an innovation of misguidance than they concede it to other non-Sufi attackers, whether jurists such as Shaykh Wahba al-Zuḥaylī who compared those who do the *ḥaḍra* to the worshippers of the Golden Calf [!] in his *Tafsīr* and other books, or out-and-out "Salafis" like the late 'Abd al-Qādir al-Arna'ūṭ and his associates. Suffice them that Sulṭān al-'Ulamā' Imām al-'Izz Ibn 'Abd al-Salām is authentically reported to have "habitually attended the *samā'* and danced in states of ecstasy" (*kāna yaḥḍuru al-samā' wa-yarquṣu wa-yatawājad*) as related by Imām al-Dhahabī in his *Siyar* (17:33) and Ibn al-'Imād in *Shadharāt al-Dhahab* (5:302). One of the most explicit proofs of the licitness of such movements while in a state of spiritual elation is the ḥadīth related by our liege-lord 'Alī ibn Abī Ṭālib: "I visited the Prophet ﷺ with Ja'far [ibn Abī Ṭālib] and Zayd [ibn Ḥāritha]. The Prophet ﷺ said to Zayd: 'You are my freedman' (*mawlāy*), whereupon Zayd began to hop on one leg around the Prophet (*ḥajila*). <The Prophet ﷺ said to Ja'far: 'You resemble me physically and morally' (*ashbahta khalqī wa-khuluqī*)>, whereupon Ja'far began to hop behind Zayd. The Prophet ﷺ then said to me: 'You are part of me and I am part of you' (*anta minnī wa-anā mink*) whereupon I began to hop behind Ja'far." A fair narration from 'Alī by Imām Aḥmad (Shākir ed. 1:537 §857 "with a *ṣaḥīḥ* chain," al-Arna'ūṭ ed. 2:213-214 §857 "with a weak chain"), al-Bayhaqī in *al-Sunan al-Kubrā* (8:6 §15548, 10:226 §20816), and al-Bazzār with a *ṣaḥīḥ* chain according to al-Haythamī (5:176). Al-Arna'ūṭ based his grading on Hāni' ibn Hāni' but overlooked that al-Bayhaqī narrates it from Hāni' **and** Hubayra ibn Yarīm, a combined narration which, as Shaykh Shu'ayb himself said elsewhere (*Musnad Aḥmad* 2:161), "makes their ḥadīth *ḥasan* as they corroborate one another." He also declares that combined chain "strong" (*jayyid*) in Ibn Ḥibbān (15:520 §7046). This authentication is confirmed by the fact that al-Ḍiyā' al-Maqdisī included the narration in his compilation of authentic narrations, *al-Aḥādīth al-Mukhtāra* (2:392, *isnād ḥasan* according to its editor). Also narrated by Ibn Abī Shayba (12:105) and Ibn Sa'd *mursal*, chapter on Ja'far ibn Abi Ṭālib. The bracketed segment is also narrated by itself from 'Alī by Ibn Ḥibbān (15:520 §7046 *ṣaḥīḥ*), Ibn Abī Shayba (1:105), al-Ḥākim (3:120) who declared it sound while al-Dhahabī concurred, and Ibn Sa'd.

These matters were innovated and injected into the Religion although they are not part of the Religion in any way whatsoever. [...]

As for the matters that were innovated and were not existent before but were not injected into the Religion, the people practiced them as habits and procedures in which they found usefulness for themselves, whether such were connected with their worldly sphere or with their Religion. [...]

There are many, many examples for this type. We can give an example for these many habits and procedures which the Muslims have innovated after the death of the Messenger of Allah ﷺ or even in his time. Among them are the innovations connected with food and drink. Also among them are the innovations connected with dwellings, their decoration and their architecture. Among them also are the matters connected with manufacture, commerce, agriculture and the like. Among them also are the matters connected with dress in all its variety. [...]

All of those are innovated matters but they were not injected into the Religion. That is, the people did not practice them as if they were part of the Religion. Hence, the definition of the legal innovation does not apply to them.

No doubt, someone is bound to ask: "What does the Law say of these innovations which entered like waves into the life of the Muslims?" Let us hear what the Messenger of Allah ﷺ said in his authentic ḥadīth: "Whoever institutes a good practice in Islam has its reward and the reward of all those who practice it until the Day of Judgment, and whoever institutes a bad practice in Islam bears its onus and the onus of all those who practice it until the Day of Judgment"[161] as part of a well-known long ḥadīth.

[161] See note 300.

Many are those who imagine a contradiction between the ḥadīth of the Messenger of Allah ﷺ "Every innovation is misguidance" and this ḥadīth. They see a problem here and act confused when in reality there is no problem at all.

Innovated matters that are injected into the Religion and are not part of it are apt to be described by his hadīth ﷺ, "Every innovation is misguidance." As for innovated matters among habits and procedures that are connected to daily life in all their varieties, without people intending them as Religion and without their being injected into the Divine Law (such matters not being part of it): they fall under the [twofold] distinction mentioned by the Messenger of Allah ﷺ ["Whoever institutes a good practice..."]. We look at the results of these habits and regimens. Whatever of them have a good effect on the life of people or their Religion are classed under the "good sunna" to which the Messenger of Allah ﷺ called. And whatever of them leaves bad effects in the Religion or in the worldly affairs of people – for Allah Most High commanded the people to take care of their religious and worldly interests – then such are classed under the "bad sunnas" against which the Messenger of Allah ﷺ warned. The Ulema of the Law have explained this at length and in great detail under the subheading of "matters of public welfare" (*maṣāliḥ al-mursala*).

When are such matters of public welfare lawful and licit even when they are "widespread" (*mursala*), since the Book and the Sunna did not say anything about them? When are such matters imaginary and corrupt, that is, part of the bad sunna? The Ulema of Islamic Law showed this. In any case, what the people innovated without injecting it into the Religion – of which it is not a part at all – is not part of the meaning of the legal innovation which is always misguidance and always a forbidden practice.

The conferences which are held here and there are among those innovated matters. How are they assessed? We look at the types of these conferences and the effect they have. Whichever of them supports the Religion is classed among the good sunnas; whichever has a harmful effect is classed among the bad sunnas. All those universities which were innovated out of non-existence; the various media including publishing houses and all kinds of means for disseminating information; all these are innovated matters that did not exist before. This development which has touched the script of the Qur'ān including dotting, vowelization, division into tenths, and so forth – and the chain of developments is endless – all these are among innovated matters. However, those that innovated them at no time claimed that they were part of the Religion or part of the Divine Law.

All of those matters are assessed on the basis of this scale of which the Messenger of Allah ﷺ informed us. Whatever part of that serves the Religion of Allah Most High or preserves the lawful worldly matters of public welfare for the people is classed together with the good sunna and one is invited to practice it, and whoever does so with sincere intention toward Allah ﷻ is rewarded. And whatever part of those newly innovated matters is harmful to the Religion or harmful to the lawful worldly matters of public welfare for the people, is classed together with the bad sunna against which the Messenger of Allah ﷺ warned.

People have this custom of celebrating the memory of their great personalities. They may do this on the occasion of the birth anniversary of one of them or on that of his death. This is among innovated matters; but no one ever said that they belong to the Religion. Nor has anyone ever said that they are an integral part of worship or of the Law which Allah Most High has commanded. They can only be described as cultural or social activities by which a certain goal is sought. We examine this goal: if this goal is good and benefits the Muslims in their Religion or in their lawful worldly matters, then it is a good sunna as the Messenger of Allah ﷺ said. [...]

Let us now look at the people's celebration of the commemoration of the birth of the Messenger of Allah ﷺ. Is it a matter that was innovated and injected into the Religion and then considered one of the types of worship that was made law for us? If anyone celebrates this event to that intention then he is an innovator! For this celebration is not an integral part of the Religion, that is, not one of the types of worship that was made law for us, nor a ruling from the Divine rulings that came down in the Qur'ān or came in the Sunna.

As for those that celebrate the commemoration of the birth of the Messenger of Allah ﷺ after the model of those who organize conferences to publicize a legitimate principle or a cause or a right which Allah Most High ordered us to uphold, or to defend something which Allah Most High allows in His Law, **this is a social activity by which good in the Religion is sought.**

This is exactly like those who organize conferences and seminars to commemorate one of their great personalities. I told you once how I was invited to a conference in one of our dear Arab countries on the occasion of the passing of this or that many years after the death of Muḥammad ibn ʿAbd al-Wahhāb. I am not among those that say that such activities are an innovation or express disapproval and warn people against them. This is because the brothers who organized this conference only did so as a social activity, like all conferences. They did it on the basis of a benefit which they considered such an activity would bring about. The criterion [of assessment] in this is the same as that for the information media or television channels – innovated matters by which is sought, when the Muslims use them well, a spiritual or temporal benefit which

Allah has allowed in His Law. What is sought in all this is the same good sought by those people who developed the writing of the Arabic language by developing the script of the Qur'ān and including in it the dotting and vowelization and division into tenths which you can see and of which all the Ulema approved. Is there any person who proceeds from a sound and meticulous basis of knowledge who will say: "A conference that is organized to commemorate the passing of this or that many years after the death of Shaykh Muḥammad ibn 'Abd al-Wahhāb is a forbidden, innovative act?" I do not think so. Not at all. And since this is the case, then **why is such an act [of commemoration] licit or even a good sunna when it is for the sake of Muḥammad ibn 'Abd al-Wahhāb, Allah have mercy on him, but then it becomes a "forbidden, innovative act" when the very same act is for the sake of Muḥammad ibn 'Abd Allah ﷺ??** There is no difference.[162] I believe that this discourse ends all noise and din over the issue.[163]

[162]There is a huge difference; however, Dr. Būṭī's statements that "there is no difference" and that commemorating Ibn 'Abd al-Wahhāb is a good sunna are, of course, free indirect speech and rhetorical conclusions to the opponents' premises *(ilzāmāt)*, not assertions in absolute terms.

[163]A *khuṭba* delivered on the Jumu'a of the 22nd of Rabī' al-Awwal 1419 (17 July 1998) in Damascus.

The Sunna Character of the Companions' Innovations

Following is a continuation of the evidence that the acts of the Companions and their excellent innovations in the Religion serve as a further basis for defining what is Sunna in Islam. They also form illustrations of the Companions' innovations that became actual Sunnas on the basis of individual *ijtihād* on the principles of the Sunna.

The Voluntary Prayer After Each *Wuḍū'*

58. The Prophet ﷺ said to Bilāl ؓ at the time of the dawn prayer: "Bilāl! Tell me about the deed for which you are most hopeful for reward in Islam for, truly, I heard the sound of your sandals in Paradise." He replied: "I did not do anything for which I am more hopeful of reward except the fact that I never perform ablution in the day or night without praying what I must pray after such ablution."[164] In another version Bilāl says: "I never raised *adhān* except I prayed two *rak'as* afterwards, nor did I ever lose my ritual purity except I performed ablution then prayed the two *rak'as* I owed Allah," whereupon the Prophet ﷺ said *bihimā*, meaning "With these two *rak'as* [you entered Paradise]."[165] Ibn Ḥajar said: "This ḥadīth signifies that *ijtihād* is permissible concerning timing in acts of worship."[166]

An Innovated Post-*Rukū'* Supplication

59. The Companion Rifā'a ibn Rāfi' al-Zuraqī's innovated invocation at the time the Prophet ﷺ was leading the sunset prayer and said: "May Allah hear whoever praises Him!" whereupon

[164] Narrated from Abū Hurayra by al-Bukhārī, Muslim, and Aḥmad.
[165] Narrated from Burayda al-Aslamī by al-Tirmidhī (*ḥasan ṣaḥīḥ gharīb*) and al-Ḥākim, who declared it *ṣaḥīḥ* and al-Dhahabī concurred.
[166] In *Fatḥ al-Bārī* (1959 ed. 3:63 §1098).

Rifāʿa said out loud: "Our Lord! To You belongs all praise, abundant, excellent, and blessed!" Later, the Prophet ﷺ asked who had said this and declared that the angels were competing to be the first to write it down.[167] Ibn Ḥajar said: "From this ḥadīth can be inferred the permissibility of innovating (*jawāz iḥdāth*) an invocation inside *ṣalāt* other than what is received from the Prophet ﷺ as long as it does not contradict what is received from the Prophet ﷺ."[168]

An Innovated Form of *Takbīrat al-Iḥrām*

60. Similar to the above evidence is the ḥadīth whereby a Companion came late to join the ranks of the people at prayer and opened his prayer with the words:

> *"Allahu akbaru kabīran*
> *wal-ḥamdu lillāhi kathīran*
> *wa-subḥān Allahi bukratan wa-aṣīlā"*

> "Allah is greater and truly great!
> Praise belongs to Allah abundantly!
> Glory to Allah morning and evening!"

After prayer the Prophet ﷺ asked who had said this. The man identified himself saying: "Messenger of Allah! I did not intend by it other than good." The Prophet ﷺ said: "I saw the gates of heaven open because of those words." Ibn ʿUmar added in his narration: "I never stopped saying them since I heard the Prophet ﷺ say this."[169]

[167]Narrated from Rifāʿa by al-Bukhārī, Mālik, al-Nasā'ī, and Aḥmad.
[168]In *Fatḥ al-Bārī* (1959 ed. 2:287 §766).
[169]Narrated from Ibn ʿUmar by Muslim, al-Tirmidhī (*ḥasan ṣaḥīḥ gharīb*), al-Nasā'ī with two chains, and Aḥmad with several chains. One of al-Nasā'ī's versions has: "I saw twelve angels compete for it," while two of Aḥmad's versions have: "I saw your words ascend to heaven until a door was opened and they entered."

Habitual Recitation of Sūrat al-Ikhlāṣ in Prayer

61. Al-Bukhārī narrates from ʿĀʾisha ﷺ that the Prophet ﷺ dispatched a man at the head of a military expedition who recited the Qur'ān for his companions at prayer, finishing each recital with al-Ikhlāṣ (Sūra 112). When they returned, they mentioned this to the Prophet ﷺ who told them to ask him why he did this. When they asked him, the man replied, "because it describes the All-Merciful, and I love to recite it." The Prophet ﷺ said to them: "Tell him Allah loves him." Another version states that this Companion would begin each recital [after the Fātiḥa] with this Sūra and then read something else. When the Prophet ﷺ asked him why, he said, "Messenger of Allah, truly I love this Sūra!" Whereupon the Prophet ﷺ told him, "Your love for it shall cause you to enter Paradise."[170] Al-Sayyid Yūsuf al-Rifāʿī commented:

> In spite of this [the Prophet's ﷺ approval (*iqrār*)], we do not know of any scholar who holds that doing the above is recommended, for the acts the Prophet ﷺ used to do regularly are superior, though his confirming the like of this illustrates his Sunna regarding his acceptance of various forms of obedience and acts of worship, and shows he did not consider the like of this to be a reprehensible innovation (*bidʿa*), as do the bigots who vie with each other to be the first to brand acts as innovation and misguidance.
>
> Further, it will be noticed that all the preceding ḥadīths are about *Ṣalāt*, which is the most important of bodily acts of worship, and of which the Prophet ﷺ said, "Pray as you have seen me pray."[171] Yet he ﷺ accepted the above examples of personal reasoning because they did not depart from the form defined by the Lawgiver, for every limit must be observed, while

[170] Narrated from Anas by al-Tirmidhī (*ḥasan gharīb ṣaḥīḥ*) and others.
[171] Narrated from Mālik ibn al-Ḥuwayrith by al-Bukhārī.

there is latitude in everything besides, as long as it is within the general category of being called for by Sacred Law. This is the Sunna of the Prophet and his way ﷺ and it is as clear as can be. Islamic scholars infer from it that every act for which there is evidence in Sacred Law that it is called for and which does not oppose an unequivocal primary text or entail harmful consequences is not included in the category of reprehensible innovation (*bid'a*), but rather, it is of the sunna, even if there should exist something whose performance is superior to it.[172]

Repetitive Recitation of Sūrat al-Ikhlāṣ in Prayer

62. Al-Bukhārī also relates from Abū Sa'īd al-Khudrī that one man heard another reciting Sūrat al-Ikhlāṣ over and over again, so when morning came he went to the Prophet ﷺ and mentioned this act to him in a disapproving way. The Prophet ﷺ said: "By Him in Whose Hand is my soul, it equals a third of the Qur'ān." Al-Dāraquṭnī recorded another version of this ḥadīth in which the man said, "I have a neighbor who prays at night and does not recite anything but al-Ikhlāṣ." Sayyid al-Rifā'ī said:

> The ḥadīth shows that the Prophet ﷺ confirmed the person restricting himself to this *sūra* while praying at night, despite its not being what the Prophet ﷺ himself did. Although the Prophet's ﷺ practice of reciting from the whole Qur'ān was superior, the man's act was within the general parameters of the Sunna and there was nothing blameworthy about it in any case.[173]

[172] Al-Rifā'ī, *al-Radd al-Muḥkam* (p. 119-133) as translated in *Reliance of the Traveller* (p. 912) with very slight editing.
[173] *Ibid.* Actually the Prophet ﷺ did sometimes practice repetitiveness as mentioned further below, section entitled "Repetitive Recitation."

Using *Ruqya* and Accepting Payment

63. Al-Bukhārī relates from Abū Saʿīd al-Khudrī that a group of the Companions of the Prophet ﷺ departed on one of their journeys, alighting at the encampment of some desert Arabs whom they asked for hospitality but who refused to host them. The leader of the encampment was stung by a scorpion and his followers tried everything to cure him. When all had failed, one of them said, "If you would approach the group camped near you, one of them might have some cure." So they came to them and said, "O band of men, our leader has been stung and we have tried everything. Do any of you have something for it?" One of the Companions replied: "Yes, by Allah! I recite healing words (*ruqya*) over people, but – by Allah! – we asked you to be our hosts and you refused, so I will not recite anything unless you give us a fee." They agreed upon a herd of sheep, so the man went and began spitting and reciting the Fātiḥa over the victim until he got up and walked as if he were a camel released from its hobble, nothing the matter with him. They paid the fee agreed upon, which some of the Companions wanted to divide up, but the man who had done the reciting told them, "Do not do so until we reach the Prophet ﷺ and tell him what has happened, to see what he may order us to do." They came to the Prophet ﷺ and told him what had occurred. He said: "How did you know it [the Fātiḥa] was among the words that heal? You were right. Divide up the herd and give me a share."

The above ḥadīth is explicit that the Companion – perhaps Abū Saʿīd himself – had no previous knowledge that reciting the Fātiḥa to heal was countenanced by Sacred Law, but rather did so because of his own personal reasoning (*ijtihād*). Since it did not contravene anything that had been legislated, the Prophet ﷺ confirmed him therein because it was of his Sunna and way to accept and confirm what contained good and did not entail harm, even if it did not proceed from the acts of the Prophet himself ﷺ as a definitive precedent.

Innovated Wordings in *Duʿāʾ*

64. Aḥmad and Ibn Ḥibbān relate from ʿAbd Allah ibn Burayda that his father said, "I entered the mosque with the Prophet ﷺ where a man was at prayer, supplicating: 'O Allah, I ask You by the fact that I testify You are Allah, there is no god but You, the One, the Ultimate, Who did not beget and was not begotten, and to Whom none is equal!' Whereupon the Prophet ﷺ said: 'By Him in Whose hand is my soul, he has asked Allah by His greatest name, which if He is asked by it He gives, and if supplicated He answers.'" Al-Sayyid Yūsuf al-Rifāʿī said:

> It is plain that this supplication came spontaneously from the Companion, and since it conformed to what the Sacred Law calls for, the Prophet ﷺ confirmed it with the highest degree of approbation and acceptance, while it is not known that the Prophet ﷺ had ever taught it to him.[174]

Tathwīb

65. *Tathwīb* consists in adding the phrase "Prayer is better than sleep" (*al-ṣalātu khayrun min al-nawm*) to the *fajr* call to prayer. It was originally spoken by Bilāl ؓ but the Prophet ﷺ included it as a permanent addition to the *adhān* of the *fajr* prayer.[175]

The *tathwīb* which al-Ṭurṭūshī (d. 520) counted among the reprehensible innovations in his book *al-Ḥawādith wal-Bidaʿ* and which al-Wansharīsī (d. 914), also a Mālikī, calls "a good innovation" (*bidʿa mustaḥsana*) is a different addition, consisting in

---

[174] *Ibid.*

[175] As stated by al-Zuhrī in Ibn Mājah and Saʿīd ibn al-Musayyab in Aḥmad, and narrated with sound chains from Bilāl by Ibn Mājah and from ʿAbd Allah ibn Zayd by Aḥmad. The report that mentions ʿUmar instead of Bilāl is in Mālik, book of the Call to Prayer, without chain.

haranguing the people to wake up and come to prayer even after the *adhān* is finished. This is still practiced by some in Syro-Palestine. As for the loud invocation of blessings and peace on the Prophet ﷺ after every *adhān*, this is an excellent innovation that was begun by the *Mujaddid Mujāhid* and glorious Sulṭān Salāḥ al-Dīn al-Ayyūbī in the countries of Egypt and Shām (present-day Syria, Lebanon, Palestine and Jordan) where it has never since been omitted, as mentioned by al-Suyūṭī in *al-Wasā'il fī Musāmarat al-Awā'il* (p. 14-15), al-Sakhāwī in *al-Qawl al-Badī'* ("It is a *bid'a ḥasana*" p. 377), al-Qasṭallānī in *Masālik al Ḥunafā* (p. 290), and al-Haytamī in *al-Durr al-Manḍūd* (p. 157).

Cutting the *Idhkhir* Plant in Makka

66. The Prophet ﷺ said on the day he conquered Makka: "Allah, truly, prevented the elephants from entering Makka and [now] gave supremacy over it to His Messenger and the Believers. Truly, it was not permitted to anyone before me and it was permitted to me for a while but will not be permitted again to anyone after me! Therefore, let no one pursue any prey in it nor uproot its plants! Nor can someone keep any lost property he finds there except after announcing and publicizing the fact. Whoever suffers manslaughter among his relatives has the choice either to receive the wergeld or for the killer to be put to death." Al-'Abbās said: "Except the mastic tree (*al-idhkhir*),[176] Messenger of Allah, for we put it in our graves and our houses." The Prophet ﷺ said, "Except the mastic tree." Then Abū Shāh got up – a Yemeni – and said, "Write it for me, Messenger of Allah!" The Prophet ﷺ said, "Write it for Abū Shāh!" Al-Awzā'ī said, "Meaning, the sermon he had just heard from the Messenger of Allah ﷺ."[177]

[176] Due to its qualities as an astringent and rose-like fragrant evergreen cf. Abū al-Khayr al-Ishbīlī, *'Umdat al-Ṭabīb fī Ma'rifat al-Nabāt* (1:46 §38).
[177] Narrated from Abū Hurayra, Ibn 'Abbās, and Ṣafiyya bint Shayba in the Six Books and Aḥmad.

The Handshake Innovated by the Yemeni Companions

67. The Prophet ﷺ said: "Tomorrow shall come to you a people more sensitive in their hearts towards Islam than you." Then the Ash'arīs came – Abū Mūsā was with them.[178] On their approach to Madīna they sang poetry, saying: "Tomorrow we meet our beloved ones, Muḥammad and his group!" Anas said: "When they arrived they began to shake hands with the people, and they were the first to innovate hand-shaking."[179]

Compiling the Qu'rān

68. Al-Bukhārī related in his *Ṣaḥīḥ* from Zayd ibn Thābit ؓ that the Prophet ﷺ died and the Qu'rān had not been compiled anywhere. 'Umar ؓ suggested to Abū Bakr ؓ to compile the Qu'rān in one volume. When a large number of Companions were killed in the battle of Yamāma, Abū Bakr wondered, "How could we do something that the Prophet ﷺ did not do?" 'Umar said, "By Allah, it is good." 'Umar persisted in asking Abū Bakr until Allah expanded his chest for it and he sent for Zayd ibn Thābit and assigned him to compile the Qu'rān. Zayd said, "By Allah! If they had asked me to move a mountain, it would not have been more difficult than to compile the Qur'ān." He also said, "How could you do something that the Prophet ﷺ did not do?" Abū Bakr said, "It is good, and 'Umar kept coming back to me until Allah expanded my chest for the matter."

---

[178] He was coming back from his land after having entered Islam in Makka and having emigrated to Abyssinia.

[179] Narrated from Anas with a sound (*ṣaḥīḥ*) chain by Aḥmad and Ibn 'Abd al-Barr in *al-Tamhīd* (21:15) as well as – without mention of the handshake – Ibn Sa'd (4:106), Aḥmad, al-Nasā'ī in *al-Kubrā* (5:92 §8352) and *Faḍā'il al-Ṣaḥāba* (p. 73 §247), Abū Ya'lā (6:454 §3845), Ibn Ḥibbān (16:164-165 §7192-7193 both *isnād ṣaḥīḥ*), and al-Bayhaqī in the *Dalā'il* (5:351).

Dotting the Qur'ānic Letters

69. The *Tābiʿī* Abū al-Aswad al-Du'alī dotted the entire *Muṣḥaf* in the rule of Muʿāwiya ﷺ and the *Tābiʿī* Ibn Sīrīn, according to al-Dānī, possessed a *Muṣḥaf* originally dotted by the *Tābiʿī* Yaḥyā ibn Yaʿmar al-Qaysī although Ibn Sīrīn (at first), Qatāda, and al-Nakhaʿī detested that practice but not al-Ḥasan nor Rabīʿa ibn Abī ʿAbd al-Raḥmān. Yaḥyā was the first to innovate it as narrated from Hārūn ibn Mūsā.[180]

The Maqām of Ibrāhīm ﷺ in relation to the *Kaʿba*

70. Al-Bayhaqī narrated with a strong chain of narrators from ʿĀ'isha: "The *Maqām* during the time of the Prophet and Abū Bakr was attached to the House, then ʿUmar moved it back." Ibn Ḥajar said in the *Fatḥ*, "The Companions did not oppose ʿUmar, neither did those who came after them, thus it became unanimous agreement." He was the first to build an enclosure (*maqṣūra*) around it.

The addition to the *Tashahhud* by Ibn Masʿūd

71. After "*wa-raḥmatullāhi wa-barakātuh,*" Ibn Masʿūd used to say, "*al-salāmu ʿalaynā min Rabbinā*" (peace upon us from our Lord).[181]

The addition to the *Tashahhud* by ʿAbd Allah ibn ʿUmar

72. Ibn ʿUmar added the *basmala* at the beginning of the *tashahhud*. He also added to the *talbiya*, "*labbayka wa-saʿdayka wal-khayru bi-yadayka wal-raghbā'u ilayka wal-ʿamalu.*" This is mentioned in al-Bukhārī and Muslim.

[180] By Ibn Abī Dāwūd in *al-Maṣāḥif* (2:521 §445), al-Dānī in *al-Nuqaṭ* (p. 125), Ibn al-Jazarī, *Ghāyat al-Nihāya* (2:381), al-Dhahabī in *Maʿrifat al-Qurrā' al-Kibār* (1:68) and the *Siyar* (Risāla ed. 4:442), and Ibn Ḥajar in *Tahdhīb al-Tahdhīb* (11:305).
[181] Narrated by al-Tabarānī in *al-Kabīr*.

Salutations on the Prophet ﷺ by our Liege-Lords ʿAlī, Ibn ʿAbbās, and Ibn Masʿūd

73. The ḥadīth Master Abū Mūsā al-Madīnī (d. 581) narrated the following formula of salutation on the Prophet ﷺ from our liege-lord ʿAlī ibn Abī Ṭālib ؓ: "The blessings of Allah, His angels, His Prophets, His Messengers, and His entire creation on Muḥammad and on the House of Muḥammad! Upon him and them peace, the mercy of Allah, and His benedictions!"[182] He also narrated from our liege-lord ʿAbd Allah ibn ʿAbbās ؓ the formula: "O Allah, Who eternally bestows favor on creation! O open-handed One with His Gift! O Owner of the loftiest presents! Bless Muḥammad, the best of creatures in his character! And forgive us, O Most Exalted One, on this night!" Shaykh Yūsuf al-Nabhānī mentioned them in his massive compilation of invocations of blessings on the Prophet ﷺ entitled *Saʿādat al-Dārayn fil-Ṣalāt ʿalā Sayyid al-Kawnayn* ﷺ (p. 245-247).

Another, longer but *mursal* version from our liege-lord ʿAlī begins with the words, "O Allah, leveler of plains and planets *(allāhumma dāḥiya al-madḥuwwāt)*!"[183] while a famous version from Ibn Masʿūd states: "When you invoke blessings on your Prophet, invoke blessings in the best possible way *(idhā ṣallaytum*

[182]We have received this formula, by the grace of Allah, from the blessed mouth of our teacher, Mawlānā al-Shaykh Muḥammad Nāẓim al-Ḥaqqānī – Allah bless and preserve him – as part of the devotions that are recited after every *Ṣalāt* and in the daily and weekly *khatm* in the Most Distinguished Naqshbandī Path.

[183]Narrated by Ibn Abī Shayba (6:66 §29520), al-Ṭabarānī in *al-Awsaṭ* (9:43 §9089), and Abū Nuʿaym in his *Man Rawā ʿan Saʿīd ibn Manṣūr ʿĀliyan* (ʿĀṣima ed. p. 54). Al-Qasṭallānī in *Masālik al-Ḥunafā'* (p. 514) said it is also narrated by al-Ṭabarī in Ṭalḥa's *Musnad* in *Tahdhīb al-Āthār*, Aḥmad ibn Sinān al-Qaṭṭān in his *Musnad*, Yaʿqūb ibn Shayba in his *Akhbār ʿAlī ibn Fāris*, and Ibn Bashkuwāl, all broken-chained cf. al-Mizzī and others cf. Ibn Kathīr, *Tafsīr* (3:510), al-Haythamī (10:163), al-ʿIrāqī, *Tuḥfat al-Taḥṣīl fī Dhikri Ruwāt al-Marāsīl* (al-Rushd ed. p. 142), al-ʿAlā'ī, *Jāmiʿ al-Taḥṣīl fī Aḥkām al-Marāsīl* (ʿĀlam al-Kutub ed. p. 193 §274), and *Fatḥ* (11:158).

fa-aḥsinū al-ṣalāta ʿalā nabiyyikum) for – you do not know – this might be shown to him. Therefore, say: 'O Allāh! Grant your *ṣalāt*, mercy, and blessings upon the Master of Messengers *(sayyid al-Mursalīn)*, the Imām of the Godfearing, and the Seal of Prophets, Muḥammad your servant and Messenger, the Imām of goodness and leader of goodness and Messenger of Mercy! O Allāh! Raise him to a glorious station for which the first and the last of creatures will yearn! O Allāh! Grant mercy to Muḥammad and to the House of Muḥammad!'" and so forth to the end of the normal wording of *tashahhud*.[184]

[184]Narrated from Ibn Masʿūd by Ibn Mājah, Abū Yaʿlā (9:175 §5267), al-Ṭabarānī in *al-Kabīr* (9:115 §8594), Abū Nuʿaym in the *Ḥilya* (1985 ed. 4:271), and al-Bayhaqī in the *Shuʿab* (2:208 §1550). Al-Mundhirī declared the chain fair in *al-Targhīb* (1997 ed. 2:329 §2588) cf. *Fatḥ* (11:158) while al-Būṣīrī in *Miṣbāḥ al-Zujāja* (1:111) said it is corroborated by an identical narration from Ibn ʿUmar by Aḥmad ibn Manīʿ in his *Musnad*. It is further corroborated by ʿAbd al-Razzāq's chains (2:213-214 §3109-3112) while al-Dāraquṭnī in his *ʿIlal* (5:15 §682) cites yet two other chains.

Companions' Innovations after the Time of the Prophet ﷺ or in His Absence

The Pre-Execution Prayer and Other

74. Similar to the above evidence is the ḥadīth of the Companion Khubayb ibn Isāf or Yasāf al-Anṣārī ؓ who, when he was captured by the disbelievers of Quraysh, asked to pray two *rak'as* before his execution as narrated in two places from Abū Hurayra ؓ in al-Bukhārī's *Ṣaḥīḥ*. Abū Hurayra then added: "Khubayb was the first to inaugurate (*sanna*) the two *rak'as* for each and every Muslim who is to be executed by his enemies." Khubayb was killed after excruciating tortures. The Companion Sa'īd ibn 'Āmir ibn Ḥidhyam said: "I witnessed the slaying of Khubayb. The Quraysh had quartered him then they placed him on his trunk and said: 'Would you not love for Muḥammad to be in your place right now [and for you to be safe and sound among your kin]?' He said: 'By Allah! I would not love for myself to be among my kin and children if Muḥammad were to be pricked by a thorn.' Then he cried out: *'Yā Muḥammad!'*"[185]

75. A man married 'Abd Allah ibn Rawāḥa's widow and said to her: "Do you know why I married you? So that you would tell me how 'Abd Allah acted in his house." She said: "He used to pray two *rak'as* before going out, and two *rak'as* after coming in. He never omitted to do this."[186]

---

[185] Narrated from Khālid ibn Ma'dān by Abū Nu'aym in *Ḥilyat al-Awliyā'* (1985 ed. 1:245-246) and Ibn al-Jawzī in *Ṣifat al-Ṣafwa* (1:621-622 and 1:666 chapters on Khubayb ibn 'Adī and Sa'īd ibn 'Āmir ibn Ḥidhyam).

[186] Narrated by Ibn al-Mubārak in *al-Zuhd* with a sound chain cf. Ibn Ḥajar, *Iṣāba* (2:306) and al-Dhahabī, *Siyar* (Fikr ed. 3:146).

Congregational *Tarāwīḥ*

76. ʿUmar during his caliphate gathered the multifarious groups praying *tarāwīḥ* into a single congregation. Ubay ibn Kaʿb said: "This was not done before!" (*inna hādhā lam yakun*). ʿUmar said: "I am fully aware of this, but it is excellent (*qad ʿalimtu wa-lākinnahu ḥasan*)!"[187] He also said: "What a fine innovation this is!" (*niʿmati al-bidʿatu hādhih*)."[188]

The Second Jumuʿa *Adhān*

77. The Companion al-Sā'ib ibn Yazīd said: "The first call for Jumuʿa Prayer was when the Imām first sat on the pulpit. This was the practice in the time of the Prophet ﷺ, Abū Bakr, and ʿUmar. But when ʿUthmān saw the multitude of the people, he introduced the second *adhān* [actually raised first], and this practice took hold."[189] Ibn Rajab said: "Ibn ʿUmar called it a *bidʿa*,[190] and he might have meant what his father meant with regard to [*tarāwīḥ*] night prayers in the month of Ramaḍān."[191]

Public Admonishers (*Quṣṣāṣ*)

78. ʿUmar gave permission to Tamīm al-Dārī to stand and address public gatherings. Al-Sā'ib ibn Yazīd said this was unprecedented in the time of the Prophet ﷺ and Abū Bakr, and calls Tamīm the first *qāṣṣ* in Islam.[192]

[187] Cited in Ibn Rajab, *Jāmiʿ al-ʿUlūm wal-Ḥikam* (2:50=al-Arna'ūṭ ed. 2:128), misspelt as "I have done it" (*ʿamiltu*) in al-Zuḥaylī's edition.
[188] Narrated from ʿAbd al-Raḥmān ibn ʿAbd by Mālik (*niʿmati al-bidʿatu hādhih*) and al-Bukhārī (*niʿma al-bidʿatu hādhih*).
[189] Narrated by al-Bukhārī, in the Four *Sunan*, and by Aḥmad.
[190] Narrated by Ibn Abī Shayba.
[191] Ibn Rajab, *Jāmiʿ al-ʿUlūm wal-Ḥikam* (2:51).
[192] Narrated by Aḥmad.

Covered Caskets for Women

79. Before Fāṭima died she complained to Asmā' bint 'Umays al-Khath'amiyya – wife of Abū Bakr[193] and half-sister of Maymūna bint al-Ḥārith the wife of the Prophet ﷺ – that she considered the open bier an unbecoming method for a woman's funeral, because the cover that was thrown over her revealed her forms. Asmā' then said: "I will show you what they use in Abyssinya," and fashioned a palm-leaf stalk covered casket after the Abyssinian custom. Fāṭima was happy and instructed her to use it for her burial. Ibn 'Abd al-Barr said: "Fāṭima was the first to use this type of casket in Islam and, after her, Zaynab bint Jaḥsh was also buried in this fashion."[194] So was Asmā' herself.

[193]He married her at the time of the battle of Ḥunayn after she was widowed of Ja'far ibn Abī Ṭālib whom she had accompanied to Abyssinia as per Ibn Ḥajar, *al-Iṣāba* (7:473 §10803). Cf. al-Dhahabī, *Tārīkh* (*Maghāzī* p. 431).

[194]Narrated by Ibn 'Abd al-Barr in *al-Istī'āb* (4:1897-1898=4:378-379) and al-Dhahabī in *Tārīkh al-Islam* (1987 ed. 3:48). Cf. Abū Nu'aym, *Ḥilya*, al-Ḥākim (entries on Fāṭima) and al-Bayhaqī cf. al-Zayla'ī, *Naṣb al-Rāya* (1:339), Ibn Ḥajar, *Talkhīṣ al-Ḥabīr* (p. 170), and al-Tahānawī, *I'lā' al-Sunan* (8:275-276 §2246).

Sunna Innovations of the *Ṣaḥāba* in Worship

The examples of Bilāl, Khubayb, the Companions who kept reciting Sūrat al-Ikhlāṣ, and their extemporaneous forms of supplication illustrate the vast leeway for acts of worship in the Sunna, particularly prayer, as spelled out by the Prophet ﷺ in his ḥadīth: "*Al-ṣalātu khayrun mawḍū'un fa-aqlil minhā aw istakthir*: Prayer is goodness at your disposal, therefore pray a little or pray much."[195] Although this ḥadīth is weak, it is agreed upon among the jurists of *Ahl al-Sunna* that the best type of physical worship (*'ibādat al-badan*) is prayer on the evidence of the Divine order {*Bow down and prostrate yourselves, and worship your Lord, and do good*} (22:77), and as elucidated by two other established narrations of the Prophet ﷺ such as "Know that the best of your good deeds is prayer"[196] and "Prayer is a light."[197] It is known that the ankles of the Holy Prophet ﷺ were swollen due to his constant station in prayer at night.[198] Accordingly, abundance in prayer by night or by day can never be termed an innovation of misguidance and many of the *Salaf* were famous for their continuous devotional exertions, as shown by the following examples

[195]Narrated from Abū Dharr by Aḥmad with three weak chains although al-Zayn declares one of them fair (16:259 §22189), by al-Quḍā'ī in *Musnad al-Shihāb* (1:378 §651), al-Ḥākim who declared it *ṣaḥīḥ* but al-Dhahabī pointed out that its chain contains Yaḥyā ibn Sa'īd Abū Zakariyyā al-Sa'dī al-Baṣrī who is weak as per Ibn 'Adī (7:244 §2142), by al-Bazzār and, as part of a very long ḥadīth, by Abū Nu'aym in *al-Ḥilya* and Ibn Ḥibbān with a very weak chain as stated by al-Arna'ūṭ (2:76 §361); also narrated from Abū Hurayra by al-Ṭabarānī, *al-Awsaṭ* with a weak chain as indicated by al-Haythamī, from Abū Umāma by Aḥmad and al-Ṭabarānī in *al-Kabīr* (8:217§7871) with a weak chain as stated by al-Haythamī (1:159). Ibn Ḥajar indicates its weakness in *Talkhīṣ al-Ḥabīr* (1964 ed. 2:21 §542) and *Fatḥ al-Bārī* (1959 ed. 2:480 §946).

[196]Narrated as part of a longer ḥadīth from Thawbān with sound chains by Ibn Mājah and Aḥmad. Mālik cites it.

[197]Part of a longer ḥadīth narrated from Abū Mālik al-Ash'arī (Ka'b ibn 'Āṣim) by Muslim, al-Tirmidhī (*ḥasan ṣaḥīḥ*), al-Nasā'ī, Ibn Mājah, Aḥmad, and al-Dārimī.

[198]Narrated from 'Ā'isha by al-Bukhārī and Muslim.

cited, among other compilations, from Imām al-Lacknawī's *Iqāmat al-Ḥujja ʿalā anna al-Ikthār min al-Taʿabbudi Laysa bi-Bidʿa* ("The Conclusive Argument that Abundance in Acts of Worship is not an Innovation").[199]

Permanent Year-Round Fast

80. Ibn Kathīr said in his *Bidāya*: "ʿUmar would pray *ʿishā* with the people then enter his house and not cease praying until dawn, and he did not die before acquiring the habit of fasting permanently."[200]

81. Ruhayma the grandmother of al-Zubayr ibn ʿAbd Allah narrated that ʿUthmān fasted the whole year and used to spend the night in prayer except for a rest in its first part.

82. ʿAbd al-Raḥmān al-Taymī narrated that he saw ʿUthmān recite the entire Qur'ān in a single *rakʿa* at the *Maqām* of Ibrāhīm, at night. Muḥammad ibn Sīrīn narrated from Nā'ila the wife of ʿUthmān that at the time he was besieged before he was murdered, "he used to spend the whole night praying, with a single *rakʿa* in which he recited the entire Qur'ān."[201]

83. Also among the Companions who fasted all year round was ʿAbd Allah ibn ʿUmar, as he revealed when he told Asmā', referring to himself: "What about someone who observes continuous fasting?"[202] If Ibn ʿUmar missed the congregational *ʿishā* prayer he would also spend the night praying until morning.[203]

[199]Translated by Zahir Mahmood under the title *Bidʿah and the Salaf's Worship* (London: al-Hamra Publications, 1999).
[200]Ibn Kathīr, *Bidāya* (7:135).
[201]All three reports narrated in Abū Nuʿaym, *Ḥilya* (1:56=1:94) cf. *Iqāmat al-Ḥujja* (p. 59-60).
[202]Narrated from ʿAbd Allah Mawlā Asmā' bint Abī Bakr by Muslim.
[203]Narrated by Abū Nuʿaym in his *Ḥilya* (1:303) cf. *Iqāmat al-Ḥujja* (p. 61-62).

84. After the Prophet's ﷺ death, Abū Ṭalḥa fasted permanently for forty years, among other Companions such as ʿĀ'isha.[204]

Perpetual fast (*ṣawm al-dahr*) is the practice of several of the Companions and *Salaf* such as ʿUmar, his son ʿAbd Allah, ʿUthmān, Abū Ṭalḥa, ʿĀ'isha, Saʿīd ibn al-Musayyab, Thābit al-Bunānī, Abū Ḥanīfa, Saʿd ibn Ibrāhīm ibn ʿAbd al-Raḥmān ibn ʿAwf al-Zuhrī, Shuʿba, al-Shāfiʿī, al-Tustarī, Manṣūr Abū ʿAttāb al-Sulamī, Wakīʿ, al-Nawawī, and countless others. Al-Bayhaqī began fasting perpetually thirty years before his death. Ibn Khuzayma and his student Ibn Ḥibbān each devoted chapters of their *Ṣaḥīḥs* to the subject.[205] Ibn Ḥibbān said, commenting on the ḥadīth of the Prophet ﷺ: "Whoever fasts all his life has neither fasted nor broken his fast"[206]:

> He means: whoever fasts all his life including the days in which one was forbidden to fast, such as the days of *tashrīq*[207] and the two ʿ*Īds*. By the words: 'he has neither fasted nor broken his fast' he means that he did not in fact fast all his life in order to reap reward for it. For he did not omit [the fasting of] the days in which he was forbidden to fast. That is why the Prophet ﷺ said: 'Whoever fasts all his life, the Fire shall straiten him for this much,' and he counted ninety on his fingers,[208] meaning the days of his life in which he was forbidden to fast. It does not apply to the person who fasts all his life – being strong enough to do so – without the prohibited days.[209]

[204] Ibn Qudāma, *al-Mughnī* (Beirut, 1994 ed. 3:119).
[205] Cf. Ibn Khuzayma (3:312-313); Ibn Ḥibbān (8:349-350). See also Ibn Ḥajar's notes on the topic in *Fatḥ al-Bārī* (1989 ed. 4:222).
[206] Narrated in the *Ṣaḥīḥayn* from ʿAbd Allah ibn ʿAmr, and from ʿAbd Allah ibn al-Shikhkhīr by Aḥmad, al-Nasā'ī, al-Ḥākim, Ibn Ḥibbān, Ibn Abī Shayba, and others.
[207] The Days of drying the meat after the sacrifice of ʿ*Īd al-Aḍḥā* = 11, 12, and 13 of *Dhūl-Ḥijja*.
[208] Narrated from Abū Mūsā al-Ashʿarī by Aḥmad (*isnād ṣaḥīḥ*) and Ibn Ḥibbān.
[209] Ibn Ḥibbān (8:349-350).

The above is confirmed by Imām Mālik in his *Muwaṭṭa'*:

> There is no harm in perpetual fasting (*ṣiyām al-dahr*) provided one breaks one's fast on the days which the Prophet ﷺ forbade fasting.[210] Mālik praised the *qāḍī* 'Abd Allah ibn 'Abd al-Raḥmān ibn Ma'mar and said he fasted perpetually.[211]

Imām al-Nawawī said on the topic:

> Ibn 'Umar fasted permanently, *i.e.* except the days of '*Id* and *tashrīq*. This perpetual fast was his way and the way of his father 'Umar ibn al-Khaṭṭāb, 'Ā'isha, Abū Ṭalḥa and others of the *Salaf* as well as al-Shāfi'ī and other scholars. Their position is that perpetual fasting is not offensive (*makrūh*).[212]

Ibn Qudāma states something similar in *al-Mughnī* and adds that the same view is related from Aḥmad and Mālik, and that after the Prophet's ﷺ death Abū Ṭalḥa fasted permanently for forty years, among other Companions.[213] Ibn Ḥajar al-Haytamī in *al-Khayrāt al-Ḥisān* similarly relates that Abū Ḥanīfa was never seen eating except at night.[214] In our time, the late Moroccan ḥadīth Master of Damascus Badr al-Dīn al-Ḥasanī also used to fast permanently, including on the day of 'Arafa on pilgrimage.[215]

[210] *Muwaṭṭa'* (1:300).
[211] Cf. Ibn 'Abd al-Barr, *al-Tamhīd* (17:416).
[212] *Sharḥ Ṣaḥīḥ Muslim, Kitāb* 37, *Bab* 2, §10.
[213] Ibn Qudāma, *al-Mughnī* (Beirut, 1994 ed. 3:119).
[214] Al-Haytamī, *al-Khayrāt al-Ḥisān fī Manāqib al-Nu'mān* (p. 40).
[215] Narrated to the author by Dr. Wahba al-Zuhaylī, class communication.

Repetitive Recitation of a Single Verse in Supererogatory Prayer

85. Ibn Sīrīn said that the Companion Tamīm al-Dārī would also recite the entire Qur'ān in a single *rak'a* and sometimes repeated a single verse all night until morning. Masrūq narrated that he saw Tamīm recite at night and until morning the single verse {*Or do those who commit ill deeds suppose that We shall make them as those who believe and do good works, the same life and death? Bad is their judgment!*} (45:21). Abū Nu'aym said that Tamīm was the first to install lighting in mosques.[216]

Reciting a single verse over and over inside supererogatory prayer is a Prophetic Sunna as narrated from Abū Dharr: the Prophet ﷺ stood in prayer and kept reciting the verse {*If You punish them, lo! they are Your slaves, and if You forgive them (lo! they are Your slaves). Lo! You, only You are the Mighty, the Wise*} (5:118).[217] Another ḥadīth further details the circumstances of this incident: "The Prophet ﷺ recited the prayer of Ibrāhīm عليه السلام: {*My Lord! Lo! They have led many of mankind astray. But whosoever follows me, he verily is of me. And whosoever disobeys me – Still, You are Forgiving, Merciful*} (14:36). Then he recited the saying of 'Īsā عليه السلام: {*If You punish them, lo! they are Your slaves, and if You forgive them (lo! they are Your slaves)*} (5:118). Then he raised his hands and said: 'My Community, my Community!' and he wept. Allah said: 'Gibrīl, go to Muḥammad and ask him what causes him to weep.' When Gibrīl came and asked him he told him, upon which Gibrīl returned and told Allah ﷻ – and Allah

[216] Narrated by al-Sim'ānī in *al-Ansāb* cf. al-Nawawī, *al-Tibyān* (p. 84), al-Haytamī, *Fatḥ al-Mubīn bi-Sharḥ al-Arba'īn* (p. 108), al-Khazrajī in his *Khulāṣa* (p. 55), and *Iqāmat al-Ḥujja* (p. 62-63).

[217] Narrated by al-Nasā'i, Ibn Mājah, Aḥmad, and others with a sound chain cf. al-Nawawī, *Tibyān* (p. 83-84), al-Būṣīrī in *Miṣbāḥ al-Zujāja* (1:437), al-Haythamī (2:273), al-'Irāqī in his *Amālī* (p. 121-125) etc.

knows better than him – and He said: 'Gibrīl, go to Muḥammad and tell him: We shall make you glad concerning your Community and We shall not displease you!"[218] Thus one of the meanings of the verse {*And verily your Lord will give unto you so that you will be content*} (93:5) is that none of the entire Muḥammadan *Umma* will remain in Hellfire but all will be taken out for the sake of the Prophet ﷺ, as explicitly stated in several reports.[219] Another time, the Prophet ﷺ kept repeating to Abū Dharr the verse {*And for those who fear Allah He prepares a way out and He provides for them from a source they never expected*} (65:2-3) until the latter became drowsy.[220]

Similarly, Asmā' and 'Ā'isha were observed reciting repeatedly in prayer the single verse {*But Allah has been gracious unto us and has preserved us from the torment of the breath of Fire*} (52:27) while Ibn Mas'ūd repeated {*My Lord! Increase me in knowledge*} (20:114); Sa'īd ibn Jubayr, {*And guard yourselves against a day in which you will be brought back to Allah. Then every soul will be paid in full that which it has earned, and they will not be wronged*} (2:181), also {*But they will come to know, when yokes are about their necks and chains*} (40:70-71) and {*O man! What has made you careless concerning your Lord, the Bountiful*} (82:6); al-Ḍaḥḥāk, {*They have an awning of fire above them and beneath them a dais (of fire)*} (39:16); and Abū Ḥanīfa, {*Nay, but the Hour (of doom) is their appointed tryst, and the Hour will be more wretched and more bitter*} (54:46) and {*But Allah has been gracious unto us and has preserved us from the torment of the breath of Fire*} (52:27).[221]

[218]Narrated by 'Abd Allah ibn 'Amr ibn al-'Āṣ by Muslim.
[219]These reports were documented in al-Zabīdī's *Itḥāf al-Sādat al-Muttaqīn* (9:175) and the *Tafsīrs*.
[220]Narrated from Abū Dharr by Aḥmad with a sound chain.
[221]Cf. al-Nawawī, *al-Tibyān* (p. 84-85) and al-Qārī, *al-Athmār al-Janiyya fī Ṭabaqāt al-Ḥanafiyya* in al-Lacknawī's *Iqāmat al-Ḥujja* (p. 80).

Praying All Night

86. Asad ibn Wadāʿa narrated that the Companion Shaddād ibn Aws, whenever he went to bed, would turn and toss over, saying: "O Allah! The Fire made all sleep leave me." Then he would get up and pray until the morning.[222] We mentioned many other examples of all-night prayer among the *Salaf*.

Singing After *Ṣalāt*

87. ʿUmar was approached by some people who complained, "We have an imām who, after praying the ʿ*aṣr* prayer with us, begins to sing!" ʿUmar went with them and asked the man to recite what he sang to them. He said:

My heart, every time I scold it
returns to pleasures that fatigue me.
I never see it occupied except
with empty pastimes all the time, harming me.
My evil companion, what childishness is this?
Life has passed and you still play?
My youth has gone and left me
before I ever put it to right use!
My soul! You and your lusts are nothing.
Fear Allah. Fear Him. Fear Him.

ʿUmar repeated the last verse over and over, weeping. Then he said, "Whoever of you must sing, let him sing such things."[223]

[222] Narrated by Abū Nuʿaym in his *Ḥilya* (1:264) cf. *Iqāmat al-Ḥujja* (p. 64).
[223] Narrated by Ibn al-Simʿānī as cited in *Kanz al-ʿUmmāl* (§8944).

Dhikr-Beads (*al-Subḥa*)

88. Abū Hurayra the Paragon of the Sunna ﷺ possessed a thread with two thousand knots and would not sleep until he had used it all for *dhikr.*[224] He said: "Verily, I make glorification (*tasbīḥ*) of Allah Almighty every day according to my ransom (*qadar diyatī*): twelve thousand times."[225]

This report shows the ignorance of those who claim that the *dhikr*-beads or rosary are a reprehensible innovation. Imām al-Suyūṭī recounted in one of his *fatwās* entitled *al-Minḥa fīl-Subḥa* ("The Profit In Dhikr-Beads") the story of 'Ikrima, who asked his teacher 'Umar al-Mālikī about *dhikr*-beads. The latter replied that he had also asked his teacher al-Ḥasan al-Baṣrī about it and was told: "Something we have used at the beginning of the road we have no desire to leave at the end. I love to remember Allah with my heart, my tongue, and my hand." Al-Suyūṭī comments: "And how should it be otherwise when the *dhikr*-beads remind one of Allah ﷻ, and a person seldom sees *dhikr*-beads except he remembers Allah, which is among the greatest of its benefits?"[226] The uncontested Imām of the Sunna and impeccable Shaykh al-Islam of the *Khalaf*, the ḥadīth Master Ibn Ḥajar al-'Asqalānī, always carried *dhikr*-beads in his hand, which he kept hidden from the sight of others according to his close student al-Sakhāwī in his biography titled *al-Jawāhir wal-Durar.*

[224]Narrated by Abū Nu'aym in the *Ḥilya* and al-Dhahabī in the *Siyar* (Risāla ed. 2:623) and *Tadhkira* (1:35).
[225]Narrated by al-Bayhaqī in the *Sunan* (8:79), Ibn Ḥazm in *al-Muḥallā* (10:396), Ibn al-Jawzī in *Ṣifat al-Ṣafwa* (1:691), and al-Dhahabī in the *Siyar.*
[226]Al-Suyūṭī, *al-Ḥāwī lil-Fatāwī.* Cf. section on *dhikr*-beads in al-Shawkānī's *Nayl al-Awṭār* (2:316-317) and al-Kāndihlawī's *Ḥayāt al-Ṣaḥāba* (3:818). Albānī's inept claim that whoever carries *dhikr*-beads in his hand to remember Allah is misguided and innovating was refuted in Maḥmūd Mamdūḥ's *Wuṣūl al-Tahānī bi-Ithbāt Sunniyyat al-Sibḥa wal-Radd 'alā al-Albānī* ("The Alighting of Mutual Benefit and the Confirmation that *Dhikr*-Beads are a Sunna in Refutation of Albānī").

Raising Hands with *Takbīr* at the *Qunūt* of the *Witr* Prayer

89. There is no evidence that the Prophet ﷺ raised his hands or made *takbīr* at the time of the *qunūt* of the *witr* prayer as is practiced in the Ḥanafī *madhhab*, however, this was practiced by some of the foremost Companions such as ʿUmar, ʿAlī, Ibn Masʿūd, Ibn ʿAbbās, Ibn ʿUmar, and al-Barāʾ ibn ʿĀzib. Consequently both are considered desirable (*mustaḥabb*) or a "desirable Sunna" (*sunna istiḥbābiyya*) by the Ḥanafīs while some of them say the *takbīr* is *wājib*.[227]

Collective Supplication

90. The collective response "*Āmīn*" to the supplication of the imām in and outside *ṣalāt* is not a new Sunna in the strict sense, but an established Prophetic and Companion Sunna, although the people of innovation reject it as something new, in line with their desire to always do less.[228]

The Imām Holding a Staff in *Khuṭba*

91. As stipulated in the three *Madhhabs* other than the Ḥanafī, this is definitely a Sunna which the Prophet ﷺ took from "the Arab practice of never addressing a public gathering except with a staff in hand" as mentioned by al-Jāḥiẓ in his *Kitāb al-Ḥayawān* ("Book of the Staff") and Usāma ibn Qunfudh in his *Kitāb al-ʿAsā*. It is confirmed by several reports, among them the ḥadīth of the Dajjāl in *Ṣaḥīḥ Muslim* from Fāṭima bint Qays that the Prophet ﷺ banged the pulpit with his staff (*mikhṣara*) during *khuṭba* one day, repeating: "This is Ṭayba [Madīna]! This is Ṭayba! This is Ṭayba!"

[227] Cf. al-Lacknawī, *Iqāmat al-Ḥujja* (p. 38-41).
[228] See below, Chapter on Collective Supplication.

Sunna Innovations of the *Tābiʿīn* in Worship

92. Masrūq ibn al-Ajdaʿ – the companion of Ibn Masʿūd – on pilgrimage was not seen sleeping except in prostration.[229]

93. Abū Muslim al-Khawlānī the Yemeni *Walī* who emigrated to Syro-Palestine and ʿUmar gave thanks to Allah for meeting him: two men looking for him found him praying, one of them counted three hundred rakʿas until he finished.[230]

94. Ṭalq ibn Ḥabīb al-ʿAnazī did not start reading Sūrat al-Baqara in prayer except he always reached Sūra 29 before the first *rukūʿ* – two thirds of the Qur'ān.[231]

95. Bilāl ibn Saʿd ibn Tamīm al-Ashʿarī – *Shaykh Ahli Dimashq* and another Yemeni who emigrated to Syro-Palestine – prayed one thousand *rakʿas* daily. He is the one who said: "Your remembering your good qualities and forgetting your bad ones is delusion."[232]

96. ʿAlī ibn ʿAbd Allah al-Imām al-Qānit had five hundred trees and prayed two *rakʿas* daily at each tree.[233]

97. Among those who recited the entire Qur'ān in a single *rakʿa* are Saʿīd ibn Jubayr and Abū Ḥanīfa. In Ramaḍān, as imām, he would recite one day according to the canonical reading of Ibn Masʿūd, another day according to that of Zayd ibn Thābit.[234]

[229] Narrated from Abū Isḥāq by Abū Nuʿaym in the *Ḥilya* (2:95), al-Dhahabī in the *ʿIbar* (1:68), al-Yāfiʿī in *Mir'āt al-Janān* (1:139), and al-Khazrajī in his *Khulāṣa* (p. 374) cf. *Iqāmat al-Ḥujja* (p. 65-66).
[230] Cited by al-Dhahabī in his notice on Abū Muslim al-Khawlānī in the *Siyar*.
[231] *Iqāmat al-Ḥujja* (p. 65-66).
[232] *Ibid.*
[233] *Ibid.*
[234] Cf. al-Nawawī, *al-Tibyān* (p. 57), al-Khaṭīb in *Tārīkh Baghdād* (13:356), al-Yāfiʿī in *Mir'āt al-Janān* (1:197), al-Dhahabī in *Manāqib Abī Ḥanīfa* (p. 22), and al-Suyūṭī in *Tabyīḍ al-Ṣaḥīfa* (p. 94-95) cf. *Iqāmat al-Ḥujja* (p. 71-72).

98. The regular practice of Mujāhid was to complete one full reading of the Qur'ān every day.

99. Al-Tirmidhī narrated in his *Sunan* that 'Umayr ibn Hāni' prayed one thousand supererogatory *rak'as* and made *tasbīḥ* one hundred thousand times every day.

100. Uways al-Qaranī in the evening would say: "This is the night of bowing" (*hādhihi laylat al-rukū'*) and he would bow until dawn; or he would say, "This is the night of prostration" (*hādhihi laylat al-sujūd*) and he would prostrate until dawn.[235]

101. 'Āmir ibn 'Abd Allah had made it obligatory for himself to pray one thousand supererogatory *rak'as* every day.[236]

102. It is narrated that al-Aswad ibn Yazīd ibn Qays al-Nakha'ī used to pray seven hundred rak'as every day and night.[237]

103. His son al-Imām ibn al-Imām 'Abd al-Raḥmān ibn al-Aswad was counted praying sixty-five *rak'as* before Jumu'a prayer alone.[238]

104. Sa'īd ibn al-Musayyab for fifty years prayed the dawn prayer with the same ablution as for the night prayer and he fasted permanently.[239]

[235] Narrated from Aṣbagh ibn Zayd by Abū Nu'aym in the *Ḥilya* (2:87) cf. *Iqāmat al-Ḥujja* (p. 64-65).
[236] Narrated from Ibn Wahb and others by Abū Nu'aym in the *Ḥilya* (2:88) cf. *Iqāmat al-Ḥujja* (p. 65).
[237] Cited by al-Dhahabī in the *'Ibar* (1:86) and al-Yāfi'ī in the *Mir'āt* (1:156) cf. *Iqāmat al-Ḥujja* (p. 67).
[238] Cited by al-Dhahabī in his notice on 'Abd al-Raḥmān ibn al-Aswad in the *Siyar*.
[239] Narrated by Abū Nu'aym in the *Ḥilya* (2:163) cf. *Iqāmat al-Ḥujja* (p. 67).

105. ʿUrwa ibn al-Zubayr ibn al-ʿAwwām recited a quarter of the Qur'ān every night and did not swerve from this devotion even the day his gangrenous foot was sawed off – without anesthetic nor anyone to hold him down.[240]

106. Abū al-Ṣahbā' Ṣila ibn Ashyam al-Baṣrī (d. 62) went on a military expedition to Kabul. On the way he retired to pray during a pause in the march, whereupon a lion appeared before him and, seeing him impavid in prayer, fled. Both he and his son died as martyrs in Kabul. His wife was the trustworthy *ʿālima* Umm al-Ṣahbā' Muʿādha bint ʿAbd Allah al-'Adawiyya al-Baṣriyya (d. 83) – ʿĀ'isha's student and Ayyūb al-Sakhtyānī's teacher. She said to the women who came to offer their condolences: "Welcome to you if you came to congratulate me; but if you came for other than that, then go back." She also said: "I am astonished at eyes that sleep at night after they know about the sleep of the grave." She related of her husband: "Abū al-Ṣahbā' would stand in prayer at night for so long that he did not come to bed except crawling." Ṣila used to conclude his prayers with the supplication: "O Allah, save me from the Fire! Can such as I ask for Paradise?"[241]

107. When Thābit ibn Aslam al-Bunānī al-Baṣrī died and was buried – he had accompanied Anas for forty years – one of the stones of his grave fell out of place and those that were present saw Thābit standing in prayer in his grave. After this, his daughter revealed that he prayed every night for fifty years, asking at the end of the night: "O Allah, if You ever granted to anyone

[240]Narrated by Ibn Khallikān, *Wafayāt al-Aʿyān* (2:419-420) cf. *Iqāmat al-Ḥujja* (p.68).

[241]Narrated by Abū Nuʿaym in the *Ḥilya* (2:240) cf. *Siyar* (Fikr ed. 5:19-20 = Risāla ed. 3:497 and Fikr ed. 5:417-418 § 567), Ibn al-Jawzī in *Ṣayd al-Khāṭir* (p. 241), and *Iqāmat al-Ḥujja* (p. 69-70).

prayer in the grave, grant it to me." Thābit was also among those who recited the entire Qur'ān every day and night, and he fasted permanently.[242]

108. ʿAlī ibn al-Ḥusayn ibn ʿAlī ibn Abī Ṭālib was titled Zayn al-ʿĀbidīn – ornament of the worshippers – for his assiduous worship. He used to pray one thousand *rakʿas* daily until his death.[243]

109. Qatāda ibn Diʿāma read the entire Qur'ān every seven days, in Ramaḍān once every three days, and in its last ten days once every night.[244]

110. Mūsā ibn Yasār said that Muḥammad ibn Wāsiʿ used to pray all night long even during night travel on top of a camel in a sitting position. To the question: "How are you this morning?" he replied: "Nearer to death, filled with vain hopes and plenty of bad deeds."[245]

111. Al-Mughīra ibn Ḥabīb said that he saw his father-in-law Mālik ibn Dīnār pray *ʿishā*, sit to eat, then get up and begin to pray. Then he said, standing and grasping his beard: "When You gather up the first and last of human beings, keep away Mālik's white hair from the Fire." He kept repeating it until the rising of dawn.[246]

112. Sulaym ibn ʿItr al-Tujībī, the *qāḍī* of Egypt, used to complete three full recitations of the Qur'ān every night inside and outside prayer while Ibn Abī Dāwūd and Abū ʿUmar al-Kindī in *Quḍāt Miṣr* said he recited four.[247]

[242] Narrated by Abū Nuʿaym in the *Ḥilya* (2:219) cf. *Iqāmat al-Ḥujja* (p. 70).
[243] Narrated by al-Dhahabī in his *ʿIbar* (1:111) cf. *Iqāmat al-Ḥujja* (p. 71).
[244] Narrated by Abū Nuʿaym in the *Ḥilya* (2:338) cf. *Iqāmat al-Ḥujja* (p. 71).
[245] Narrated by Abū Nuʿaym in the *Ḥilya* (2:346) cf. *Iqāmat al-Ḥujja* (p. 72).
[246] Narrated by Abū Nuʿaym in the *Ḥilya* (3:361) cf. *Iqāmat al-Ḥujja* (p. 73).
[247] Narrated by Ibn Kathīr in *al-Bidāya* (9:118) after Ibn ʿAsākir cf. *Iqāmat al-Ḥujja* (p. 96 and p. 99) and al-Nawawī, *Tibyān* (p.55)

113. Sulaymān ibn Ṭarkhān al-Taymī al-Baṣrī was imām of the mosque in Baṣra for forty years, during which he prayed both the *ʿishā* and the *fajr* prayers with a single ablution.[248]

114. Manṣūr ibn Zādhān in the month of Ramaḍān would recite the entire Qur'ān between *maghrib* and *ʿishā* and begin another reading until Sūrat al-Naḥl [16]. He once recited it in its entirety twice and began a third reading until the Ṭah Sīn Sūras (*al-ṭawāsīn*) [26-27-28] at a time they used to delay the *ʿishā* prayer until one quarter of the night had passed. He was seen praying eleven *rakʿas* between the *adhān* and *iqāma* of the *ẓuhr* prayer.[249]

115. ʿAlī ibn ʿAbd Allah ibn ʿAbbās ibn ʿAbd al-Muṭṭalib was nicknamed the Oft-Prostrate (*al-Sajjād*) due to his abundant worship. ʿAlī ibn Abī Ḥamala, al-Awzāʿī, and Aḥmad ibn Muḥammad ibn Kurayb said he made one thousand prostrations a day, *i.e.* five hundred *rakʿas* while Maymūn ibn Zyād al-ʿAdawī said he prayed one thousand *rakʿas* daily.[250]

116. Abū Ḥanīfa al-Nuʿmān ibn Thābit al-Kūfī the Imām and *Faqīh al-Milla* prayed both the *ʿishā* and the *fajr* prayer with a single ablution for between thirty and fifty years, prayed one thousand *rakʿas* per night, recited the entire Qur'ān once a day and night – twice in the month of Ramaḍān – and was nicknamed the Column (*al-watad*) due to his abundant worship. He is among those who recited the entire Qur'ān in a single *rakʿa*. Sufyān ibn ʿUyayna said: "No one in Makka prayed more than him in our time" while Yaḥyā ibn Ayyūb al-Zāhid said Abū Ḥanīfa did not sleep at night but only sitting, after the *ẓuhr* prayer, briefly.[251]

[248] Narrated by Abū Nuʿaym in the *Ḥilya* (3:29) cf. *Iqāmat al-Ḥujja* (p. 73).
[249] Narrated by Abū Nuʿaym in the *Ḥilya* (3:57) cf. *Iqāmat al-Ḥujja* (p. 73-74).
[250] Narrated by Abū Nuʿaym in the *Ḥilya* (3:207), al-Dhahabī in the *ʿIbar* (1:148), and Ibn Ḥajar in *Tahdhīb al-Tahdhīb* (7:358) cf. *Iqāmat al-Ḥujja* (p. 74-75).

117. Another junior *Tābiʿī*, Saʿd ibn Ibrāhīm ibn ʿAbd al-Raḥmān ibn ʿAwf al-Zuhrī, would fast and recite the entire Qur'ān daily.[252]

[251]Narrated by al-Nawawī in *Tahdhīb al-Asmā'* (2:220), al-Marghīnānī in *Mukhtārāt al-Nawāzil*, al-Dhahabī in *al-ʿIbar*, al-Kafawī in *Aʿlām al-Akhyār*, al-Yāfiʿī in *Mir'āt al-Janān* (1:310), al-Suyūṭī in *Tabyīḍ al-Ṣaḥīfa*, al-Shaʿrānī in *al-Mīzān al-Kubrā* (1:75), al-Haytamī in *Maʿdan al-Yawāqīt al-Multamiʿa fī Manāqib al-A'immat al-Arbaʿa*, Ibn Khallikān in *Wafayāt al-Aʿyān*, and al-Kardarī in *Manāqib Abī Ḥanīfa* (1:241-242) cf. *Iqāmat al-Ḥujja* (p. 76-82).

[252]Narrated by Abū Nuʿaym in the *Ḥilya* (3:170), al-Dhahabī in the *ʿIbar* (1:165), and al-Yāfiʿī in *Mir'āt al-Janān* (1:269) cf. *Iqāmat al-Ḥujja* (p. 90).

Sunna Innovations of the Later *Salaf* in Worship

118. Mis'ar ibn Kidām did not sleep at night before he had read half of the Qur'ān.[253]

119. Ibn al-Qāsim narrated from Imām Mālik's servant that Mālik prayed the dawn prayer with the ablution of the preceding *'ishā* prayer for forty-nine years.[254]

120. Al-Ḥasan ibn Ṣāliḥ ibn Ḥay al-Thawrī al-Hamdānī, his brother 'Alī, and their mother would each take turns to read one third of the Qur'ān while the other two slept so that they recited all of it every night. When their mother died each of them recited half and when 'Alī died, al-Ḥasan recited it entirely every night.[255]

121. Imām Bishr ibn Manṣūr al-Ḥannāṭ prayed five hundred *rak'as* daily.[256]

122. The daily *wird* or devotional practice of Qāḍī Abū Yūsuf was two hundred *rak'as*.[257]

123. Sahl al-Tustarī used to practice perpetual fasting and prayed all night. He reached a point where he broke his fast only once every twenty-five nights on one dirham's worth of barley bread. He did this for twenty years. Hence, his saying: "Hunger is the secret of Allah on His earth. He does not confide it to one who divulges it."[258]

253 Narrated by Ibn Ḥajar, *Tahdhīb al-Tahdhīb* (10:115) cf. *Iqāmat al-Ḥujja* (p. 96).
254 'Iyāḍ, *Tartīb* (2:438) cf. 'Awwāma, *Adab al-Ikhtilāf* (p. 148).
255 Narrated by Ibn Ḥajar in *Tahdhīb al-Tahdhīb* (2:288) cf. *Iqāmat al-Ḥujja* (p. 96).
256 Cited by al-Dhahabī in his chapter on Bishr ibn Manṣūr in the *Siyar*.
257 *Iqāmat al-Ḥujja* (p. 96).
258 Al-Qushayrī, *Risāla* (p.16-17); *Ḥilya* (10:198-222 §544); *Siyar* (10:647-649 §2369).

124. Muṣʿab ibn Thābit ibn ʿAbd Allah ibn al-Zubayr al-Madanī (d. 157) used to fast permanently and pray one thousand *rakʿas* daily.[259]

125. Abū ʿUthmān al-Maghribī said that the Ṣūfī Shaykh Ibn al-Kātib (d. after 340) would recite four *khatamāt* in the day and four *khatamāt* at night. Al-Nawawī said: "This is the most that we ever heard that someone recited in a single day and night."[260] All such reports imply an exceptional and miraculous kind of recitation that does not harm correct and reflective recitation, as the Sunna normally dictates that it is reprehensible to recite the entire Qur'ān in less than three days.

126. Among those who recited the entire Qur'ān every single day and night were al-Shāfiʿī and al-Bukhārī, twice daily in Ramaḍān as per Ibn al-Subkī in *Ṭabaqāt al-Shāfiʿiyya al-Kubrā.*

127. Abū Isḥāq al-Fazārī said that Ibrāhīm ibn Ad-ham in the month of Ramaḍān would not sleep at all for the whole month but harvest grain in the daytime and pray at night.[261]

128. The "Commander of the believers in ḥadīth" Shuʿba ibn al-Ḥajjāj fasted permanently and prayed until his feet became swollen.[262]

129. Imam Aḥmad never once missed praying in the night, and used to recite the entire Qur'ān daily. He said, "I saw the Lord of Power in my sleep, and said, 'O Lord, what is the best act through which those near to You draw nearer?' and He answered, 'Through [reciting] My word, O Aḥmad.' I asked, 'With under-

[259] Ibn Ḥajar, *Iṣāba* (2:326), chapter on al-Khaḍir.
[260] Al-Nawawī, *al-Tibyān* (p. 56).
[261] Narrated by Abū Nuʿaym in the *Ḥilya* (7:378) cf. *Iqāmat al-Ḥujja* (p. 90).
[262] Narrated by Abū Nuʿaym in the *Ḥilya* (7:145) and al-Dhahabī in the *ʿIbar* (1:225) cf. *Iqāmat al-Ḥujja* (p. 90-91).

standing or without?' and He answered; 'With understanding and without.'"[263]

130. Fatḥ ibn Sa'īd al-Mawṣilī was afflicted with a migraine and said: "You have tried me with the trial of the Prophets and in thanksgiving I shall pray four hundred *rak'as* tonight."[264]

131. Imām al-Shāfi'ī used to complete sixty integral readings of the Qur'ān in the month of Ramaḍān, all of which in *ṣalāt*.[265]

132. Imām Aḥmad used to pray three hundred *rak'as* daily then one hundred and fifty after his twenty-eight month imprisonment and lashing. After a light sleep right after the '*ishā* prayer he would wake up, praying and supplicating until dawn.[266]

133. Abū al-'Abbās Aḥmad ibn Muḥammad ibn Sahl ibn 'Aṭā' used to recite the entire Qur'ān once every day and night, and three times every day and night in the month of Ramaḍān.[267]

134. 'Abd al-Raḥmān ibn al-Qāsim ibn Khālid al-'Utaqī's (d. 191) daily wird included two *khatmas* of the glorious Qur'ān.[268]

135. The ḥadīth Master Manṣūr Abū 'Attāb al-Sulamī al-Kūfī fasted permanently for forty years and used to spend the night weeping.[269]

[263]Notice on Imām Aḥmad in *The Reliance of the Traveller* (x72).
[264]Narrated by Abū Nu'aym in the *Ḥilya* (7:292) cf. *Iqāmat al-Ḥujja* (p. 91).
[265]Narrated by Abū Nu'aym in the *Ḥilya* (9:134) and al-Nawawī, *Tahdhīb al-Asmā'* (1:54) cf. *Iqāmat al-Ḥujja* (p. 91-92).
[266]Narrated by Abū Nu'aym in the *Ḥilya* (9:181) and Ibn al-Jawzī in *Manāqib Aḥmad* (p. 286) cf. *Iqāmat al-Ḥujja* (p. 92).
[267]Narrated by Abū Nu'aym in the *Ḥilya* (10:302) cf. *Iqāmat al-Ḥujja* (p. 94).
[268]As narrated by al-Dhahabī in the *Siyar* (9:15), chapter on Asad ibn al-Furāt.
[269]Narrated by al-Dhahabī in the '*Ibar* (1:177) cf. *Iqāmat al-Ḥujja* (p. 94-95).

136. Abū Dāwūd al-Ṭayālisī said that Wāṣil ibn ʿAbd al-Raḥmān al-Baṣrī used to recite the entire Qur'ān once every day and night.[270]

137. Abū al-Ḥārith al-Madanī Muḥammad ibn ʿAbd al-Raḥmān ibn al-Mughīra used to pray all night long and fasted every other day at first, then permanently.[271]

138. Wakīʿ ibn al-Jarrāḥ the student of Abū Ḥanīfa and teacher of Aḥmad, fasted permanently and completed the recitation of the Qur'ān daily.[272]

139. ʿAbd Allah ibn Idrīs ibn Yazīd al-Awdī al-Kūfī said to his daughter on his deathbed: "Do not weep, I have completed the Qur'ān in this very house four thousand times."[273]

140. Abū Bakr ibn ʿAyyāsh was reported by his son Ibrāhīm to have completed the Qur'ān every single day for thirty years, and he recommended to his children the use of a certain room in which he had completed twelve thousand or twenty thousand readings.[274] Ibn Ḥajar said: "He fasted for seventy years during which he prayed all night, and he was not known to sleep at night."[275]

141. Abū Bishr Aḥmad ibn Muḥammad ibn Ḥasnūyah al-Ḥasnawī al-Naysābūrī used to complete the full recitation of the Qur'ān nightly.[276]

[270] Narrated by al-Dhahabī in the *ʿIbar* (1:218) cf. *Iqāmat al-Ḥujja* (p. 95).
[271] Narrated by al-Dhahabī in the *ʿIbar* (1:231) and al-Yāfiʿī in *Mir'āt al-Janān* (1:340) cf. *Iqāmat al-Ḥujja* (p. 95).
[272] Narrated by al-Kafawī in *Aʿlām al-Akhyār* cf. *Iqāmat al-Ḥujja* (p. 95).
[273] Narrated by al-Nawawī in *Sharḥ Ṣaḥīḥ Muslim* (1:78-79) cf. *Iqāmat al-Ḥujja* (p.97).
[274] Narrated by al-Nawawī in *Sharḥ Ṣaḥīḥ Muslim* (1:79) cf. *Iqāmat al-Ḥujja* (p. 97).
[275] Ibn Ḥajar, *Tahdhīb al-Tahdhīb* (12:39).
[276] Narrated by Ibn al-Athīr in *al-Lubāb fī Tahdhīb al-Ansāb* (1:300) cf. *Iqāmat al-Ḥujja* (p. 97).

142. The Ḥanbalī Ṣūfī and jurist Jaʿfar ibn al-Ḥasan al-Darzījānī al-Muqri' fasted, prayed, and recited Qur'ān until he would recite it in its entirety in a single *rakʿa*. He died praying, while in prostration.[277]

143. The Imām, Shaykh al-Islam, and ḥadīth Master Baqī ibn Makhlad read the entire Qur'ān every night in thirteen *rakʿas*, prayed one hundred *rakʿas* daily, and fasted permanently.[278]

144. Al-Ḥusayn ibn al-Faḍl the foremost learned authority of his time prayed six hundred *rakʿas* daily.[279]

145. Imām al-Junayd's daily *wird* was three hundred *rakʿas*.[280]

146. Abū Qilāba ʿAbd al-Mālik ibn Muḥammad al-Raqāshī al-Baṣrī (d. 276), one of the shaykhs of Ibn Mājah, used to pray four hundred *rakʿa* in every twenty-four hours.[281]

There are many more such examples. May Allah forgive us for the sake of His friends for falling so short of these magnificent examples of ʿ*ubūdiyya*! All of these are cases of Sunna innovations in worship which the Prophet ﷺ never did; yet, in no way do they contradict, but rather illustrate the principles of the Qur'ān and Sunna and they are amply supported by the Consensus and qualified juridical analogy.

[277] Narrated by Ibn Rajab in *Dhayl Ṭabaqāt al-Ḥanābila* (1:110) cf. *Iqāmat al-Ḥujja* (p. 98).
[278] Cited by al-Dhahabī in his chapter on Baqī ibn Makhlad in the *Siyar*.
[279] *Iqāmat al-Ḥujja* (p. 98).
[280] *Ibid*.
[281] Cf. Ibn Abī Yaʿlā, *Ṭabaqāt al-Ḥanābila* (1:216 §283) and al-Dhahabī, *Siyar* (10:549 §2322).

The Misconstrued Ḥadīth "Every Innovation is Misguidance"

In *al-Sunna wal-Bidʿa*, al-Sayyid ʿAbd Allah Maḥfūẓ al-Ḥaddād adduces more than three hundred and fifty narrations of the Prophet ﷺ and the Companions in refutation of the "Salafī" Muḥammad al-Shuqayrī and his book entitled *al-Sunna wal-Mubtadaʿāt*. In the latter book al-Shuqayrī displays blind fanaticism and attacks the Ulema of the Community as innovators on the misconceived basis of the Prophetic ḥadīth:

> **"Every newfangled matter (*kullu muḥdathatin*) is an innovation (*bidʿa*) and every innovation is misguidance (*ḍalāla*) <and every misguidance is in the Fire>."[282]**

[282]The full ḥadīth states that Jābir رضي الله عنه said: "When the Messenger of Allah ﷺ gave a public address his eyes would redden, his voice would rise, and his anger flare, as if he were haranguing an army. He would say: 'To proceed: Truly the most truthful of all speech is the Book of Allah, and truly the best guidance is the guidance of Muḥammad. The worst of all matters are newfangled matters. Every newfangled matter is an innovation, and every innovation is misguidance, and every misguidance is in the Fire. The Hour is about to come to you suddenly. I was sent together with the Final Hour like these [two fingers]. The Hour is coming to you in the morning, it is already touching you! I am nearer to every believer than his own soul. Whoever leaves behind property, it belongs to his dependents. Whoever leaves behind a debt or destitute dependents, the debt is on me and so is the expense of his dependents. I am the patron/protecting friend (*walī*) of the believers.'" Narrated from Jābir by al-Nasā'ī and Aḥmad respectively with a sound and a weak chain and from Ibn Masʿūd by Ibn Mājah with a weak chain. The ḥadīth is also sound in Muslim's narration from Jābir with the wording: "Every newfangled matter is an innovation and every innovation is misguidance" without mention of the Fire. Ibn Taymiyya stated in his *Minhāj al-Uṣūl* in *Majmūʿ al-Fatāwā* (19:191) that the phrase "every misguidance is in the Fire" is not a sound (*ṣaḥīḥ*) narration from the Prophet ﷺ. See the discussion of the various narrations of that ḥadīth adduced by Abū Ghudda and the latter's confirmation of Ibn Taymiyya's remark in his appendices on al-Lacknawī's *Tuḥfat al-Akhyār* (p. 139-144). See also below, n. 326.

Al-Shuqayrī and a few others systematically misconstrue the above ḥadīth to mean "every innovation without exception," misleading their followers from the path of the *Jumhūr* in disregard of the Prophet's ﷺ ḥadīth concerning the variances of scholars.

147. The Prophet ﷺ said: "If the judge (*al-ḥākim*) rules by exerting his mind and hits the mark, he has two rewards; if he rules by exerting his mind and misses the mark, he has but one reward."[283]

Accordingly, the near-totality of the scholars – including Ibn Taymiyya, the putative Imām of the Wahhābī movement – have understood, in the light of the ḥadīth of the *mujtahid's* reward and contrary to the claims of latter-day "*Salafīs*," that **the findings of *ijtihād* on the principles of the Sunna is part of the Law and not an innovation in the Religion.**

As Sayyid ʿAlī ibn Muḥammad Bā ʿAlawī said in his introduction to al-Ḥaddād's *al-Sunna wal-Bidʿa*:

> All of the Imāms are correctly guided and have their reward with Allah for their inferences and individual exertions in their diligent pursuit of the truth.... As for the likes of [Muḥammad al-Shuqayrī] the author of *al-Sunan wal-Mubtadaʿāt*, their knowledge is limited to [the letter of] one ḥadīth of the Prophet ﷺ, "Every new matter is an innovation," while they toss away every other ḥadīth of his that indicates the procurement of every good and provides the rulings that concern all new matters.... Whereas what is meant by the ḥadīth "Every new matter is an innovation" is the innovation that contravenes the texts of the Law. That, and that alone, is the innovation of misguidance.[284]

[283]Narrated from ʿAmr ibn al-ʿĀṣ and Abū Hurayra in the Six Books and Aḥmad.
[284]In al-Ḥaddād, *al-Sunna wal-Bidʿa* (p. 5-6).

All-Inclusive Expressions Implying Exceptions

Sayyid ʿAbd Allah goes on to cite several verses of the Qur'ān as proofs for the lexical understanding of expressions that outwardly denote universal inclusivity such as *kull* ("every"), each of which allows for exceptions to the rule of all-inclusiveness. This indicates, among other lexical facts, that *kull* in Arabic may mean "most" or "very many" and not necessarily "all without exception":

- {*We opened unto them the gates of all* (*kull*) *things*} (6:44) except the gates of Divine mercy.

- {*Destroying all* (*kull*) *things by commandment of its Lord*} (46:25) except the dwellings, and also the mountains, the heavens, and the earth.

- {*And she has been given (abundance) of all* (*kull*) *things*} (27:23) except the throne of Sulaymān ﷺ.

- {*And that man has only that for which he makes effort*} (53:39). However, there are proofs that reach the level of mass transmission in meaning (*tawātur maʿnawī*) whereby the Muslim can benefit from the deeds of others among his brethren and the supplication of the angels, in evidence of which Ibn Taymiyya gathered over twenty proofs which were quoted by al-Jamal in his supercommentary on *Tafsīr al-Jalālayn* for this verse.

- {*Those unto whom men* (*al-nās*) *said: Lo! the people* (*al-nās*) *have gathered against you*} (3:173), in which case both mentions of *al-nās* patently refer to a limited number and not to the totality of human beings.

- {*Lo! you (idolaters) and that (mā) which you worship beside Allah are fuel of hell*} (21:98), but ʿĪsā ﷵ, his mother, and the angels, although they were all worshipped beside Allah, are not meant by this verse.
- {*And consult with them upon the conduct of affairs*} (3:159). Ibn ʿAbbās said: "That is: in some of the affairs."[285] The Prophet ﷺ did not consult them for law-giving and legal rulings.
- {*That every (kull) soul may be requited for that which it strives (to achieve)*} (20:15). "Every soul" is here meant in the sense of what Allah does not forgive; as for what He forgives, it is excluded from the expression of universality.

[285] Narrated by Saʿīd ibn Manṣūr in his *Sunan*, al-Bukhārī in *al-Adab al-Mufrad*, and Ibn al-Mundhir with a fair chain as stated by al-Suyūṭī in *al-Durr al-Manthūr*.

The Universal Understood in Terms of the Specific

The terminology of the scholars of *Uṣūl* for the lexical and juridical rule applied in the above examples is "the universal is understood in the sense of the specific" (*al-ʿumūm bi-maʿnā al-khuṣūṣ*). Following are examples of this rule in the ḥadīth:

- The Prophet ﷺ sent a military detachment under the command of one of the Companions after ordering those who were with him to obey him faithfully. In the course of the expedition the commander became angry with them. He lit a fire and ordered them to enter it. They refused, saying: "We have fled to the Messenger of Allah ﷺ to get away from the fire (*fararnā ilā Rasūlillāhi min al-nār*)!" When the Prophet ﷺ heard about the incident he said: "Had they entered it they would not have come out of it until the Day of Resurrection. Obedience is only in good matters."[286]

- Similarly, the verse {*Obey Allah, and obey the Messenger and those of you who are in authority*} (4:59), although couched in absolute terms, is meant in absolute terms for Allah and His Messenger ﷺ only but in conditional terms for {*those of you who are in authority*} as stipulated by the Prophet's ﷺ ḥadīth: "No obedience whatsoever is due to creatures in disobedience of Allah."[287] These two ḥadīths show that, inversely, one must obey one's leaders in all good matters. Explanations of the *Salaf* for {*those who are in authority*} (4:59) include "the knowledgeable scholars of the Religion" (*al-ʿulamā'*),[288] and "the people of Religion and knowledge,"[289] particularly "the

[286] Narrated from ʿAlī by al-Bukhārī and Muslim. The leader was ʿAbd Allah ibn Ḥudhayfa al-Sahmī cf. al-Mubārakfūrī, *Tuḥfat al-Aḥwadhī* (5:259).
[287] Narrated from ʿAlī, Ibn Masʿūd, and ʿImrān ibn Ḥuṣayn by Aḥmad with sound chains.
[288] Narrated from Mujāhid and ʿAṭā' by Ibn Kathīr in his *Tafsīr* under this verse.
[289] Narrated from Ibn ʿAbbās by al-Ḥākim, Ibn al-Mundhir, al-Ṭabarī, Ibn Abī

Companions of Muḥammad who are the people of intelligence, superlative understanding, and Religion"[290], specifically the Four Rightly-Guided Caliphs and Ibn Mas'ūd,[291] and more specifically Abū Bakr and 'Umar.[292] We mentioned some of this in the chapter from al-Bayhaqī's *Madkhal*.

- The Prophet ﷺ said: "Every human being shall be consumed by the earth but for the coccyx (*'ajb al-dhanab*)."[293] Ibn 'Abd al-Barr said: "The letter of this ḥadīth and its general meaning necessitate that human beings are all undifferentiated in this case, except that it was narrated that the earth does not consume the bodies of Prophets and martyrs."[294]

Ḥātim, and Ibn Kathīr in his *Tafsīr* under this verse; and from Jābir ibn 'Abd Allah by Ibn Abī Shayba, 'Abd ibn Ḥumayd, al-Ḥakīm al-Tirmidhī, al-Ṭabarī, Ibn al-Mundhir, al-Ḥākim, and Ibn Abī Ḥātim, both as related by al-Suyūṭī in *al-Durr al-Manthūr* for this verse. Cf. above, p. 27-29.

[290]Narrated from Mujāhid by Ibn Abī Shayba, 'Abd ibn Ḥumayd, al-Ṭabarī, and Ibn al-Mundhir as related by al-Lacknawī in *Tuḥfat al-Akhyār* (p. 66); and from al-Daḥḥāk by Ibn Abī Ḥātim as related by al-Suyūṭī in *al-Durr al-Manthūr*.

[291]Narrated from al-Kalbī by 'Abd ibn Ḥumayd as related by al-Lacknawī in *Tuḥfat al-Akhyār* (p. 66) and al-Suyūṭī in *al-Durr al-Manthūr*. Cf. p. 62-63 above.

[292]Narrated from 'Ikrima by 'Abd ibn Ḥumayd, al-Ṭabarī, Ibn Abī Ḥātim, and Ibn 'Asākir as related by al-Lacknawī in *Tuḥfat al-Akhyār* (p. 66) and al-Suyūṭī in *al-Durr al-Manthūr*. Cf. above, p. 62-70.

[293]Narrated from Abū Hurayra in the Nine Books except al-Tirmidhī.

[294]Ibn 'Abd al-Barr, *al-Tamhīd* (18:173). The ḥadīth that the earth does not consume the bodies of Prophets is narrated from Aws ibn Aws al-Thaqafi by Aḥmad with a sound chain according to al-Zayn (12:474 §16107), Ibn Abī Shayba (2:516), Abū Dāwūd, al-Nasā'ī, Ibn Mājah, al-Dārimī with a sound chain as stated by Shaykh Ḥusayn Asad, Abū Nu'aym in *Ma'rifat al-Ṣaḥāba* (§976), Ibn Khuzayma with a sound chain according to al-A'ẓamī (3:118 §1733), Ibn Ḥibbān, *ṣaḥīḥ* by Muslim's criterion according to Shu'ayb al-Arna'ūṭ (3:190-191 §910), al-Ḥākim (*ṣaḥīḥ*, confirmed by al-Dhahabī 1:278, 4:560=1990 ed. 1:413, 4:604), al-Qāḍī Ismā'īl in *Faḍl al-Ṣalāt*, (*ṣaḥīḥ* p. 35), al-Ṭabarānī in his *Kabīr* (1:216 §589), al-Bayhaqī in his *Sunan* (3:248), *Shu'ab al-Īmān* (3:109-110), and *Faḍā'il al-Awqāt* (p. 497), and Ibn al-Qayyim who declared its chain "*ṣaḥīḥ* without doubt" in *Jalā' al-Afhām* (p.66-74 =42-48). As'ad Tayyim alone weakened Aws' narration and went so far as to declare it *munkar* in *Takhrīj Ḥadīth Aws al-Thaqafi* (p. 5-66) which

- The Prophet ﷺ forbade the shunning (*al-hajr*) of one Muslim by another for a period of over three days.[295] Yet he ordered the Muslims to ostracize the three Companions who had stayed back during the campaign of Tabūk, and this ostracism lasted for fifty days as narrated by Ka'b ibn Mālik al-Anṣārī – one of the three – in the two *Ṣaḥīḥs*.[296] Thus, the ḥadīth of prohibition is open to specific interpretations.

- The Prophet ﷺ said: "Truly this black seed (*al-ḥabbat al-sawdā'*) is a cure for every (*kull*) disease except death."[297] The consensus of the commentators is that the universal was named in the sense of the specific in this ḥadīth to mean that many diseases are cured by the black seed, although an all-inclusive wording was used.

- The Prophet ﷺ said: "None enters Hellfire who prays before sunrise and before sunset."[298] This ḥadīth is worded all-inclusively although it is not meant to include those who abandon the prayers of *ẓuhr*, *maghrib*, and '*ishā'*. Ibn Ḥajar confirmed al-Ṭībī's ruling that sound germane narrations must be taken together as one ḥadīth, the absolute being interpreted in light of the conditional (*yuḥmalu muṭlaquhā 'alā muqayyaduhā*) so that practice can conform with the totality of their contents.[299]

follows his *Bayān Awhām al-Albānī*. Also narrated with the wording: "Verily, among your best days is the day of Jumu'a" (*inna min afḍali ayyāmikum yawma al-jumu'a*). Cf. Ibn Ḥajar in *Fatḥ al-Bārī* (1989 ed. 6:379= 1959 ed. 6:488) and al-Nawawī as cited in Ibn 'Allān's *al-Futūḥāt al-Rabbāniyya* (3:309).

[295] Narrated from Anas by al-Bukhārī, Mālik, al-Tirmidhī, Abū Dāwūd, al-Nasā'ī.

[296] This long ḥadīth is translated in the *Encyclopedia of Islamic Doctrine* in the section listing the ḥadīths of the Companions' kissing of the Prophet's ﷺ hand.

[297] Narrated from 'Ā'isha and Abū Hurayra by al-Bukhārī, Muslim, al-Tirmidhī, Ibn Mājah, and Aḥmad through nineteen chains. Al-Zuhrī said: "The black seed is black cumin (*al-shūnīz*)." Latin name: *Nigella sativa*.

[298] Narrated from 'Umāra ibn Ru'ayba al-Thaqafī by Muslim, al-Nasā'ī, Abū Dāwūd, and Aḥmad.

[299] In *Fatḥ al-Bārī* (1959 ed. 11:271 §6080).

The "Good New Sunna" and the "Innovation of Misguidance"

What the Companions have termed "the judgment of the righteous" (§ 33-44) and "whatever the Muslims consider right" (§ 43), their innovations in practice and worship, whether in the institution of specific timings or quantities of supererogatory prayers or new supplication formulas inside and outside *ṣalāt*, or that of cures through use of the Qur'ān – all this has been termed "instituted sunnas" by the Prophet ﷺ himself in the famous ḥadīth:

148. "Whoever institutes a good practice in Islam (*man sanna fīl-islāmi sunnatan ḥasana*) has its reward and the reward of all those who practice it until the Day of Judgment without lessening the rewards of the latter. And whoever institutes a bad practice in Islam (*wa-man sanna fīl-islāmi sunnatan sayyi'atan*) bears its onus and the onus of all those who practice it until the Day of Judgment without lessening the onus of the latter."[300] The meaning of *sanna* in this ḥadīth is to start an act without precedent, as proved by the ḥadīths of Khubayb, the two narrations of Mu'ādh and Ibn Mas'ūd who "started a Sunna for you," and the narration in al-Bukhārī and Muslim stating that the son of Ādam was the first to commit murder (*awwalu man sanna al-qatl*).

The objection is heard from certain quarters that "the context of this ḥadīth is in reference to spending in the way of Allah." This is correct but irrelevant to the evidentiary aspect of the ḥadīth as the scholars of *Uṣūl* unanimously agree on the rule (*qā'ida*) in *tafsīr* as well as ḥadīth that *al-'ibratu lil-'umūm lā li-asbāb al-wurūd*, "The import of the evidence is its generality, not [limited to] the context in which it took place." Otherwise, so many verses of Qur'ān and so many ḥadīths would form rulings

[300]Narrated from Jarīr ibn 'Abd Allah al-Bajalī by Muslim, al-Tirmidhī, al-Nasā'ī, Ibn Mājah, Aḥmad, and al-Dārimī.

only for the specific Companion(s) for whom they were revealed, and be irrelevant to all others forever.

It is true that some evidence is in fact confined to the circumstances of its revelation. However, this requires (a) explicit wording to that effect in the body of the evidence, and (b) the understanding of the Scholars to that effect. These two conditions are absent from the ḥadīth in question and its commentaries. Even if they were present, the ḥadīth would form enough proof that innovations in spending *ṣadaqa* – which is a kind of worship – are good. Otherwise, anyone who claims that the ḥadīth is limited to the context of *ṣadaqa* has to provide clear and explicit evidence to that effect – and none of the Ulema has done so – short of which such an interpreter is himself a person of *bidʿa*. As for the claim that since it is connected with *ṣadaqa* then it is merely an enactment of a pre-existing Sunna, this is invalidation (*taʿṭīl*) of the meaning of the words of the Prophet ﷺ where *sanna* means "to innovate without precedent," as we discuss further below.

Further, similar narrations from different Companions suggest that the new Sunna is meant in general terms unrestricted to a specific type of act, or that the Prophet ﷺ said this on several different occasions:

149. "Whoever begins something good then others practice it (*man istanna khayran fastunna bih*), will have his reward in full as well as the rewards of those who followed his practice. Nothing of their reward will diminish. And whoever begins something bad then others practice it (*wa-man istanna sunnatan sayyiʾatan fastunna bih*), will bear its onus in full as well as the onus of those who followed his practice. Nothing of their onus will diminish.[301]

[301] Narrated from Abū Hurayra by Ibn Mājah and Aḥmad.

150. "Whoever institutes a good practice that is practiced after him (*man sanna sunnatan ḥasanatan fa'umila bihā ba'dah*) has its reward and the like of their rewards without lessening the rewards of the latter in the least. And whoever institutes a bad practice in Islam (*wa-man sanna sunnatan sayyi'atan fa'umila bihā ba'dah*) bears its onus and the like of their onus without lessening the onus of the latter in the least."[302]

151. "Whoever begins something good then others practice it (*man sanna khayran fastunna bih*), will have his reward as well as part of the rewards of those who followed him without lessening their reward in the least. And whoever begins something bad then others practice it (*wa-man sanna sharran fastunna bih*), will bear its onus as well as part of the onus of those who followed him without lessening their onus in the least."[303]

Another whispering emanates from naysayers, namely, that *sanna* in the above narrations "means that a pre-existing Sunna has been revived." Thus, they not only speak without proof but falsify and allegorize the words of the Best of creation ﷺ so as to misrepresent him as incapable of expressing himself clearly on a most simple matter – instead needing them to come after 1,400 years to clarify what he meant! We have already mentioned the proofs that the meaning of *sanna* in the above ḥadīth is to start an act without precedent. Further, the ḥadīths are clear that the new Sunna is put into practice after the person who initiated it. Further, if the Prophet ﷺ wanted to say "Whoever revives a Sunna" (*man aḥyā sunnatan*) he would have said "Whoever revives a Sunna" just as he did in several other cases! In addition, if we were to follow their misinterpretation then we would have to apply it to the second half of the ḥadīth also, and end up saying that it means "whoever revives a bad practice in Islam,"

302 Narrated from Ḥudhayfa by Aḥmad.
303 Narrated from Abū Juḥayfa by Ibn Mājah.

thus eliminating from its compass all strictly new innovations – a patently incorrect conclusion.

The ḥadīth "Whoever institutes a good practice" thus forms the strongest explicit evidence for what the scholars of the foundations of Jurisprudence have called the "excellent innovation" (*al-bid'atu al-ḥasana*) which is more correctly called a "good new sunna." They concur that the ḥadīth forms an explicit Prophetic sanction as to the division of new matters into good and bad in the matter of legal rulings, the criteria being, as al-Shāfi'ī said, the Qur'ān and the Sunna.

This understanding is confirmed by two other ḥadīths: (a) one in which the Prophet ﷺ allusively endorses good innovations in Islamic Law by specifically condemning innovations that are not part of the Law; and (b) one in which he explicitly uses the precise term "innovation of misguidance" or *bid'a ḍalala* and restrictively defines it as "an innovation that displeases Allah and His Messenger," both ḥadīths implying a twofold classification of innovations that was put into practice by the Companions, the *Salaf*, and the *Khalaf* as shown below:

152. "Whoever innovates in this Matter of ours something that does not belong in it, this is rejected" (*man aḥdatha fī amrinā hādhā mā laysa minhu fahuwa radd*).[304] Meaning: whoever innovates in this Matter of ours something that does belong in it, it is accepted. Shaykh Nūr al-Dīn 'Itr said **this ḥadīth is the clearest proof for the innovation of guidance.**[305]

[304]Narrated from 'Ā'isha by al-Bukhārī, Muslim, Abū Dāwūd, Ibn Mājah, and Aḥmad.

[305]Beware of those that massacre this ḥadīth as: "Nabi ﷺ said, 'Whosoever initiates a new action in our Deen, it is rejected.' (*Mishkaat*)," as found on the site http:/ /www.islam.tc/ask-imam/view.php?q=5246. Whether deliberately or out of ignorance, some people misquote it then pose as dispensers of *fatwā* to defend the exact opposite of the principle the ḥadīth supports!

153. "Whoever innovates an **innovation of misguidance** which does not please Allah and His Messenger (*man ibtadaʿa bidʿatan ḍalālatan lā turḍī Allaha wa-rasūlah*), there will be placed upon him the like of the sins of whoever practices it, and this shall not diminish their own sins in the least."[306]

The above narrations elucidate and accompany the narrations that mention only the reprehensible type of innovations, such as "Every innovation is a misguidance" and the ḥadīth, "Whoever innovates something new (*aḥdatha ḥādithan*) or abets someone who does (*aw āwā muḥdithan*), upon him is the curse of Allah, the angels, and that of all people! There shall be accepted from him neither barter (*ṣarf*) nor balance (*ʿadal*)."[307] These reports do not comprise nor refer to innovations of guidance but only to innovations that make one fall outside the fold of the massive congregation of the Muslims which is *Ahl al-Sunna wal-Jamāʿa*. Such reports indirectly support innovations of guidance.

154. ʿUmar's words about the *tarāwīḥ* or congregational supererogatory night prayers in the month of Ramaḍān explicitly reflect this twofold definition of innovations: "What a fine innovation (*niʿmati al-bidʿa*) this is!"[308] Meaning: the unified congregational prayer of twenty or more rakʿas, which was **not** done in the time of the Prophet ﷺ but which was innovated on grounds entirely sanctioned and supported by the Law. This is the essence of *al-bidʿatu al-ḥasana* and this is how our liege-lord ʿUmar, the Companions and *Tābiʿīn*, al-Shāfiʿī, and the totality of the Sunni Ulema of this *Umma* understood it as indicated, for example, by

[306] Narrated from ʿAmr ibn ʿAwf al-Muzanī by al-Tirmidhī (*ḥasan*). Cf. Ibn al-ʿArabī, *ʿĀriḍat al-Aḥwadhī* (10:148).
[307] Part of a longer ḥadīth narrated from ʿAlī by al-Bukhārī, Abū Dāwūd, Aḥmad, and others.
[308] Narrated from ʿAbd al-Raḥmān ibn ʿAbd by Mālik (*niʿmati al-bidʿatu hādhih*) and al-Bukhārī (*niʿma al-bidʿatu hādhih*).

al-Suyūṭī in his *fatwā* on *tarāwīḥ* – although he opens it with the words that the Prophet ﷺ never prayed more than eight *rak'as*, – al-'Askārī, who stated in *al-Awā'il* or "the book of Firsts" that "the first who innovated (*sanna*) the [congregational] prayer of Ramaḍān is 'Umar in the year 14" and al-Ṣan'ānī in *Subul al-Salām*.[309] All of this understanding is confirmed in the report of 'Urwa ibn al-Zubayr:

155. "'Umar ibn al-Khaṭṭāb was the first to gather the people for the [congregational] night prayer of the month of Ramaḍān; the men behind Ubay ibn Ka'b and the women behind Sulaymān ibn Abī Khathma."[310]

Thus, none of the reliable authorities of the *Salaf* and *Khalaf* allegorized the words of 'Umar as referring merely to "a lexical innovation as opposed to a legal innovation" as some quarters claim today, concluding that 'Umar said *bid'a* but did not mean *bid'a*! On the contrary, they all understood, on the one hand, that 'Umar meant an actual innovation by his words and, on the other, that it was a praiseworthy innovation sanctioned by Allah ﷻ and His Prophet ﷺ.

Accordingly, the Consensus of the Companions formed during the last three of the four Rightly-Guided caliphates, that the number of *rak'as* in the congregational *tarāwīḥ* is twenty or more even though [1] it is not established that the Prophet ﷺ ever prayed more than eight or ten, and [2] it is established that he prayed eight or ten in Ramaḍān and outside it. However, as the impeccable Shaykh al-Islām al-Taqī al-Subkī, al-Zarkashī, and al-Suyūṭī stated, **nowhere in the *Ṣaḥīḥ* is the number of rak'as prayed by the Prophet ﷺ in the first three nights of Ramaḍān,**

[309]Cf. al Suyūṭī, *al-Maṣābīḥ fī Ṣalāt al-Tarāwīḥ* (p. 12-13), al-'Askarī, *al-Awā'il* (1:225-226), and al-Ṣan'ānī, *Subul al-Salām* (2:10).

[310]Narrated from 'Urwa by al-Bayhaqī in *al-Sunan al-Kubrā* (2:494) cf. al-Suyūṭī, *al-Maṣābīḥ* (p. 17-18).

before he stopped, specified.[311] Those who, in our time, incorrectly inferred from the above facts that the Sunna in congregational *tarāwīḥ* prayers should necessarily be kept to eight *rak'as* (in keeping with their desire to always do less – less *ṣalāt*, less *du'ā'*, less *dhikr*, less *ṣalawāt*) have therefore spoken without knowledge, violated the Prophetic instruction to adhere to the Sunna of the Rightly-Guided Caliphs, broken the ranks of *ijmā'*, and committed misguided innovation. Al-Suyūṭī said: "Surely, if the exact number of the *tarāwīḥ* had been a subject of textual stipulation, it would have been impermissible to the first generations to add anything to it. The people of Madīna and the early Muslims were certainly more scrupulous than to commit such an act!"[312]

156. Similarly, Abū Umāma al-Bāhilī ﷺ said: "Truly Allah ordained for you the fast of Ramaḍān but He did not ordain for you its standing in prayer. Its standing in prayer is only something which you all innovated, therefore, persist in it and do not abandon it, for certain people among the Israelites innovated something in pursuit of the good pleasure of Allah, then Allah reproached them for abandoning it. Then he recited: {*Monasticism they invented – We ordained it not for them – only seeking the pleasure of Allah, and they observed it not with right observance*} (57:27)."[313] This is an explicit comparison between two innovations showing that the *Salaf* understood that the innovation of monasticism was not bad in itself but only because it was not observed properly by those who had innovated it.

157. Similarly, Ibn 'Umar replied, when asked about praying the midmorning *ḍuḥā* prayer in congregation (as is sometimes done today in Southeast Asia) or in the mosque (as the Yemeni

[311] Al-Suyūṭī, *al-Maṣābīḥ* (p. 9, 19).
[312] *Ibid.* (p. 14).
[313] Narrated from Zakariyyā ibn Abī Maryam by al-Ṭabarī in his *Tafsīr* (27:240).

Shuyūkh stress): "It is an innovation and what a fine innovation it is!" (*bidʿatun wa-niʿmati al-bidʿatu hiya*).[314]

158. Another reply to the same question by Ibn ʿUmar: "At the time ʿUthmān was killed no one considered it desirable [in the Religion] (*mā aḥadun yastaḥibbuhā*), and the people did not innovate anything that is dearer to me than that prayer."[315] Both this and the preceding report refer to *ṣalāt al-ḍuḥā* as prayed in congregation or on a regular basis in the Mosque or both. (See detailed study further below.)

159. Abū Khaythama narrated that Ismāʿīl ibn ʿUlayya gathered the people and said to them: "The Qur'ān is the Speech of Allah, and whoever says that the Qur'ān is created is an innovator (*mubtadiʿ*)." They said: "Abū Bishr! [Do you mean] an innovation of misguidance (*bidʿa ḍalāla*)?" He replied: "Yes, an innovation of misguidance."[316]

Ibn ʿUlayya did not reply to them: "All innovations are innovations of misguidance!" Rather, he acknowledged what everyone knew at the time and what his younger contemporary al-Shāfiʿī and others also acknowledged, namely, that there are two different types of innovations, those of guidance, and those of misguidance. Thus did Imām al-Shāfiʿī understand it in his famous statement "Innovations are of two kinds" which Ibn ʿAbd al-Salām elaborated in his fivefold classification of innovations – adopted by the *jumhūr* – in his book *al-Iḥkām fī Uṣūl al-Aḥkām*, and other Imāms of the Law.

[314]Narrated from al-Ḥakam ibn al-Aʿraj by Ibn Abī Shayba (2:172) with a sound chain according to Ibn Ḥajar, *Fatḥ al-Bārī* (1959 ed. 3:52) and from Mujāhid by Ibn al-Jaʿd in his *Musnad* (p. 314) and al-Ṭabarānī in *al-Muʿjam al-Kabīr* (12:424).

[315]Narrated from Sālim ibn ʿAbd Allah ibn ʿUmar by ʿAbd al-Razzāq with a sound chain according to Ibn Ḥajar in *Fatḥ al-Bārī* (3:52).

[316]In Ibn Maʿīn, *Min Kalām Abī Zakariyyā Yaḥyā ibn Maʿīn fil-Rijāl* (Ed. Aḥmad Muḥammad Nūr Sayf, Damascus: Dār al-Ma'mūn lil-Turāth, 1980, p. 124).

Al-Shāfiʿī's Definition of Innovation as Either "Good" or "Bad"

A major contribution of Imām al-Shāfiʿī ﵁ in the Foundations of Jurisprudence (*Uṣūl al-fiqh*) is his division of innovation (*al-bidʿa*) and innovated matters (*al-muḥdathāt*) into "good" and "bad" depending on their conformity or non-conformity to the guidelines of the Religion. This is authentically narrated from al-Shāfiʿī from two of his most prestigious students in the latter period of his life, the Egyptian ḥadīth Masters Ḥarmala ibn Yaḥyā al-Tujaybī and al-Rabīʿ ibn Sulaymān al-Murādī:

160. Ḥarmala said, "I heard al-Shāfiʿī say: 'Innovation is two types (*al-bidʿatu bidʿatān*): praiseworthy innovation (*bidʿa maḥmūda*) and blameworthy innovation (*bidʿa madhmūma*). Whatever conforms to the Sunna is approved (*maḥmūd*) and whatever opposes it is abominable (*madhmūm*).' He used as his proof the statement of ʿUmar ibn al-Khaṭṭāb about the [congregational] supererogatory night prayers in the month of Ramaḍān: "What a fine innovation this is!"[317] This shows that al-Shāfiʿī never interpreted ʿUmar's words figuratively the way the "Salafi" *muʿaṭṭila* do.

161. Al-Rabīʿ said, "Al-Shāfiʿī said to us: 'Innovated matters are of two kinds (*al-muḥdathātu min al-umūri ḍarbān*): one is an innovation that contravenes (*mā uḥditha yukhālifu*) something in the Qur'ān or the Sunna or a Companion-report (*athar*) or the Consensus (*ijmāʿ*): **that** innovation is misguidance (*fahādhihi al-bidʿatu ḍalāla*). The other kind is the innovation of any and all good

[317]Narrated from Ḥarmala by Abū Nuʿaym with his chain through Abū Bakr al-Ājurrī in *Ḥilyat al-Awliyā'* (9:121 §13315=1985 ed. 9:113) and cited by Abū Shāma in *al-Bāʿith ʿalā Inkār al-Bidʿa wal-Ḥawādith* (Ryadh 1990 ed. p. 93), Ibn Rajab in *Jāmiʿ al-ʿUlūm wal-Ḥikam* (p. 267=Zuḥaylī ed. 2:52= Arna'ūṭ ed. 2:131 *ṣaḥīḥ*), Ibn Ḥajar in *Fatḥ al-Bārī* (1959 ed. 13:253), al-Ṭurṭūshī in *al-Ḥawādith wal-Bidaʿ* (p. 158-159), and al-Shawkānī, *al-Qawl al-Mufīd fī Adillat al-Ijtihād wal-Taqlīd* (1347/1929 ed. p. 36).

things (*mā uḥditha min al-khayr*) contravening none of the above, and this is a blameless innovation (*wa-hādhihi muḥdathatun ghayru madhmūma*). ʿUmar said of the prayers of Ramaḍān: 'What a fine *bidʿa* this is!', meaning that it was innovated without having existed before and, even so, there was nothing in it that contradicted the above.'"[318]

Thus al-Shāfiʿī set forth the essential, indispensable criterion for the determination of true *bidʿa*, as defined, as already cited, by Imām al-Haytamī, Qāḍī Abū Bakr Ibn al-ʿArabī, Imām al-Lacknawī, and others.

Consequently, as we already said, **it is not enough for something merely to be novel to be a *bidʿa*; it must also contradict the Religion.**

Al-Bayhaqī commented on al-Rabīʿs report thus:

> Similarly, debating with the people of innovations – when they make public their innovations or bring up their insinuations – to refute them and expose their fallacies: even if this is an innovation, nevertheless, it is a praiseworthy one because it consists in refuting what we just mentioned. The Prophet ﷺ was asked about Divine foreordainment (*al-qadar*) and so were some of the Companions, and they replied with the answers that were narrated to us from them. At that time, they contented themselves with the words of the Prophet ﷺ and, thereafter, with the reports to that effect. However, in our time, the innovators do not content themselves with such reports nor

[318]Narrated from al-Rabīʿ by al-Bayhaqī in his *Madkhal* (§253) and *Manāqib al-Shāfiʿī* (1:469) with a sound chain as stated by Ibn Taymiyya in his *Darʾ Taʿāruḍ al-ʿAql wal-Naql* (p. 171) and through al-Bayhaqī by Ibn ʿAsākir in *Tabyīn Kadhib al-Muftarī* (Kawtharī ed. p. 97). Cited by al-Dhahabī in the *Siyar* (8:408), Ibn Rajab in *Jāmiʿ al-ʿUlūm wal-Ḥikam* (p. 267=Zuḥaylī ed. 2:52-53=Arnaʾūṭ ed. 2:131 *ṣaḥīḥ*), and Ibn Ḥajar in *Fatḥ al-Bārī* (1959 ed. 13:253).

> do they accept them. Therefore, it is necessary to refute their insinuations – when they make them public – with what they themselves consider proofs. And success is through Allah.[319]

This is a clear-cut defense of the necessity and Sunna character of *kalām* in the defense against innovators on the part of Imām al-Bayhaqī. Something similar is reported from al-Qushayrī, Ibn ʿAsākir, Ibn al-Ṣalāḥ, al-Nawawī, Ibn al-Subkī, Ibn ʿĀbidīn, and others of the great Imāms we cited in our chapter on Imām Aḥmad in *The Four Imāms and Their Schools.*

[319] Al-Bayhaqī, *Manāqib al-Shāfiʿī* (1:469).

Division of *Bid'a* into Good and Bad among *Ahl al-Sunna* and Ẓāhirīs

Al-Ghazzālī's Identical Definition

Ḥujjat al-Islam al-Ghazzālī said in his discussion of the adding of dots to the Qur'ānic script:

> The fact that this is innovated (*muḥdath*) forms no impediment to this. How many innovated matters are excellent! As it was said [by al-Shāfiʿī] concerning the establishing of congregations in *tarāwīḥ*, that it was among the innovations of ʿUmar ⚭ and that it was an excellent innovation (*bidʿa ḥasana*): the blameworthy *bidʿa* is only what opposes the ancient Sunna or might lead to changing it.[320]

Ibn al-ʿArabī al-Mālikī's Identical Definition

The *Qāḍī* Abū Bakr Ibn al-ʿArabī said in his discussion of *bidʿa*:

> Know – may Allah grant you knowledge! – that innovated matters are two kinds (*al-muḥdathātu ḍarbān*). [1] An innovated matter that has no basis other than lust and arbitrary practice. Such is categorically invalid. And [2] an innovated matter understood to correspond to something [established]. Such is the Sunna of the Caliphs and that of the eminent Imāms. **Innovated matters and innovations are not blameworthy merely for being called *muḥdath* and *bidʿa* nor because of their meaning!** Allah Most High said, {*Never comes there unto them a new (muḥdath) reminder from their Lord*} (21:2) and ʿUmar ⚭ said: 'What a fine *bidʿa* this is!' Rather, **only the *bidʿa* that contradicts the Sunna is blameworthy and only the innovated matters that invite to misguidance are blameworthy.**[321]

---

[320] Al-Ghazzālī, *Iḥyāʾ ʿUlūm al-Dīn* (1:276).
[321] Ibn al-ʿArabī, *ʿĀriḍat al-Aḥwadhī* (10:146-147).

Ibn Ḥazm and Ibn al-Jawzī's Identical Definitions

Ibn Ḥazm al-Ẓāhirī said:

> *Bidʿa* in the Religion is everything that did not come to us in the Qurʾān nor from the Messenger of Allah ﷺ, except that **one is rewarded for some of it and those who do this are excused if they have good intentions.**[322] Of it is the rewardable and excellent (*ḥasan*), namely, what is basically permitted (*mā kāna aṣluhu al-ibāḥa*) as was narrated from ʿUmar ؓ: "What a fine *bidʿa* this is!" Such refers to **all good deeds which the texts stipulated in general terms of desirability even if their practice was not fixed in the text.** And of it is the blameworthy for which there is no excuse such as what has proofs against its invalidity.[323]

Ibn al-Jawzī speaks in similar terms in the beginning of his *Talbīs Iblīs*:

> Certain innovated matters (*muḥdathāt*) have taken place which do not oppose the Sacred Law nor contradict it, so they [the *Salaf*] saw no harm in practicing them, such as the convening of the people by ʿUmar ؓ for the night prayer in Ramaḍān, after which he saw them and said: "What a fine *bidʿa* this is!"

Basic desirability despite innovative modality is the concept summed up by Shaykh al-Islām Zakariyyā al-Anṣārī in his expression: "The basis is sunna while the 'how' is an innovation (*al-aṣlu sunnatun wal-kayfu bidʿa*)."[324]

---

[322] Ibn Taymiyya repeated those very words in his discussion of *Mawlid*. See our booklet *Mawlid: Celebrating the Birth of the Holy Prophet* ﷺ.
[323] Ibn Ḥazm, *al-Iḥkām fī Uṣūl al-Aḥkām* (1:47).
[324] Cited by al-Haytamī in *al-Durr al-Manḍūd* (p. 157)

Ibn al-Athīr al-Jazarī's Identical Definition

The lexicographer Ibn al-Athīr said in his masterpiece, *al-Nihāya fī Gharīb al-Ḥādīth wal-Athar*:

> *Bid'a* is two kinds: the *bid'a* of guidance and the *bid'a* of misguidance (*bid'atu hudā wa-bid'atu ḍalāla*). Whatever contravenes the command of Allah and His Messenger ﷺ falls within the sphere of blame and condemnation. And whatever enters into the generality of what Allah or His Prophet ﷺ commended or stressed falls within the sphere of praise. Whatever has no precedent such as extreme generosity or goodness – such are among the praiseworthy acts. It is impermissible that such be deemed to contravene the Law because the Prophet ﷺ has stipulated that such would carry reward when he said: "Whoever institutes a good practice in Islam has its reward and the reward of all those who practice it." And he said, conversely, "whoever institutes a bad practice in Islam bears its onus and the onus of all those who practice it."[325]
>
> Such is when the act goes against what Allah and His Messenger ﷺ commanded. [...] It is in this sense that the ḥadīth "every innovation is misguidance"[326] is understood: he means,

[325] See note 300 above.

[326] Narrated from al-'Irbāḍ ibn Sāriya by al-Tirmidhī (*ḥasan ṣaḥīḥ*), Abū Dāwūd, Ibn Mājah, Aḥmad, al-Dārimī, Ibn Ḥibbān (1:178-179 §5 *ṣaḥīḥ*), al-Ḥākim (1:95-97=1990 ed. 1:174-177) – declaring it *ṣaḥīḥ* while al-Dhahabī confirmed it – and in *al-Madkhal ilā al-Ṣaḥīḥ* (p. 80-81), al-Ājurrī in *al-Sharī'a* (p. 54-55 §79-82=p. 46 *ṣaḥīḥ*), Ibn Abī 'Āṣim in *al-Sunna* (p. 29 §54 *ṣaḥīḥ*), al-Ṭaḥāwī in *Mushkil al-Āthār* (2:69=3:221-224 §1185-1187 *ṣaḥīḥ*), Muḥammad ibn Naṣr al-Marwazī in *al-Sunna* (p. 26-27 §69-72 *ṣaḥīḥ*), al-Ḥārith ibn Abī Usāma in his *Musnad* (1:197-198), al-Rūyānī in his *Musnad* (1:439), Abū Nu'aym in *Ḥilyat al-Awliyā'* (1985 ed. 5:220-221, 10:115), al-Ṭabarānī in *Musnad al-Shāmiyyīn* (1:254, 1:402, 1:446, 2:197, 2:298) and *al-Kabīr* (18:245-257), al-Bayhaqī in *al-Sunan al-Kubrā* (10:114), *al-Madkhal* (p. 115-116), *al-I'tiqād* (p. 229), and *Shu'ab al-Īmān* (6:67), al-Baghawī who declared it *ḥasan* in *Sharḥ al-Sunna* (1:205 §102 *isnād ṣaḥīḥ*), Ibn al-Athīr in *Jāmi' al-Uṣūl* (1:187, 1:279), Ibn 'Asākir in *al-Arba'īn al-*

whatever contravenes the bases of the Law and does not concur with the Sunna.[327]

Ibn ʿAbd al-Salām's Final Fivefold Classification

Shaykh al-Islam, Sulṭān al-ʿUlāmā', Imām al-ʿIzz Ibn ʿAbd al-Salām similarly said:

> There are different types of innovations (*bidʿa*). The first type is whatever the Law indicated as praiseworthy or obligatory and the like of which was not done in the first period of Islam. The second type is whatever the Law indicated as forbidden or disliked, and which was not done in the first period of Islam. The third type is whatever the Law indicated as indifferently permitted and which was not done in the first period of Islam.[328]

Elsewhere he states that the categories of *bidʿa* are five, identical to the jurists' classification of deeds: "obligatory" (*wājib*), "forbidden" (*ḥarām*), "recommended" (*mandūb*), "disliked" (*makrūh*), and "indifferently permitted" (*mubāḥ*).[329]

Al-Nawawī's Endorsement of the Fivefold Classification

Shaykh al-Islam, Imām al-Nawawī said:

> *Al-bidʿa* in the Law is the innovating of what did not exist in the time of the Messenger of Allah ﷺ and is divided into

Buldāniyya (p. 121), Ibn ʿAbd al-Barr in *al-Tamhīd* (21:278-279) and *Jāmiʿ Bayān al-ʿIlm* (2:924 §1758) where he declared it *ṣaḥīḥ*, and others. Cf. note 282 above.

[327] Ibn al-Athīr, *al-Nihāya* (1:79 entry *b-d-ʿ*).

[328] Ibn ʿAbd al-Salām, *al-Fatāwā al-Mawṣiliyya* (p. 129).

[329] Ibn ʿAbd al-Salām, *al-Qawāʿid al-Kubrā* (2:337-339) cf. al-Nawawī in *al-Adhkār* (Thaqāfiyya ed. p. 237) and *Tahdhīb al-Asmā' wal-Lughāt* (3:20-22) al-Kirmānī in *al-Kawākib al-Darārī* (9:54), Ibn Ḥajar in *Fatḥ al-Bārī* (13:253-254), al-Suyūṭī, introduction to *Ḥusn al-Maqṣid* in *al-Ḥāwī lil-Fatāwī*, al-Haytamī, *Fatāwā Ḥadīthiyya* (p. 150), Ibn ʿĀbidīn, *Radd al-Muḥtār* (1:376) etc.

"excellent" and "bad" (*wa-hiya munqasimatun ilā ḥasanatin wa-qabīḥa*). The Shaykh, the Imām on whose foremost leadership, greatness, standing, and brilliance in all kinds of Islamic sciences there is consensus, Abū Muḥammad ʿAbd al-ʿAzīz ibn ʿAbd al-Salām – Allah have mercy on him and be well-pleased with him! – said toward the end of his book, *al-Qawāʿid* [*al-Kubrā*]: "Innovation is divided into 'obligatory' (*wājiba*), 'forbidden' (*muḥarrama*), 'recommended' (*mandūba*), 'offensive' (*makrūha*), and 'indifferent' (*mubāḥa*). The way [to discern what applies] in this is that the innovation be examined in the light of the regulations of the Law (*qawāʿid al-sharīʿa*). If it falls under the regulations of obligatoriness (*ījāb*) then it is obligatory; under the regulations of prohibitiveness (*taḥrīm*) then it is prohibited; recommendability, then recommended; offensiveness, then offensive; indifference, then indifferent.[330]

Ibn Ḥajar's Endorsement of the Fivefold Classification

The Ḥāfiẓ Ibn Ḥajar said:

> The root meaning of innovation is what is produced without precedent. It is applied in the law in opposition to the Sunna and is, in that case, blameworthy. Strictly speaking, if it is part of what is classified as commendable by the law then it is an excellent innovation (*ḥasana*), while if it is part of what is classified as blameworthy by the law then it is blameworthy (*mustaqbaḥa*), otherwise it falls in the category of what is indifferently permitted (*mubāḥ*). It can be divided into the known five categories.[331]

[330] Al-Nawawī, *Tahdhīb al-Asmā' wal-Lughāt* (3:20-22).
[331] Ibn Hajar, *Fatḥ al-Bārī* (1959 ed. 4:253=1989 ed. 4:318). See epigraph.

Agreement of the Schools over the Fivefold Classification

Agreement formed in the Four Schools around the fivefold classification of *bid'a* as illustrated by the endorsement of the major later authorities in each School.

[1] Among the Ḥanafīs: al-Kirmānī, Ibn ʿĀbidīn, al-Turkmānī, al-ʿAynī, Ibrāhīm al-Ḥalabī, and al-Tahānawī.[332]

[2] Among the Mālikīs: al-Ṭurṭūshī, Ibn al-Ḥājj, al-Qarāfī, and al-Zarqānī, while al-Shāṭibī objected that the fivefold classification was "an invented matter without proof in the Law"![333]

[3] Consensus among the Shāfiʿīs.[334]

[4] Reluctant acceptance among later Ḥanbalīs, some of whom altered al-Shāfiʿī and Ibn ʿAbd al-Salām's terminology to read "lexical innovation" (*bidʿa lughawiyya*) and "legal innovation" (*bidʿa sharʿiyya*), respectively matching al-Shāfiʿī's "approved" and "abominable."[335] This manner of splitting hairs has become

[332] Al-Kirmānī, *al-Kawākib al-Darārī Sharḥ Ṣaḥīḥ al-Bukhārī* (9:54), Ibn ʿĀbidīn, *Ḥāshiya* (1:376, 1:560); al-Turkmānī, *al-Lumaʿ fil-Ḥawādith wal-Bidaʿ* (Stuttgart, 1986, 1:37); al-Tahānawī, *Kashshāf Iṣṭilāḥat al-Funūn* (Beirut, 1966, 1:133-135); al-ʿAynī, *ʿUmdat al-Qārī* in al-Ḥimyarī, *al-Bidʿat al-Ḥasana* (p. 152-153), Ibrāhīm ibn Muḥammad al-Ḥalabī in *al-Rahṣ li-Mustaḥill al-Raqṣ*.

[333] Al-Ṭurṭūshī, *Kitāb al-Ḥawādith wal-Bidaʿ* (p. 15, p. 158-159); Ibn al-Ḥājj, *Madkhal al-Sharʿ al-Sharīf* (Cairo, 1336/1918 2:115); al-Qarāfī, *al-Furūq* (4:219); al-Shāṭibī, *al-Iʿtiṣām* (1:188-191) and his *Fatāwā* (p. 234-235); al-Zarqānī, *Sharḥ al-Muwaṭṭa'* (1:238). Al-Shāṭibī's *Iʿtiṣām* was recirculated by two Wahhābīs: Rashīd Riḍā then Salīm Hilālī. A third, Muḥammad ʿAbd al-Salām Khaḍir al-Shuqayrī, Riḍā's student, authored *al-Sunan wal-Mubtadaʿāt al-Mutaʿalliqa bil-Adhkār wal-Ṣalawāt* which he filled with unverifiable tales he proceeds to denounce with much ado as we already mentioned.

[334] Abū Shāma, *al-Bāʿith ʿalā Inkār al-Bidaʿ wal-Ḥawādith* (Riyaḍ: Dār al-Rāya, 1990 p. 93, Cairo ed. p. 12-13) as well as those already mentioned.

[335] Ibn Rajab, *al-Jāmiʿ fil-ʿUlūm wal-Ḥikam* (2:50-53), and Ibn Taymiyya's section on *bidʿa* in his *Iqtiḍā' al-Ṣirāṭ al-Mustaqīm Mukhālafat Aṣḥāb al-Jaḥīm*. This is also the position of Ibn Kathīr: see his *Tafsīr* on the verse: {*The Originator of the heavens and the earth!*} (2:117). He followed in this his teacher Ibn Taymiyya.

the shibboleth of Wahhābism in every micro-debate on *bid'a* although the correct way – as usual – is patently that of the *Jumhūr*.

Shaykh Muḥammad Bakhīt al-Muṭī'ī said that "The legal *bid'a* is the one that is misguidance and condemned; as for the *bid'a* that the Ulema divided into obligatory and forbidden and so forth, such is the lexical *bid'a* which is more inclusive than the legal because the legal is only part of it."[336]

Al-Shawkānī said in *Nayl al-Awṭār* that the foundational division of innovations into "good" and "bad" is the soundest and most correct position.[337]

It is enough that a major *Mujtahid* Imām of the *Salaf* said so on the basis of the Qur'ān and Sunna regardless of the argumentations of later centuries – whether from a *murajjiḥ* like al-Shawkānī or a censor like al-Shāṭibī – in the light of concurrence of the *Jumhūr* around al-Shāfi'ī's explanation and the Divine and Prophetic injunctions to follow the path of the Believers and stay with their greatest mass. And Allah knows best.

[336] Bakhīt, *Fatāwā Ḥadīthiyya* (p. 205).
[337] Al-Shawkānī, *Nayl al-Awṭār* (4:60).

Conclusion: The Prophet ﷺ Distinguished Between Good *Bid'a* and Bad *Bid'a*

In conclusion, there are three divisions of the terminology of the Prophet ﷺ on matters of innovation:

a) The Prophet ﷺ generally condemned all innovations in the ḥadīth: "*Kullu bid'atin ḍalāla*." This is a general, unspecific (*'āmm*) phrasing and there is no disagreement over this.

b) The Prophet ﷺ explicitly condemned bad innovations in the ḥadīth narrated by al-Tirmidhī from 'Amr ibn 'Awf, "Whoever innovates an innovation of misguidance..."

c) The Prophet ﷺ explicitly praised good innovations in the ḥadīth of Jarīr ibn 'Abd Allah al-Bajalī, "Whoever innovates a good Sunna..."

Thus, the Prophet ﷺ (a) generally condemned all innovations; (b) specifically condemned bad innovations; and (c) explicitly praised good innovations. The rule that must be applied according to the principles of jurisprudence (*qā'ida uṣūliyya*) states: *al-lafẓu al-khāṣṣ muqaddamun 'alā al-'āmm*, meaning, "Specific terminology takes precedence over the general one." Therefore, the ḥadīth of general terminology, *kullu bid'atin ḍalāla*, must be understood in the light of the ḥadīths of specific terminology in (b) and (c) and not vice-versa.

The terms used in the second part of the ḥadīth of Jarīr is confirmed by the ḥadīth of 'Amr, namely *sanna sunnatan sayyi'a* = *ibtada'a bid'atan ḍalala*. This is enough evidence from the blessed mouth of the Prophet ﷺ, by contrapositive proof, that *sanna sunnatan ḥasana* = *ibtada'a bid'atan ḥasana* and that there is no difference between the *bid'a ḥasana* and the excellent sunna other than the classification of the Prophet's ﷺ sunna as a *sunna tashrīʿiyya* or "law-making sunna," while the sunna of the Companions and all subsequent sunnas are called *sunna qiyāsiyya* or "analogical sunna." It is on these principles that "the good innovation is," as Shaykh ʿĪsā al-Ḥimyarī said, "one of the foundations of the Law."[338]

If the above were not enough evidence for the twofold classification of *bidʿa*, it would be enough evidence for the people of truth and sound hearts that the massive majority of the Ulema of the four Sunni Schools accept that twofold classification, and the Prophet ﷺ said: "You must stay with the greatest mass."[339]

There are numerous additional verses and sound ḥadīths that similarly illustrate the above principles. It is therefore a mark of ignorance of the foundations of the Law and of the Islamic sciences – as well as a patent contravention of the practice of the *Salaf* and *Khalaf* of *Ahl al-Sunna* – to interpret the ḥadīth "Every new matter is an innovation" in the absolute sense and refuse to subject it to the established rules provided by the *Sharīʿa* in such a case!

Imām al-Nawawī in *Sharḥ Ṣaḥīḥ Muslim* said of the ḥadīth "Every new matter is an innovation":

> This is an universal rule understood specifically (*ʿāmmun makhṣūṣ*). What is meant by it is **new matters that are not validated by the Sharīʿa. That – and that alone – is what is meant by innovations** (*al-bidaʿ*).[340]

[338] Al-Ḥimyarī, *al-Bidʿatu al-Ḥasana Aṣlun min Uṣūl al-Tashrīʿ*.
[339] See above, § 45.
[340] Al-Nawawī, *Sharḥ Ṣaḥīḥ Muslim* (1972 ed. 6:154).

Part Two

Case Studies

Collective Supplication (*al-Du'ā'u Jamā'atan*)

Imām al-Jazarī in his book *al-Ḥiṣn al-Ḥaṣīn* ("The Impregnable Fortress") which he wrote at the time Syria was under attack by the Mongols, includes congregational participation in the etiquette of *du'ā*: "Let both the supplicant and the listener say *Āmīn*." Al-Shawkānī said in his commentary on that work titled *Tuḥfat al-Dhākirīn* (p. 59): "Something is mentioned in the *ṣaḥīḥ* ḥadīth which guides [us] to this [practice]. Abū Dāwūd narrated that the Prophet ﷺ heard a man supplicating whereupon he said: 'He must conclude it with *Āmīn*.' Al-Ḥākim narrated – grading its chain sound (*ṣaḥīḥ*) – from Umm Salama ﵂ that the Prophet ﷺ said *Āmīn* in his supplication. Al-Ḥākim narrated – grading its chain sound – that the Prophet ﷺ said: 'No group assembles, one of them supplicating while others say *Āmīn*, except Allah answers them.'"

Evidence

There are many proofs for the collective *du'ā* in the Qur'ān and Sunna both inside and outside *ṣalāt*.

Its proofs for the first case (inside *ṣalāt*) need not be listed here other than to say that the congregation must say *Āmīn* together with and at the same time as the *imām* after the words, "*wa-lā al-ḍāllīn*" in other than the day prayers, whether out loud as in the Three Schools, or silently as in the Ḥanafī; out loud repeatedly during the (Shāfi'ī) imām's *qunūt* supplication in the *fajr ṣalāt*; outloud during the (other than Ḥanafī) imām's *qunūt* in the *witr ṣalāt* in the second half of Ramaḍān; and out loud during the imām's supplication in the prayer for rain (*istisqā'*).

Some of the proofs for the collective *du'ā* outside *ṣalāt* are:

In the Qur'ān:

1. Sūrat Yūnus, 89: {*The supplication of the two of you has been answered*}. The reports from the Companions and *Salaf* concur that the modality of this supplication was that Mūsā ﷺ supplicated while Hārūn ﷺ said *Āmīn*, as narrated by the Imāms of *Tafsīr* from Ibn 'Abbās, Abū al-'Āliya, Abū Ṣāliḥ, 'Ikrima, Muḥammad ibn Ka'b al-Quraẓī, al-Rabī' ibn Anas and others.[341]

In the Sunna:

2. As mentioned already, the Prophet ﷺ said: "No group assembles (*lā yajtami'u qawmun/mala'un*), one of them supplicating while others say *Āmīn*, except Allah answers them."[342] This ḥadīth is *ṣaḥīḥ* and clearly stipulates that the collective *du'ā* has better chances of being accepted by Allah ﷻ than the individual *du'ā*. This ḥadīth was used by the Muslim armies to achieve victory over their enemies. On the basis of this ḥadīth and the ruling based on it, whoever bans or opposes collective supplication is opposing the Sunna, committing *bid'a*, and weakening the *Umma*!

[341] See the *Tafsīrs* of al-Ṭabarī, Ibn Kathīr (2:656) and al-Suyūṭī's *al-Durr al-Manthūr* (3:315). Cf. al-Ḥākim, *Ma'rifat 'Ulūm al-Ḥadīth* (p. 91).

[342] Narrated from Ḥabīb ibn Maslama al-Fihrī by al-Ṭabarānī in *al-Kabīr* (4:21-22), al-Ḥākim (3:347=1990 ed. 3:390 *ṣaḥīḥ*), and al-Dāraquṭnī. Al-Haythamī (10:170) said: "The narrators in its chain are those of al-Bukhārī and Muslim except for Ibn Lahī'a and he is fair in his narrations." However, the Ḥadīth Masters said that Ibn Lahī'a's narrations are sound (*ṣaḥīḥ*) when he narrates from certain narrators: 'Abd Allah ibn al-Mubārak, 'Abd Allah ibn Wahb, 'Abd Allah ibn Yazīd al-Muqri' (as is the case here), 'Abd Allah ibn Maslama al-Qa'nabī, Sa'īd ibn Abī Sa'īd Kaysān al-Maqburī and his father Kaysān cf. Ibn Ḥajar, *Tahdhīb al-Tahdhīb* (5:330) and al-Arna'ūṭ, *Taḥrīr al-Taqrīb* (2:258-259 §3563). So the ḥadīth is *ṣaḥīḥ* as stated by al-Ḥākim.

3. Zayd ibn Thābit said: "While I, Abū Hurayra, and a third man were in the mosque one day, supplicating Allah ﷻ and remembering our Lord, the Prophet ﷺ came out to us and sat with us. When he sat we fell silent. He said: 'Continue what you were doing.' So I supplicated, then my friend, before Abū Hurayra, while the Prophet ﷺ said *Āmīn* to our supplication. Then Abū Hurayra supplicated saying: 'O Allah! I ask you all that my two friends asked of you and I ask you for knowledge that shall not be forgotten.' The Messenger of Allah ﷺ said *Āmīn*. We said: 'Messenger of Allah! We, too, ask for knowledge that shall not be forgotten.' He replied: 'The boy from Daws asked for it before you (*sabaqakumā/sabaqakum ghulāmu daws/al-ghulāmu al-dawsī*).'"[343]

4. From Abū Shaddād while ʿUbāda ibn al-Ṣāmit was present and confirmed him: "We were in the house of the Prophet ﷺ when he said: 'Is there any stranger among you?' He meant one of the People of the Book. We said, 'No, Messenger of Allah.' He ordered for the door to be shut and said: 'Raise your hands and say *Lā ilāha illAllah*. We raised our hands and said *Lā ilāha illAllah* for a while. Then he ﷺ lowered his hands and said: 'Glory and praise to Allah! O Allah, my Lord! Truly You have sent me with this phrase and commanded me to say it and promised me Paradise for it. Truly You do not break the trust.' Then he said: 'Be glad, for Allah has forgiven you.'"[344]

[343]Narrated by al-Nasā'ī in *al-Sunan al-Kubrā* (3:440 §5835) and al-Ṭabarānī in *al-Awsaṭ* with a chain of trustworthy narrators except for Qays al-Madanī who is of unknown reliability as indicated by al-Haythamī (9:361), while Ibn Ḥajar declared "good" (*jayyid*) al-Nasā'ī's chain in *al-Iṣāba* (7:438 §10674) and *Tahdhīb al-Tahdhīb* (12:291). Al-Ḥākim (3:508=1990 ed. 3:582) also narrated it with a chain he declared sound (*ṣaḥīḥ*) but al-Dhahabī cited the weakness of one of its narrators, Ḥammād ibn Shuʿayb. However, in the *Siyar* (4:197=al-Arna'ūṭ ed. 2:616) he cites Qays's chain [cf. al-Mizzī in *Tahdhīb al-Kamāl* (24:94)] with al-Faḍl ibn al-ʿAlā' in lieu of Ḥammād, adding: "Ibn al-ʿAlā' is truthful (*ṣadūq*)," which makes this a strong narration *in shā' Allah*, and Ibn Ḥajar cites it in his *Fatḥ* (1959 ed. 1:215).

[344]Al-Haythamī (1:18-19) said: "Aḥmad, al-Ṭabarānī [in *al-Kabīr* (7:290 §7163) and

5. ʿĀ'isha ﵂ related that the Prophet ﷺ said: "The Jews do not envy you for anything as much as they envy you for *Salām* and *Āmīn*."[345] Another version from Ibn ʿAbbās mentions only *Āmīn* and adds, "Therefore say it frequently," also in Ibn Mājah but with a weak chain because of Ṭalḥa ibn ʿAmr.[346] Although this narration's immediate context indicates that it refers to the Jumuʿa prayer, yet its probative force is general, just as the import of the prayer for rain during Jumuʿa in the next narration is general. And what is the difference between those that oppose collective *duʿā'* in the mosques and the disbelievers that envy the Muslims for saying *Āmīn*?

6. From Anas ﵁ in al-Bukhārī's *Ṣaḥīḥ*: A desert Arab came to the Messenger of Allah ﷺ the Day of Jumuʿa saying: "Messenger of Allah, the beasts of burden are dying, the dependents are dying, the people are dying!" Whereupon the Messenger of Allah ﷺ raised his hands in supplication and the people raised their hands in supplication with the Messenger of Allah ﷺ. The desirability of raising one's hands in supplication in general is firmly established in the sunna except for the *khaṭīb* in Jumuʿa.[347] By the

Musnad al-Shāmiyyīn (2:158 §1104)], and al-Bazzār narrated it and its narrators have been declared trustworthy." Elsewhere (10:81) he said: "Aḥmad narrated it and its chain contains Rāshid ibn Dāwūd who was declared trustworthy by more than one [authority] although there is some weakness in him, and the rest of its narrators are trustworthy." Al-Ḥākim narrated it (1:501=1990 ed. 1:679) grading it *ṣaḥīḥ* but al-Dhahabī disagreed because of Rāshid, while al-Mundhirī in *al-Targhīb* (2:330 §2288) and Ḥamza al-Zayn in his edition of the *Musnad* (13:271 §17057) both declared its chain fair (*ḥasan*) but Shuʿayb al-Arna'ūṭ in his edition (28:348-349 §17121) said its chain was weak (*ḍaʿīf*) due to the same narrator. Also narrated by al-Dūlābī in *al-Kunā* (1:93).

[345] Narrated by Ibn Mājah with a sound chain per Muslim's criterion, al-Bukhārī in *al-Adab al-Mufrad* (p. 242), and Ibn Khuzayma (1:287-288, 3:38).

[346] Ibn Ḥajar cited them both in *Fatḥ al-Bārī* (1959 ed. 11:4, 11:200) cf. al-Būṣīrī, *Miṣbāḥ al-Zujājā* (1:106-107).

[347] See the collected narrations to that effect in al-Ṭabarānī's *al-Duʿā'* (p. 84-86) and Ibn Ḥajar's discussion in the *Fatḥ* (11:142-143) among others.

same token, collective supplication is lawful both inside and outside *istisqā'*, and Allah knows best.

7. From Abū Usayd al-Sāʿidī: The Messenger of Allah said to al-ʿAbbās ibn ʿAbd al-Muṭṭalib: "Do not leave your house tomorrow morning with your children [al-Faḍl, ʿAbd Allah, ʿUbayd Allah, Qutham, Maʿbad, ʿAbd al-Raḥmān, and Umm Ḥabība] until I come and visit you for I have some need to ask of you." So they waited for him until midmorning, at which time he came in to see them, saying *al-Salāmu ʿalaykum*. They replied, *ʿalaykum al-Salām, wa-raḥmatullāh, wa-barakātuh*. He said: "How are you this morning?" They replied, "We give thanks and praise to Allah!" [Ibn Mājah narrates it only to here.] He said: "Come close together, all of you," until they let him gather them all into his cloak (*ishtamala ʿalayhim bi-mulāʾatihi*). Then he said, "O my Lord! Here is my paternal uncle and the brother and double of my father (*ṣinwu abī*), and these are the Folk of my House (*wa-hāʾulāʾi ahlu baytī*)! Therefore shield them from the Fire just as I am shielding them with this cloak of mine." Whereupon the doorsill (*uskuffatu al-bāb*) and the walls of the house began to say "*Āmīn, āmīn, āmīn!*"[348]

8. From Umm Salama the Prophet said: "When you visit a sick person or a dead one, say something good, for the angels say *Āmīn* to whatever you say." Narrated by Muslim in his *Ṣaḥīḥ*. Imām al-Nawawī said in his commentary: "In this there is a recommendation for saying something good at that time, such as supplication or asking forgiveness for him, asking kindness and

---

[348] Al-Ṭabarānī narrated it in *al-Kabīr* (19:263) and *al-Awsaṭ* with a fair (*ḥasan*) chain according to al-Haythamī (9:270), Abū Nuʿaym in *Dalāʾil al-Nubuwwa* (p. 432-433 §339) and al-Bayhaqī in *Dalāʾil al-Nubuwwa* (6:71), and in part, Ibn Mājah, all of them with a chain containing ʿAbd Allah ibn ʿUthmān ibn Isḥāq ibn Saʿd ibn Abī Waqqāṣ who is weak. ʿIyāḍ cites it in *al-Shifāʾ* (p. 374 §781 and p. 529 §1278), al-Suyūṭī in *al-Khaṣāʾiṣ al-Kubrā* (2:309), Ibn Kathīr in *al-Bidāya*, and al-Nabhānī in the *Ḥujjatullāh* (p. 450) and *Nujūm al-Muhtadīn* (p. 82).

relief for him and the like. In it also is a proof for the presence of the angels at that time, and their saying *Āmīn*." Another narration in *Ṣaḥīḥ Muslim* from Abū Hurayra states that the Prophet ﷺ said: "If one of you says *Āmīn* and the angels in the heaven say *Āmīn*, and the two coincide, all his past sins are forgiven."

9. From al-Aswad ibn Hilāl al-Muḥāribī: When 'Umar ؓ was made Caliph he stood on the pulpit and said: "People! I am going to invoke Allah, therefore say *Āmīn* in witness to it (*hayminū lahā*)! Allah, my Lord! I am rough, so make me soft, and I am stingy, so make me generous, and I am weak, so make me strong!"[349] Where are those who would tell 'Umar that collective *du'ā* is banned in Islam?

10. Abū Sa'īd the Mawlā of Abū Sa'īd al-Khudrī said that 'Umar patrolled the mosque after '*ishā*' and would allow no one to remain inside except lone worshippers standing at prayer. One night, he saw a group of the Companions of the Prophet ﷺ sitting together, among them Ubay ibn Ka'b. He asked: "Who are you?" Ubay replied: "A group of your relatives, Commander of the Believers." "And what is keeping you now that the *ṣalāt* is over?" "We sat down to remember Allah ﷻ." 'Umar joined them and said to the man nearest to him: "Go ahead." The man began to supplicate. Then he told each one to supplicate, one by one until he ended up at me, as I was sitting by his side. He said: "Let us hear it." I became tongue-tied and began to shake. He noticed this and said: "Just say, Allah, our Lord, forgive us! Allah, our Lord, show us mercy!" Then 'Umar himself supplicated. No one in that gathering wept more than him. Then he said: "Good! Now, all of you, leave!"[350]

---

[349] Narrated by Abū Nu'aym in *Ḥilyat al-Awliyā'* (1985 ed. 1:53) and Ibn Sa'd (3:275) cf. al-Zamakhsharī, *al-Fā'iq* (4:113).
[350] Narrated by Ibn Sa'd (3:294) and Ibn al-Jawzī in *Manāqib 'Umar* (p. 76) cf. al-Ṭanṭāwī, *Akhbār 'Umar* (p. 304).

11. These and the following reports show that Ibn ʿUmar, like his father, ‎ supplicated together with others: From Wahb: "I saw Ibn ʿUmar and Ibn al-Zubayr supplicating [*i.e.* together] and rubbing their hands against their faces."[351] This event may have taken place at the highly dramatic time following the death of al-Ḥusayn ibn ʿAlī at the hands of Yazīd ibn Muʿāwiya, after which Ibn ʿUmar told ʿAbd Allah ibn al-Zubayr: "Al-Ḥusayn has beaten us" *i.e.* with martyrdom, and they wept.

12. ʿAbd al-Razzāq narrated with his chain from Yaḥyā ibn Saʿīd al-Anṣārī the Qāḍī of al-Madīna that "Ibn ʿUmar used to supplicate together with al-Qāṣṣ" (*kāna yabsuṭu yadayhi maʿa al-Qāṣṣ*) and that "they [*i.e.* the senior Successors] mentioned that those that came before them [*i.e.* the Companions] would supplicate and then place back their hands on their faces so as to place back the *duʿā'* and its *baraka*."[352] Al-Qāṣṣ is the *Tābiʿī* ʿUbayd ibn ʿUmayr ibn Qatāda al-Laythī al-Makkī the admonisher and Qur'ānic commentator. Shaykh Abū Ghudda said: "This is frank evidence to the effect that wiping the face with the two hands after raising them in supplication was practiced in the first generations."[353] Ibn Ḥajar in the chapter on wiping the face in *Bulūgh al-Maram* said that the narrations related from the Prophet to its licitness, even if individually weak, collectively attain the rank of "fair" – that is, authentic.

[351]Narrated by al-Bukhārī in *al-Adab al-Mufrad* (2:68) with a sound chain according to Shaykh ʿAbd al-Fattāḥ Abū Ghudda in his *Thalāth Rasā'il fī Istiḥbāb al-Duʿā wa-Rafʿ al-Yadayn baʿd al-Ṣalawāt al-Maktūba* (p. 93).

[352]Narrated by ʿAbd al-Razzāq (2:252-253).

[353]Abū Ghudda, *Thalāth Rasā'il* (p. 94). Cf. al-Sakhāwī, *al-Fatāwā al-Ḥadīthiyya* (p. 306-309 §67).

As for the ḥadīth of the Prophet ﷺ: "Truly, Allah is most modest and noble, He shies, when a man raises his two hands to Him [in supplication], from returning them empty,"[354] Ibn Ḥajar declared it fair (*ḥasan*) in *al-Amālī al-Ḥalabiyya*.

Additional Reports

13. A *marfū*ʿ report with a very weak chain from Anas states: "I was given three things: I was given prayer in ranks; I was given '*al-salām* [ʿ*alaykum*],' which is the greeting of the dwellers of Paradise; and I was given '*Āmīn*' which none was given before your time except that Allah gave it to Hārūn. For Mūsā would supplicate while Hārūn would say *Āmīn*."[355]

14. Another *marfū*ʿ report with a very weak chain from Ibn ʿAbbās by al-Daylamī in *al-Firdaws* states in part: "The supplicant and the one who says *Āmīn* are two partners in reward."[356]

15. In the *marfū*ʿ ḥadīth from Ḥudhayfa ibn al-Yamān narrated by al-Ṭabarī: After the coming out of Ya'jūj and Ma'jūj, ʿĪsā عليه السلام shall supplicate for help and the Muslims shall say *Āmīn*, whereupon Allah shall send against them a beast called *al-naghaf* = black earthworms. Al-Suyūṭī cited it in *al-Durr al-Manthūr*.

16. Shahr ibn Ḥawshab relates that one day Abū al-Dardā' entered the mosque of Bayt al-Maqdis and saw people gathered around their admonisher (*mudhakkir*) who was admonishing them, and they were raising their voices, weeping, and making invocations. Abū al-Dardā' said: "My father's life and my mother's be sacrificed for those who moan over their state before the Day

[354]Narrated from Salmān al-Fārisī by al-Tirmidhī, Abū Dāwūd, Ibn Mājah, and Aḥmad. Ibn Ḥajar declared it fair (*ḥasan*) in *al-Amālī al-Ḥalabiyya* (p. 26).
[355]Ibn Mardūyah narrated it in his *Tafsīr*, al-Ḥārith ibn Abī Usāma in his *Musnad*, Ibn ʿAdī in *al-Ḍuʿāfa*', and al-Bayhaqī in *Shuʿab al-Īmān* as cited by al-Suyūṭī in *al-Jāmiʿ al-Ṣaghīr wa-Ziyādātuh*. Cf. al-Ghumārī, *al-Mudāwī* (1:638 §577/ 1173).
[356]Cf. al-Ghumārī, *al-Mudāwī* (4:43 §1782/4245).

of Moaning!" Then he said: "Ibn Ḥawshab, let us hurry and sit with those people. I heard the Prophet ﷺ say: 'If you see the groves of Paradise, graze in them,' and we said: 'Messenger of Allah, what are the groves of Paradise?' He said: 'The circles of remembrance; by the One in Whose hand is my soul, no people gather for the remembrance of Allah Almighty except the angels surround them closely, mercy covers them, Allah mentions them in His presence, and when they desire to get up and leave, a herald calls them saying: 'Rise forgiven, your evil deeds have been changed into good deeds!'"[357] Then Abū al-Dardā' went towards them and sat with them eagerly.[358]

17. A very weak long ḥadīth on the *mubāhala* of the Prophet ﷺ with the Christian delegation of Najrān ends with the mention of ʿAlī, al-Ḥasan, al-Ḥusayn, and Fāṭima to whom the Prophet ﷺ is related to say: "When I supplicate, you all say *Āmīn*," whereupon the Banū Najrān refused to enter the mutual cursing and agreed to pay the *jizya*.[359]

18. ʿImrān ibn Ḥuṣayn saw a storyteller *(qāṣṣ)* and exclaimed, "We belong to Allah and to Him do we return! I heard the Messenger of Allah ﷺ say, 'Recite [pl.] the Qur'ān and ask Allah with it before a people appear that will ask people with it!'"[360]

[357]Narrated from Abū Hurayra and Abū Saʿīd al-Khudrī by Muslim, al-Tirmidhī, Ibn Mājah, and Aḥmad.

[358]Ibn al-Jawzī relates it with his chain in the chapter entitled: "Mention of those of the elite who used to attend the gatherings of story-tellers" in his book *al-Quṣṣāṣ wal-Mudhakkirīn* (p. 31).

[359]Narrated by Abū Nuʿaym in *Dalā'il al-Nubuwwa* with a chain containing Abū al-Naḍr al-Kalbī who is accused of forgery.

[360]Narrated by al-Tirmidhī (*ḥasan*) and Aḥmad.

Recent *Fatwās*

1. Following is an excerpt from Dr. Wahba al-Zuhaylī's *al-Bidaʿ al-Munkara* ("Condemned Innovations") in which he took care to differentiate between the real innovations and the lawful practices which some misguided people have falsely branded as innovations, in the section titled "Innovations of Worship" (p. 46-48):

Supplication (*al-duʿā*) is lawful whether individually or collectively (*fardiyyan wa-jamāʿiyyan*) due to what Muslim narrated from Abū Hurayra ◈ who said that the Prophet ◈ said: "No people gather for the remembrance of Allah Almighty except the angels surround them closely, and mercy covers them, and Allah mentions them in His presence." Al-Ṣanʿānī said in *Subul al-Salām* (2:213): "This ḥadīth indicates the merit of the gatherings of *dhikr* and the rememberers, and the immense merit of gathering for the purpose of *dhikr*."

The ḥadīth Master al-Mundhirī devoted a section to what he titled *al-Targhīb fī Ḥuḍūr Majālis al-Dhikr wal-Ijtimāʿ ʿalā Dhikr Allah Taʿālā* ("The Encouragement to Attend the Gatherings of Dhikr and Assembling for the Purpose of Remembering Allah ◈"). He cited narrations, among them that narrated by al-Bukhārī and Muslim from Abū Hurayra that the Messenger of Allah ◈ said: "Allah has angels roaming the roads to find the people of *dhikr*, and when they find such a group of people, they call each other and encompass them in layers until the first heaven... [ending with the words:] They are the folk [= the true believers] and even those that sit with them shall obtain felicity."

Similarly, [al-Tirmidhī (*ḥasan gharīb*), Aḥmad,] Ibn Abī al-Dunyā, Abū Yaʿlā, al-Bazzār, al-Ṭabarānī, al-Ḥākim – he declared it *ṣaḥīḥ* – and al-Bayhaqī narrated: "...What are the groves of Paradise?" to which he ◈ replied: "The gatherings of *dhikr*."

There might be in the gathering a righteous servant because of whom Allah answers the supplication of the whole gathering.

The Ulema of the Muslim cities used to gather in the mosques the night before ʿArafa for *duʿā'* and *dhikr*. Imām Aḥmad approved of this, saying, "I hope there is no harm in it, several [of the *Salaf*] did it." Its basis in the Sunna is the encouragement towards *duʿā'* and *dhikr* in the days of fragrant Divine gifts and the seasons that are high in acts of worship and obedience. The ḥadīth mentions: "Truly your Lord gives, on certain of your days, fragrant gifts. Lo! Avail yourselves of the fragrant gifts of your Lord."[361]

[361]Narrated from [1] Muḥammad ibn Maslama al-Anṣārī by al-Ṭabarānī in *al-Awsaṭ* (3:180) and *al-Kabīr* (19:233-234) with a weak chain cf. al-Haythamī (10:231) and al-Suyūṭī in *al-Jāmiʿ al-Ṣaghīr* (§2398); also by al-Rāmahurmuzī in *al-Muḥaddith al-Fāṣil* (p. 497 §615) – cf. Ibn Kathīr in his *Tafsīr* (4:87) – with another chain, also weak. Something close is narrated [2] from Anas by al-Ḥakīm al-Tirmidhī in *Nawādir al-Uṣūl* (*Aṣl* §185), al-Ṭabarānī in *al-Kabīr* (1:250) and *al-Duʿā'* (§26); through him Abū Nuʿaym who said it is single-chained *(gharīb)* from 'Amr ibn al-Rabī' and Ṣafwān in the *Ḥilya* (3:162) as did al-Baghawī in *Sharḥ al-Sunna* (5:179 §1378); al-Bayhaqī in *al-Asmā'* (Ḥāshidī ed. 1:378-379 §306 *isnād ḍaʿīf*) and the *Shuʿab* (2:42 §1121-1122); Ibn ʿAbd al-Barr in *al-Tamhīd* (5:339); al-Quḍāʿī in *Musnad al-Shihāb* (1:407); Ibn ʿAsākir (24:123 and 52:5) cf. Ibn Kathīr, *Tafsīr* (2:435); and al-Rāfiʿī in *al-Tadwīn* (3:192), all with a better chain according to al-Haythamī (10:231) though *mursal* since Ṣafwān ibn Sulaym never met Anas, hence al-Suyūṭī also indicated its weakness in *al-Jāmiʿ al-Ṣaghīr* (§1108). Also [3] from Abū Hurayra by Baqī ibn Makhlad in his *Musnad* cf. al-Zabīdī, *Itḥāf al-Sādat al-Muttaqīn* (5:40); Ibn Abī al-Dunyā in *al-Faraj baʿd al-Shidda* (§27); al-Ṭabarānī in *al-Duʿā'* (§27); Ibn ʿAsākir (24:123); and al-Bayhaqī in the *Shuʿab* (2:43 §1123) cf. Ibn Rajab, *Laṭā'if* (p. 40-41). Also narrated [4] from Abū al-Dardā' by Ibn Abī Shayba (7:111) and through him Abū Nuʿaym in the *Ḥilya* (1:221), both with a good *mawqūf* chain but possibly *mursal* between Zayd ibn Aslam and Abū al-Dardā'. Cf. also al-Zabīdī, *Itḥāf* (3:280-281) and al-Ghumārī's *Mudāwī* (1:600-602 and 2:518). The Yemeni Scholar al-Sayyid ʿAlī ibn Ibrāhīm ibn Muḥammad ibn Ismāʿīl al-Ṣanʿānī (1171-1219) authored a monograph on this ḥadīth titled *Sūq al-Shawq li-Ahli al-Dhawq min Taḥt ilā Fawq* ("The Market of Desire for the People of Taste from Below to Above"). The Indian Sufi Wahhabi Ṣiddīq Ḥasan Khan al-Qinnawjī cites it in his *Abjad al-ʿUlūm* (3:184).

> So it is incorrect to declare as an innovation the collective supplication after *ṣalāt* in the mosques and elsewhere, because supplication is desirable at that time even if one does not persist in it. Among the states of the Messenger of Allah ﷺ, he sometimes isolated or singled himself out apart from those present in supplication so as to teach the formula of the supplications transmitted from him[362] while the practice of latter-day Muslims has settled on collective supplication.
>
> However, al-Qarāfī counted collective supplication among the blameworthy innovations according to the Mālikī School.

The Mālikis objected to collective supplication only to prevent conceit (*ʿujb*) on the part of the imām, and Allah knows best.[363]

2. From the *Encyclopedia of Islamic Doctrine* (7:108-110):

> Some "Salafis" try to propagate the notion that collective *duʿā* is wrong, that is: *duʿā* led by the *imām* to which the congregation responds "*Āmīn*." This is a false notion, as just proven by the mention of the ḥadīth of Zayd ibn Arqam whereby the Prophet ﷺ said: "O Allah! **Our Lord**" after every prayer. ["I heard the Messenger of Allah ﷺ making *duʿā* after every prayer (*dubura kulli ṣalāt*): *Allahumma rabbanā wa-rabba kulli shay'*, O Allah! Our Lord and the Lord of everything!" Narrated by Abū Dāwūd and Aḥmad with a good chain.]
>
> The principle for collective *duʿā* is entirely based on the Qur'ān and Sunna. Someone asked: I am inquiring about the permissibility of making congregational *duʿā* in general and congregational *duʿā* after the obligatory *ṣalāt* in specific. Many contemporary "Salafis" label this practice a blameworthy and unlawful innovation.

[362] Cf. al-Shāṭibī, *al-Iʿtiṣām* (2:349-356).
[363] Cf. Ibn Nājī in al-ʿAdawī's *Ḥāshiya* on Ibn Abī Zayd's *Risāla* (1:275)

The answer is: There is decisive evidence (*ḥujja qāṭiʿa*) for loud *duʿā* in *jamāʿa*:

Al-Ḥākim relates from Ḥabīb ibn Maslama al-Fihrī: I heard the Messenger of Allah ﷺ say: "No people gather while some of them make invocation and others say *Āmīn* except Allah answers them."

The Sunna of collective invocations specifically after the *ṣalāt* is established from the Sunna of *dhikr* directly after the *ṣalāt* as described by the ḥadīth of Ibn ʿAbbās in al-Bukhārī and Muslim whereby he knew from outside the mosque that the *ṣalāt* had ended by the sound of the collective t*akbīr*, and *dhikr* is a form of *duʿā* as are all forms of worship according to the *ṣaḥīḥ* ḥadīth in al-Tirmidhī: "The *duʿā* is *ʿibāda* itself."

The Qur'ān is replete with collective invocations by a group of Muslims, as the following one which Anas in al-Bukhārī said the Prophet ﷺ repeated the most: {*O our Lord, grant us goodness in this life, and grant us goodness in the next life, and protect us from the Fire*} (2:201). Also the *duʿā* of the *Ḥawāriyyūn* or disciples of ʿĪsā عليه السلام: {*O our Lord, we believe in what you have revealed and do follow the Messenger, therefore write us among the witnesses*} (3:53) and the *duʿā* of the young men of the *aṣḥāb al-kahf*: {*Our Lord! Give us mercy from Thy presence, and shape for us right conduct in our plight*} (18:10).

The congregational *duʿā* hinges on the *duʿā* of the imām of a people. Tirmidhī narrates from Thawbān and he said it is *ḥasan*: The Prophet ﷺ said that the imām who makes his *duʿā* particular to himself has betrayed his people. Abū Dāwūd, Ibn Mājah, and Aḥmad also narrate it.

When ʿUmar, as the Imām of Muslims, made his *duʿā* through al-ʿAbbās, it was a collective *duʿā* as established by the plural wording employed. As Muslim narrated, the Prophet ﷺ said,

"The [greater] imām is a shield from behind which the rest of the people fight."

The evidence is clear to the effect that congregational *du'ā* is ordered by the Prophet ﷺ in the ḥadīth that says: "When you hear in (loud) congregational prayer the Imām say: *wa-lā al-ḍāllīn*, say: *Āmīn*" (al-Bukhārī, Muslim and others). Ibn Ḥajar said in commenting on this ḥadīth: "The meaning of the unmodified order 'say' is 'say out loud.'" This does not make it incorrect to say it silently according to other interpretations. At any rate this is clearly a plain congregational *du'ā* as the noble *Fātiḥa* is the highest and best *du'ā* of all. The fact that it is inside or outside *ṣalāt* is irrelevant, as utterances of *dhikr* and *du'ā* that are *ḥalāl* inside *ṣalāt* do not become *ḥarām* outside it!

Another clear evidence is the *du'ā* of *Qunūt* in the congregational *fajr* prayer, whereby the imām stands after *rukū'* in the second *rak'a* and makes loud *du'ā* with his hands raised palms up, and the congregation repeatedly says *Āmīn* until he goes into prostration. This is the position of the Shāfi'ī school as set forth in their books. It is recommended to make the same kind of loud *qunūt* in prayers other than *fajr* in certain circumstances. Al-Nawawī in *al-Adhkār* cites the ḥadīth of Anas whereby "The Prophet ﷺ did not cease to make *qunūt* in the Dawn (prayer) until he left this world." Al-Ḥākim narrates it and said it is *ṣaḥīḥ*, and Ibn Ḥajar: *ḥasan*. He then cites the *ṣaḥīḥ* ḥadīth of al-Ḥasan ibn 'Alī stipulating the words taught by the Prophet ﷺ for that *qunūt*. Abū Hurayra used to recite *qunūt* in the Dawn prayer.[364] And Allah knows best.

[364] Cf. Ibn al-Qayyim, *Zād al-Ma'ād* (1:274).

Collective Loud Recitation of the Qur'ān

The "Darussalam" Ryādh and Texas publishing house produced a glossy two-volume English edition of al-Nawawī's *Riyāḍ al-Ṣāliḥīn* then distributed it for free to Islamic schools around the world, apparently in order to propagate "Salafī" ideology among English-speaking Muslim students. This ideology is couched within a "commentary" inserted into the book chapters and authored by a "Hafiz Ṣalāḥuddīn Yūsuf of Pakistan", "revised and edited" by a "Maḥmūd Riḍā Murād" (1:7). Among their tamperings is their rephrasing of a ḥadīth (2:810-811) supporting collective loud recitation of the Qur'ān in al-Nawawī's chapter 184 of *Riyāḍ al-Ṣāliḥīn* titled "Desirability of Assembling for Qur'ān-Recitation" so as to promote their own claim that collective loud Qur'ānic recitation is prohibited.

Al-Nawawī cites the ḥadīth of Muslim whereby the Prophet ﷺ said: "No group of people assemble in one of the Houses of Allah, all of them reciting [plural pronoun] the Book of Allah (*yatlūna kitāb Allah*) and studying It among themselves except Serenity (*al-sakīna*) shall descend upon them...."

The editor/commentator(s) of *Riyāḍ al-Ṣāliḥīn* rephrased the ḥadīth thus: "Any group of people that assemble in one of the Houses of Allah to study the Qur'ān, tranquility will descend upon them..." omitting the key words: "all of them reciting the Book of Allah and studying it together." Then the same editor/commentator(s) had the gall to comment: "This ḥadīth... does not tell us in any way that this group of people recite the Qur'ān all at once. This is *bid'ah* for this was not the practice of the Messenger of Allah ﷺ." This is tampering compounded with a shameless lie. Imām al-Nawawī said in *al-Tibyān fī Ādāb Ḥamalat al-Qur'ān*, in the chapter on loud group recital of the Qur'ān:

Know that a group reciting together is recommended, according to obvious evidence and according to the actions of the pure *Salaf* and *Khalaf*. It is rigorously authenticated from the relations of Abū Hurayra and Abū Saʿīd al-Khudrī – Allah be well-pleased with them both – that the Prophet ﷺ said: "No group remembers Allah save that the angels encompass them, mercy envelops them, tranquility descends upon them, and Allah mentions them to those in His presence." Al-Tirmidhī said this is a *ḥasan ṣaḥīḥ* ḥadīth. Abū Hurayra ؓ said that the Prophet ﷺ said: "A group does not gather in one of the Houses of Allah Most High reciting the Qurʾān and studying it together, except that tranquility descends upon them, mercy envelops them, the angels encompass them, and Allah mentions them with those in His presence." Muslim related it; Abū Dāwūd related it with a rigorously authenticated chain meeting the conditions of al-Bukhārī and Muslim. [...]

Ibn Abī Dāwūd related that Abū al-Dardāʾ ؓ would study the Qurʾān with a group, all of them reciting together. The superiority of studying together is related from groups of the superior *Salaf*, *Khalaf*, and judges (*quḍāt*) of the early generations. Ḥasān ibn ʿAṭiyya and al-Awzāʿī both said: "The first one to initiate studies in the mosque of Damascus is Hishām ibn Ismāʿīl upon his coming to ʿAbd al-Malik [ibn Marwān ibn al-Ḥakam]."

As for what Ibn Abī Dāwūd related from al-Ḍaḥḥāk ibn ʿAbd al-Raḥmān ibn ʿArzab that he censured these studies and said: "I did not see [it] nor hear [it], and I have met the Companions of the Messenger of Allah ﷺ," it means: I did not see anyone do this. And Ibn Wahb said: "I said to Mālik, 'What do you think about a people gathering and reading a single chapter together until they finish it?' He rejected this and censured it, saying, 'This is not how people do it. It was only that a man

> would recite it to another.'" But this denial of theirs is contrary to the actions of the *Salaf* and *Khalaf* and contrary to what the evidence implies. However, collective recitation has conditions [related to etiquette] that we previously mentioned that should be given attention. And Allah knows best.[365]

The "Darussalam" edition of *Riyāḍ al-Ṣāliḥīn* and their misinterpretation and false claim of *bid'a* is, of course, directed at the Maghribī style of Qur'ānic recitation that relies heavily on collective *tilāwa* in order to strengthen memorization. Another hidden purpose behind their propaganda is the desire to prevent the prevalent way of conveying the reward of reciting the entire Qur'ān to the deceased. The Qur'ān is read in such style in gatherings of Sunni Muslims all over the Indian Subcontinent and elsewhere. The thirty parts of the Qur'ān are distributed to all those present who then read them within a brief span of time and the merit or reward (*thawāb*) is then conveyed to the deceased. Those who oppose this as an innovation of misguidance are themselves misguided innovators. {*And the disbelievers said, Do not listen to this Qur'ān and engulf it in noise – perhaps you may be victorious this way*} (41:26).

[365] Al-Nawawī, *al-Tibyān*, translation by Shaykh Mūsā Furber. Cf. *Etiquette with the Quran* (p. 52-54). For more on the "Darussalam" edition of *Riyāḍ al-Ṣāliḥīn* see the chapter on Bin Bāz in our *Albānī and His Friends.*

Partitions for Women in Mosques

Two types of behavior can be observed in connection with the presence of female worshippers in mosques. The first consists in absolutely preventing women from attending mosques and misconstruing evidence to support this position. The second extreme consists in declaring it an innovation (*bid'a*) to put up a partition between the main hall and the women's section of the mosque, on the grounds that the Prophet ﷺ and Companions never did, also misconstruing evidence to support this position.

Those interested in banning women from mosques claim that our Master 'Umar ibn al-Khaṭṭāb banned them during his Caliphate. However, this is not true, as he only banned loiterers – men and women – from the Mosque after the last prayer of the day, not worshippers, as clearly shown by the evidence. Khawla bint Qays said: "We were women, in the Mosque [in Madīna al-Munawwara], who may have mixed with the men at times and perhaps even flirted (*ghazalna*) and even harmed themselves in this intermixing; so 'Umar said: 'I swear I shall make free women of you again.' So he brought us out (*akhrajanā*) of the Mosque."[366] Abū Sa'īd the Mawlā of Abū Sa'īd al-Khudrī said: "'Umar patrolled the mosque after '*ishā*' and would leave no-one inside except he got them out but for lone worshippers standing in prayer."[367]

'Umar never prevented nor forbade women from attending the mosque for prayers. This general permission and conditional prohibition is how he understood the meaning of the ḥadīth of the Prophet ﷺ: "Do not forbid the bondswomen of Allah from [going to] the mosques of Allah!"[368] 'Umar also narrated that the Prophet ﷺ said more explicitly, "If your women ask permission to

[366] *Kanz al-'Ummāl* (§23131) from Ibn Sa'd's *Ṭabaqāt*.
[367] Narrated by Ibn Sa'd (3:294).
[368] Narrated from Ibn 'Umar by al-Bukhārī, Muslim, and others.

go out to *ṣalāt*, do not forbid them!"[369] (On condition they come out *tafilāt*, *i.e.* without any perfume on their persons, as per the Prophet's ﷺ ḥadīth related by Zaynab bint Mu'āwiya al-Thaqafiyya the wife of Ibn Mas'ūd in Muslim and the narration of Abū Hurayra in Abū Dāwūd and the *Musnad*.) Its continuation is, "And prayer in their own homes is better for them."

Accordingly, 'Umar permitted women to attend the mosque for the five obligatory prayers and the Sunna prayers of *tarāwīḥ*. To that end, he made sure they had a separate entrance and exit to the Mosque – which he forbade men from using – and separate ablution facilities.[370] He had them pray *tarāwīḥ* prayers in the Mosque separately from the men and ordered Sulaymān ibn Abī Khathma to be *imām* for them at the far end of the Mosque, while Ubay ibn Ka'b and Tamīm al-Dārī were *imāms* for the men. Then 'Uthmān had men and women all pray behind a single *imām*, but he took measures to prevent women from leaving until the men had left first.[371]

Yes, 'Umar disliked for women to go the mosque. Whenever his wife 'Ātika bint Zayd asked him permission to go to *ṣalāt* in the Mosque, he would remain silent. She would continue, "I swear I will go out unless you forbid me." She used to go out for *ṣalāt al-'ishā* and *ṣalāt al-fajr*. She was asked once: "Why do you go out like that, knowing how jealous 'Umar is?" She replied: "And what prevents him from forbidding us?" The reply came: "What prevents him is the ḥadīth of the Prophet ﷺ: 'Do not forbid the bondswomen of Allah from [going to] the mosques of Allah.'"[372] Ibn Ḥajar said the latter ḥadīth, although apparently narrated from 'Abd Allah ibn 'Umar, is considered part of the narrations of 'Umar himself although it is also possible the exchange took

[369] Narrated by Aḥmad.
[370] Ibn Ḥazm, *al-Muḥallā* (3:131 and 4:119).
[371] Narrated by Ibn Sa'd (5:26) and Ibn Ḥazm, *al-Muḥallā* (3:139) cf. § 155 above.
[372] Narrated from Ibn 'Umar by al-Bukhārī. Cf. Ibn Abī Shayba (1:106).

place between his wife and his son.[373] 'Umar once said to 'Ātika: "I swear that you know very well I dislike it." She said: "By Allah! I shall not stop until you forbid me." 'Umar replied: "I certainly do not forbid you." The day 'Umar was stabbed to death in the mosque, she was present.[374]

It is 'Ā'isha – Allah be well-pleased with her – that forbade the women from going to the mosques, including for the five obligatory prayers let alone *tarāwīḥ*. She gave her reason in the famous statement: "If the Messenger of Allah had seen what the women of our time do, he would have forbidden them to go to the mosques just as the Israelite women were forbidden!"[375] It is on this basis, among other evidence, that Imām Abū Ḥanīfa and his School consider it prohibitively offensive (*makrūh taḥrīmī*) for women to pray in congregation other than the '*Īd* prayer, especially the day prayers when they come in full sight. Nevertheless, it is established that 'Ā'isha did pray *tarāwīḥ* in congregation – at home.

The majority of the Ulema, if not their Consensus, agree – and Allah knows best – that if women go to mosques, for obligatory prayers or otherwise, then there should be (1) a separate entrance for them and (2) space for prayer and facilities they can use in isolation from mixing with and view by the men. The use of a partition for the women's section in the mosque serves both of these conditions.

Those that object to the use of a partition sometimes cite a disclaimed report whereby "A truly beautiful woman used to pray behind the Prophet ﷺ. Some of the people used to go to pray in the front row to ensure they would not see her. Others would pray in the last row of the men, and during *rukū'* [or *sujūd*] they would look from underneath their armpits to see her. Because of

[373] Ibn Ḥajar, *Fatḥ al-Bārī* (2:383-384).
[374] Ibn Ḥazm, *al-Muḥallā* (3:139).
[375] Narrated by al-Bukhārī, Muslim, and in the books of *Sunan*.

this, Allah revealed: {*And verily We know those of you who hasten forward, and those who lag behind*} (15:24)."[376] Such a report, even if it were not weak, cannot serve as a basis to claim that the partition goes against the objectives of the *sharīʿa*, which is a condition *sine qua non* for something to be declared a *bidʿa*.

Another odd argument is that the Prophet ﷺ was discontent at the sight of the women's tents in the mosque in the ḥadīth of *iʿtikāf* because, it is claimed, he ﷺ "considered it inappropriate for them to hide themselves from public view"! However, it is obvious from the wording of the ḥadīth itself that the Prophet ﷺ was actually criticizing the women for being motivated by rivalry among themselves rather than piety: "Is it righteousness?" Then he ﷺ himself walked out of his *iʿtikāf*.[377] And how could the Prophet ﷺ possibly consider it inappropriate for women to hide from public view when Allah ﷻ commanded the Mothers of the Believers to {*remain quietly in your houses*} (33:33) and the Prophet ﷺ warned that "Woman is nakedness (*al-mar'atu ʿawra*), so when she goes out the devil is facing her, and the nearest she is to her Lord's countenance is in the privacy of her house?"[378]

[376]Narrated by al-Tirmidhī, Ibn Mājah, al-Nasāʾī, and others, all of them with the same chain through Abū al-Jawzāʾ, from Ibn ʿAbbās. Contrary to the claim of authenticity forwarded by the author of *al-Silsila al-Ṣaḥīḥa* (§2472), this hadith is weak (*ḍaʿīf*) since it appears to be a *maqṭūʿ* narration of the *Ṭābiʿī* Abū al-Jawzāʾ without any mention of Ibn ʿAbbās, as stated by al-Tirmidhī himself, while Ibn Kathīr in his *Tafsīr* (2:551) says it is "very much disclaimed" (*fīhi nakāra shadīda*)! Further, al-Ṭabarī in his *Tafsīr* (14:26) considers that this ḥadīth is the least probable of two explanations narrated for the Qur'anic verse cited and that the most correct explanation is that the verse refers to those who are eager to meet their Lord as opposed to those who wish to live long in the world.

[377]Narrated from ʿĀʾisha in the *Ṣaḥīḥayn* and *Sunan*.

[378]Narrated from Ibn Masʿūd by Ibn Khuzayma (3:93 §1685) and Ibn Ḥibbān (12:413 §5599) with a sound chain meeting Muslim's criterion according to al-Arna'ūṭ. As for the narration in which the Prophet ﷺ is related to say to Asmāʾ: "If the woman reaches the age of puberty, no part of her body should be seen but this – and he pointed to his face and hands," it should not be adduced as sole evidence in a ruling as it is a weak ḥadīth as indicated by Abū Dāwūd himself as well

It is true that in the time of the Prophet ﷺ there was no curtain separating men from women. The men prayed directly behind the Prophet ﷺ, then the boys, then the women starting behind the last row of the boys. However, numerous precautions were taken that made the use of a curtain superfluous. Among them, the Prophet ﷺ designated a door exclusively for women to enter and leave the mosque. The Prophet ﷺ said: "Let us restrict this door to women only." Nāfiʿ narrated that after hearing this, Ibn ʿUmar did not use that door until his death.[379] When he saw intermixing upon leaving the mosque the Prophet ﷺ reportedly said to the women: "Hang back! You may not walk in the middle of the road but bear to the sides of the road," after which a lady would walk so close to the walls along the road that her clothes would touch the walls.[380] The Prophet ﷺ himself used to defer his departure so that the ladies might leave the mosque first, as narrated in *Ṣaḥīḥ al-Bukhārī* from Umm Salama. The evidence also shows that the women who prayed *tarāwīḥ* in the mosque in the time of ʿUmar were sufficiently far enough from the men to have their own *imām* without interference with the male *jamāʿa*, an arrangement that strongly suggests they were also out of men's sights. ʿUthmān prevented the female *jamāʿa* from budging until the male *jamāʿa* had left the mosque after *tarāwīḥ*. All this goes to show that the curtain is not against the Sunna but, on the contrary, is a way to prevent sexual enticement (*fitna*) – which prevention is *farḍ* and a prerequisite of obligatory and recommended practices. There is a basic principle that "the prevention

as Ibn Ḥajar in *al-Dirāya fī Takhrīj Aḥādīth al-Hidāya* (1:173). Narrated *mursal* with a chain missing the Successor-link from ʿĀʾisha by Abū Dāwūd, al-Bayhaqī in *al-Sunan al-Kubrā* (1:187) and *Shuʿab al-Īmān* (6:165).

[379]Narrated from ʿUmar and Ibn ʿUmar by Abū Dāwūd with three *ṣaḥīḥ* chains.

[380]Narrated from Ḥamza ibn Abī Usayd's father by Abū Dāwūd and al-Bukhārī in *al-Kunā* (p. 55 §476) with a weak chain cf. Ibn Ḥajar, *Tahdhīb al-Tahdhīb* (4:279 §554).

of evil takes precedence over the obtainment of good." Such prevention, in other words, applies before everything else.

In view of this, the Prophet ﷺ said that the best place for a woman's *ṣalāt* is in the privacy of her house or, in another narration, the privacy of her room.[381] He ﷺ also approved of his daughter Fāṭima's answer when, asked what women were best, she replied: "The best women are those who do not see men nor do men see them."[382] If something facilitating modesty and approaching the function and purposes of this private space can be duplicated in the mosque, it should be welcome as something close to *wājib*, not fought against. Thus, the curtain should be accepted, allowing men and women to pray on alternate sides if space does not allow for front rows for men and back rows for women, which is a better arrangement. Together with this, there should be separate facilities for ablution and separate entrances.

This conclusion reunites the basic stipulations of the texts on the issue of women praying in the Mosque, not on the allegation that "ʿUmar banned women from the mosque" but in order that believing men and women can obtain the benefits of *Jamāʿa* without Shayṭān interfering with them. And Allah knows best.

[381] Narrated from Ibn Masʿūd by Abū Dāwūd and from Umm Ḥumayd al-Anṣāriyya and Umm Salama by Aḥmad.

[382] ʿAlī was with the Prophet ﷺ when the latter asked: "What is the best trait in women?" but no one spoke. ʿAlī said: "When I returned, I asked Fāṭima and she replied: 'That men do not see them.' I mentioned this to the Prophet ﷺ and he said: 'Truly, Fāṭima comes from me.'" Narrated by al-Bazzār (2:159-160 §526) and by Abū Nuʿaym in the *Ḥilya* (1985 ed. 2:175) with a chain containing Qays ibn al-Rabīʿ al-Asadī who is "truthful" (*ṣadūq)* to "weak" (*ḍaʿīf*) as in *Taḥrīr Taqrīb al-Tahdhīb* (3:186 §5573) and ʿAlī ibn Zayd who is weak. Cf. Ibn Ḥajar, *Mukhtaṣar* (1:567 §1001), al-Haythamī (4:255; 9:203), and *Kanz al-ʿUmmāl* (§46012). However, this is also narrated from Anas through a strong chain by al-Dāraquṭnī in *Su'ālāt Ḥamzat al-Sahmī* (p. 280 §409) and Abū Nuʿaym in the *Ḥilya* (1985 ed. 2:40-41) with the wording, "That they do not see men nor do men see them."

The *Ḍuḥā* Prayer[383]

The midmorning prayer (*ṣalāt al-ḍuḥā*) is an emphasized Sunna that was narrated from the Prophet ﷺ through paths that reach mass-narration levels – from nineteen to over thirty Companions – according to al-Ṭabarī, al-ʿAynī in *ʿUmdat al-Qārī*, al-Haytamī in *Sharḥ al-Shamā'il*, al-Munāwī in *Sharḥ al-Shamā'il*, al-Qārī in *Sharḥ al-Shamā'il*, Ibn Ḥajar in *Fatḥ al-Bārī*, al-Kattānī in *Naẓm al-Mutanāthir*, the monographs compiled by al-Ḥākim and al-Suyūṭī, as well as the recensions of Abū Zurʿa al-ʿIrāqī in *Ṭarḥ al-Tathrīb*, Ibn al-Qayyim in *Zād al-Maʿād*, and al-Shawkānī in *Nayl al-Awṭār*. According to the vast majority of the Ulema of the *Salaf* and *Khalaf* it is a desirable and recom-mended prayer. The following is an overview of the name, legal status, time, length, and immense merit of this important voluntary prayer.

I. Its name

The supererogatory morning prayer has many names. Among them:

a) *Ṣalāt al-ḍuḥā* or *sibḥat al-ḍuḥā*, *sibḥa* meaning a supererogatory prayer in general while *ḍuḥā* means morning, midmorning, or late morning. This is the name that recurs the most in the narrations.

b) *Ṣalāt al-awwābīn* ("Prayer of the Oft-Returning"), thus specified by the Prophet ﷺ for the late morning prayer when the sun is very hot according to the narration of Zayd ibn Arqam in *Ṣaḥīḥ Muslim* cited below; the narration of ʿAlī who saw a group of people praying *ḍuḥā* immediately after sunrise and

[383] See also the Ḥadīth Master Burhān al-Dīn al-Nājī's (810-900) monograph on *ṣalāt al-ḍuḥā* published by Niẓām al-Yaʿqūbī and Ramzī Dimashqiyya under the title *Muṣannafun fī Ṣalāt al-Ḍuḥā hiya Ṣalāt al-Awwābīn* (Beirut: Dār al-Bashā'ir al-Islāmiyya, 1998).

advised them to delay it, saying: "It would be best if they left it until the sun was one or two spear-lengths high for that is *ṣalāt al-awwābīn*."[384] ʿAwn al-ʿUqaylī also said in explanation of the verse {*innahu kāna lil-awwābīna ghafūrā – verily He is most forgiving to those who turn to him again and again* (*in true penitence*)} (17:25): "Its meaning is those who pray *ṣalāt al-ḍuḥā*."[385] More evidence for this appellation is adduced below [II. 6 (a-e)]. The reason for this name is that one leaves *dunyā* at that time to return to Allah Most High and makes up for the Night prayer that he missed. Hence, *ṣalāt al-ḍuḥā* is even more stressed for those who miss *tahajjud* and is its replacement[386] since the Prophet ﷺ said: "Whoever missed something of his regular nightly devotion ('his *wird* or his *ḥizb*') then recites it between the *fajr* prayer and *ẓuhr*, it is as if he had recited it in the previous night."[387] ʿUbayd ibn ʿUmayr defined *al-awwābīn* as "Those who remember their sins when all alone then ask Allah forgiveness."[388] The post-*maghrib* supererogatory prayers are also called by the same name.

c) *Ṣalāt al-Ishrāq* or *Ṣalāt al-Shurūq* ("Sunrise Prayer"), *i.e.* very shortly after sunrise, and this is its Qur'ānic name according to the narration of Ibn ʿAbbās in the *Sunan* of Saʿīd ibn Manṣūr: "I searched for *ṣalāt al-ḍuḥā* in the Qur'ān and found it in the verse {*yusabbiḥna bil-ʿashiyyi wal-ishrāq – Lo! We subdued the*

[384] Ibn Abī Shayba and al-Ṭabarī, cf. *Kanz al-ʿUmmāl* (§23437, 23461).
[385] Narrated by al-Aṣbahānī in *al-Targhīb* as cited by al-Shawkānī in *Nayl al-Awṭār*.
[386] Cf. Ibn al-Qayyim, *Zād al-Maʿād* (1:356) as cited in ʿItr, *Iʿlām al-Anām* (1:628).
[387] Narrated from ʿUmar in Muslim, the *Sunan*, and Aḥmad. This is one of the narrations that come through a Companion (al-Sā'ib ibn Yazīd), from a *Tābiʿī* (ʿAbd al-Raḥmān ibn ʿAbdin al-Qārī), from a Companion (ʿUmar ibn al-Khaṭṭāb) cf. al-Suyūṭī, *al-Fānīd fī Ḥalāwat al-Asānīd* (p. 41 §5).
[388] In al-Qurṭubī's commentary on the verse {*Rabbukum aʿlamu bimā fī nufūsikum in takūnū ṣāliḥīna fa'innahu kāna lil-awwābīna ghafūrā – Your Lord is best aware of what is in your minds. If you are righteous, then lo! He was ever Forgiving unto those who turn (unto Him)*} (17:25).

hills to hymn the praises (of their Lord) with him [*Dāwūd*] *at nightfall and sunrise*} (38:18). Ibn Abī Shayba and al-Bayhaqī in *Shu'ab al-Īmān* also narrate from Ibn 'Abbās: "Verily it [*ṣalāt al-ḍuḥā*] is in the Book of Allah, nor can they penetrate it who attempt to penetrate it [without knowledge]! Then he recited: {*In houses which Allah has allowed to be exalted and that His name shall be remembered therein. Therein do they offer praise to Him at morn and evening*} (24:36)."

d) *Ṣalāt al-Fatḥ* ("The Victory Prayer") because it is established that the Prophet ﷺ prayed it the morning he entered Makka (in al-Bukhārī and Muslim) and this has become the Sunna of military leaders upon entering a newly-conquered region.

II. Its legal status and time

1. "*Ṣalāt al-ḍuḥā* has the status of a *sunna mu'akkada* (emphasized Sunna)... and its time is from the rising of the sun a spear-length from the horizon until it passes its zenith, while the preferred time is that one begins it after one-quarter of the day has passed due to the ḥadīth of Zayd ibn Arqam [see below]."[389]

2. "*Ṣalāt al-ḍuḥā* is a Sunna acording to three of the Imāms while the Mālikīs differed and said it is a stressed *mandūb* prayer but not a Sunna. Its time is from the rising of the sun about a spear-length from the horizon until it passes its zenith, but the preferred time is that one begins it after one-quarter of the day has passed, while the Mālikīs prefer its delay for the same span of time as passes between the beginning of '*aṣr* and sunset."[390]

[389] *Fiqh al-'Ibādāt 'alā al-Madhhab al-Shāfi'ī, Kitāb al-Ṣalāt, al-Ṣalawāt al-Masnūna.*
[390] *Al-Fiqh 'alā al-Madhāhib al-Arba'a, Kitāb al-Ṣalāt, Ṣalāt al-Taṭawwu', Ṣalāt al-Ḍuḥā.*

3. On the Day of *ʿĪd* the preferred time for *ṣalāt al-ḍuḥā* is the earliest time according to the Shāfiʿīs: "*ṣalāt al-ʿīd* does not dispense from *ṣalāt al-ḍuḥā* but the latter remains sunna whether before or after *ṣalāt al-ʿīd*; however, it is preferable to pray it before *ṣalāt al-ʿīd*, so as to avoid the difference of opinion of the Ulema."[391]

4. One of the most complete collections of narrations on the subject is in al-Shawkānī's book *Nayl al-Awṭār*:[392]

> The Prophet ﷺ said: "Whoever prays the dawn prayer in congregation then waits patiently until he offers the *ḍuḥā* prayer, there shall be for him the reward of a pilgrim for both the major and minor pilgrimages, complete and not missing anything."[393] Another wording states: "Whoever prays the dawn prayer in congregation then sits remembering Allah until the sun rises, after which he prays two *rakʿas*, there shall be for him something like the reward of a major and minor pilgrimage (*ḥajj wa-ʿumra*), complete, complete, complete!"[394]
>
> The Prophet ﷺ also said: "Whoever prays the *fajr* prayer then sits in his place of prayer remembering Allah until sunrise, then prays two *rakʿas* of *ḍuḥā*, Allah shall make him forbidden to the Fire, nor shall it touch him nor consume him."[395]
>
> The Prophet ﷺ also said: "Your Lord said: 'Son of Ādam, pray for Me four *rakʿas* at the beginning of the day and I shall take care of your needs for the rest of it.'"[396] Al-ʿIrāqī said: "The beginning of the day is the dawn and so is the time of sunrise,

[391] *Fiqh al-ʿIbādāt ʿalā al-Madhhab al-Shāfiʿī, Kitāb al-Ṣalāt, al-Ṣalawāt al-Masnūna.*
[392] *Nayl al-Awṭār* (2:73-74): *Kitāb al- Ṣalāt, Ṣalāt al-Taṭawwuʿ, Ṣalāt al-Ḍuḥā.*
[393] Narrated from ʿUtba ibn ʿAbd by al-Ṭabarānī and from Abū Umāma in Abū Dāwūd.
[394] Narrated from Anas in al-Tirmidhī (*ḥasan gharīb*).
[395] Narrated from al-Ḥasan ibn ʿAlī by al-Bayhaqī.
[396] Narrated from Nuʿaym ibn Ḥammār by Abū Dāwūd, Aḥmad, and al-Dārimī; and from Abū Dharr or Abū al-Dardā' by al-Tirmidhī (*ḥasan gharīb*).

the latter being the apparent meaning of this narration, and those four *rak'as* being *ṣalāt al-ḍuḥā*."[397]

The Prophet ﷺ said: "Whoever gets up when the sun is before his eyes, performs a thorough ablution then stands and prays two *rak'as*, his sins are forgiven as when his mother gave birth to him."[398]

5. Al-'Irāqī in *Ṭarḥ al-Tathrīb* (3:61) said: "The time of *ḍuḥā* is the beginning of the day". Al-Nawawī in *al-Rawḍa* narrated from al-Shāfi'ī's companions that the time of *ḍuḥā* enters upon sunrise, together with the desirability of waiting for it to elevate a little. This shows that it is permissible not to wait for the sun to rise a spear-length before praying, although it is preferable. However, al-Rāfi'ī, Ibn al-Rif'a, and others of the Shāfi'ī authorities asserted that *ḍuḥā* enters only from the time the sun is elevated [from the horizon] and 'Itr in *I'lām al-Anām* (1:629) adduces the ḥadīth of Zayd ibn Arqam to state that the preferred time is midmorning while the permitted time is when the sun is one or two spear-lengths above the horizon.

6. The name *Awwābīn* applies more specifically to it when it is prayed at its midmorning time *i.e.* before *ẓuhr* by one or two hours:

a) The ḥadīth of the Prophet ﷺ in *Ṣaḥīḥ Muslim* from Zayd ibn Arqam with two chains: "*Ṣalāt al-awwābīn* is when the young camels' hoofs burn from the heat (*ḥīna tarmaḍu al-fiṣāl*)." The occasion for this ḥadīth was Zayd's reminder to those he had seen pray it early, that it was preferable to wait until later for greater merit.

[397] In *Ṭarḥ al-Tathrīb*, which contains a most thorough discussion on the topic (3:60-72).

[398] Narrated by Abū Ya'lā as cited by Shaykh 'Abd Allah Sirāj al-Dīn in the chapter on *ṣalāt al-ḍuḥā* of his book *al-Ṣalāt fil-Islām* (p. 129).

b) The Prophet ﷺ also said: "None is assiduous in keeping *ṣalāt al-ḍuḥā* except one who is oft-repentent (*awwāb*), and it is the prayer of the oft-repentent (*wa-hiya ṣalāt al-awwābīn*)."[399]

c) "My Beloved instructed me never to leave three things until I die: fasting three days of the month, praying *ṣalāt al-witr* before sleep, and praying the two *rak'as* of *ṣalāt al-ḍuḥā*." Aḥmad's version adds, "which is *ṣalāt al-awwābīn*."[400]

d) Something similar is narrated from Anas by al-Aṣbahānī in *al-Targhīb* and al-Bazzār in his *Musnad*.[401]

e) Abū Sufyān related that the Prophet ﷺ said: "When the shadows lean and the souls go forth [in search of sustenance], ask for your needs from Allah for it is the hour of the oft-repentent (*fa'innahā sā'at al-awwābīn*), and he recited: {*innahu kāna lil-awwābīna ghafūrā – verily He is most forgiving to those who turn to him again and again (in true penitence)*} (17:25)."[402]

7. Al-Haytamī said in *al-Minhāj al-Qawīm* (p. 249): "Its time is after the elevation of the sun from the horizon about a spear-length and until it reaches its zenith, while waiting for the end of the first quarter of the day is best due to a sound ḥadīth to that effect." He means the ḥadīth of Zayd ibn Arqam. Al-Ghazzālī in the *Iḥyā'* pointed out that this preference is in keeping with the concern that all four quarters of the day and night contain a prayer.

[399] Narrated from Abū Hurayra by Ibn Khuzayma, al-Ḥākim who graded it *ṣaḥīḥ* as per Muslim's criterion, al-Ṭabarānī in *al-Awsaṭ*, al-Bukharī in his *Tārīkh*, and Ibn Mardūyah.
[400] Narrated from Abū Hurayra by al-Bukhārī, Muslim, and Aḥmad.
[401] As cited by Ibn Kathīr in his *Tafsīr* and al-Suyūṭī in *al-Jāmi' al-Ṣaghīr* (§5012).
[402] Narrated by 'Abd al-Razzāq (3:66) while Ibn Abī Shayba (7:228) narrates it *mawqūf* from 'Alī ؓ.

8. Abū Zurʿa al-ʿIrāqī said in *Ṭarḥ al-Tathrīb* (3:71): "Our Shāfiʿī colleagues said that *ḍuḥā* is the best voluntary prayer after those regularly offered with the *farḍ* prayers (*rawātib*) but al-Nawawī in *al-Majmūʿ* put *tarāwīḥ* before it, *i.e.* between the *rawātib* and *ḍuḥā*." So did al-Ḥaḍramī in his *Muqaddima*. Shaykh al-Islam al-Haytamī in his commentary on *al-Muqaddima al-Ḥaḍramiyya* entitled *al-Minhāj al-Qawīm* (p. 248-249) explained that this is due to the fact that *tarāwīḥ* is prayed in congregation.

III. Its length

Its length is between two as in most of the narrations – and this is its minimum by Consensus – to 12 *rakʿas*, although the basis seems to be four as per the ḥadīth of ʿĀ'isha in Muslim, Ibn Mājah, Aḥmad, and others: "Yes, the Messenger of Allah ﷺ used to pray *ḍuḥā* in four *rakʿas*. After that he might add whatever Allah wished" and other narrations, and this is the best number according to a number of the Imāms of ḥadīth, among them al-Ḥākim and al-Kattānī; eight – as per the ḥadīth of Umm Hāni' in al-Bukharī and Muslim – being the best number according to the majority of the *Fuqahā'* and the maximum for most of the Shāfiʿīs according to al-Nawawī in *al-Majmūʿ* and for the Ḥanbalīs according to Ibn Qudāma in *al-Mughnī*; while the *Jumhūr* said it is up to twelve as chosen by al-Rūwyānī in *al-Ḥilya*, al-Rāfiʿī in *al-Sharḥ al-Ṣaghīr* and *al-Muḥarrar*, al-Nawawī in *al-Rawḍa* and *al-Minhāj*, and others taking into consideration the weak *marfūʿ* narrations that mention twelve *rakʿas* from Abū Dharr, Abū al-Dardā', and Anas narrated by al-Tirmidhī (*gharīb*), Ibn Mājah, al-Bayhaqī, al-Ṭabarānī, and others,[403] while al-Ṭabarī narrates from al-Aswad that there is no limit to their number, attributing this to a number of the *Salaf*. Allah knows best.

[403] Cf. *Ṭarḥ* (3:71), *Iʿlām* (1:624), *Nayl* and *Fatḥ al-Bārī*.

IV. Its immense merit and required character

There is a *ṣadaqa* incumbent upon every limb and joint of a servant who wakes up in the morning, which is remitted by praying *ṣalāt al-ḍuḥā* according to the following narrations:

a) The Prophet ﷺ said: "In the morning every single joint of yours must pay a *ṣadaqa*. Every *tasbīḥ* is a *ṣadaqa*, every *taḥmīd* is a *ṣadaqa*, every *tahlīl* is a *ṣadaqa*, every *takbīr* is a *ṣadaqa*, every commanding good is a *ṣadaqa*, and every forbidding evil is a *ṣadaqa*, and all this is accomplished through two *rakʿas* one can pray in *ḍuḥā*."[404]

b) Abū Dāwūd and Aḥmad from Abū Burayda: The Prophet ﷺ said: "There are three hundred and sixty joints in a human being, and he must[405] pay a *ṣadaqa* for each one of them." They said: "Who can do such a thing, Messenger of Allah?" He replied: "Bury the dirt [lit. sputum] you see in the Mosque; remove a dangerous object from the road; and, if you are unable, then the two *rakʿas* of *ḍuḥā* accomplish it for you."[406]

The above two ḥadīths are proofs of the huge merit of the *ḍuḥā* prayer as they indicate that it fulfills the performance of three hundred and sixty charities. Ibn ʿAbd al-Barr said these ḥadīths are the most emphatic evidence that has reached us concerning the immense merit of *ṣalāt al-ḍuḥā*.[407]

c) The Prophet ﷺ said: "Whoever regularly prays the two *rakʿas* of *ḍuḥā*, his sins are forgiven even if they are as numerous as the foam of the sea."[408]

[404] Narrated from Abū Dharr by Muslim.
[405] *I.e.* it is *mustaḥabb* as stated in *Ṭarḥ al-Tathrīb* (3:69).
[406] Its chain is strong as per Shuʿayb al-Arna'ūṭ in Ibn Ḥibbān (4:520 §1642) and al-Taḥāwī's *Sharḥ Mushkil al-Āthār* (§99).
[407] Cf. al-ʿIrāqī, *Ṭarḥ al-Tathrīb* (3:71).
[408] Narrated from Abū Hurayra by al-Tirmidhī, Ibn Mājah, and Aḥmad.

d) It is a Sunna of the Prophets as narrated in explanation of the verse {*And Ibrāhīm who paid his debt*} (53:37): *i.e.* he paid his daily debt with four *rak'as* which he prayed in *ḍuḥā*. Narrated by al-Ṭabarī and Ibn Abī Ḥātim in their *Tafsīrs*. Similarly, al-Qāḍī Ibn al-ʿArabī al-Mālikī in *ʿĀriḍat al-Aḥwadhī* adduced the verse of Dāwūd ﷺ already cited above [I (c)] to conclude: "It used to be the prayer of all the Prophets before Muḥammad ﷺ after which Allah ﷻ let the *ʿaṣr* prayer remain in the evening and abrogated the sunrise prayer."[409] Dāwūd, Sulaymān, and Ayyūb are all called *awwāb* in the Qur'ān – upon our Prophet and upon them blessings and peace.

V. Addressing some misunderstandings

Some people with scant knowledge of ḥadīth assert that *ṣalāt al-ḍuḥā* is an innovation (*bidʿa*) on the basis of the reports from ʿĀ'isha in al-Bukharī and Muslim that "I never saw the Prophet ﷺ pray *ṣalāt al-ḍuḥā*" and from Ibn ʿUmar also in the *Ṣaḥīḥayn*: "It is a *bidʿa*." However, these only mean that they did not see the Prophet ﷺ pray it (a) in the Mosque (b) on a regular basis (c) in congregation (d) for more than two or four *rakʿas* lest it be imposed on the *Umma* as an obligation. In addition, the two principles must be applied that "the narrations of affirmation take precedence over those of negation" and that "those who know are a proof over those who do not know." This view was expounded by the Imāms of *Fiqh* and ḥadīth Masters such as al-Bayhaqī in *al-Sunan al-Kubrā*, al-Qāḍī ʿIyāḍ in *Sharḥ Ṣaḥīḥ Muslim*, al-Nawawī in *Khulāṣat al-Aḥkām* and *Sharḥ Ṣaḥīḥ Muslim*, al-Zayn al-ʿIrāqī in *Sharḥ Sunan al-Tirmidhī*, Abū Zurʿa al-ʿIrāqī in *Ṭarḥ al-Tathrīb*, and others. This is established by the following evidence:

[409] Cf. *Ṭarḥ al-Tathrīb* (3:64).

1. ʿĀʾisha not only did narrate its performance by the Prophet ﷺ as cited above [sec. III] but also prayed it assiduously herself as narrated in the *Muwaṭṭaʾ*: "I would not leave the eight *rakʿas* of *ṣalāt al-ḍuḥā* even if my father and mother rose from the dead." The same maximum emphasis is narrated in the famous narrations from Abū Hurayra in al-Bukharī, Muslim, al-Tirmidhī, al-Nasāʾī, Abū Dāwūd, Aḥmad, and al-Dārimī and from Abū al-Dardāʾ in Muslim, Abū Dāwūd, al-Nasāʾī, and Aḥmad: "My Beloved instructed me never to leave three things until I die: fasting three days of the month, praying *ṣalāt al-witr* before sleep, and praying *ṣalāt al-ḍuḥā*." Some versions add after the last clause: "both at home and in travel." On that basis alone, praying it can never be declared a *bidʿa* in absolute terms.

2. Both ʿĀʾisha and Ibn ʿUmar stated that "the Prophet ﷺ would not pray *ḍuḥā* except when returning from a trip."[410] Ibn Ḥibbān explained that "this means he did not pray *ḍuḥā* in the mosque among people rather than in the house except upon returning from a trip." This clarification is vital in view of his ﷺ prohibition to travelers from returning to their homes at night – the Prophet ﷺ returned from his trips mostly in the early part of the day – and his emphasis in the Nine Books – except Ibn Mājah – that "Your best *ṣalāt* is that prayed in your homes other than the prescribed one." That is, other than at that time, he ﷺ would pray *ḍuḥā* at home, in private. However, the *marfūʿ* narrations of ʿUtba ibn ʿAbd, Abū Umāma, and al-Ḥasan ibn ʿAlī cited above are clear – if authentic – as to the desirability of praying the two *rakʿas* of *ḍuḥā* in the same place as the congregational *fajr* prayer.

[410]Narrated among others by Muslim, Abū Dāwūd, Aḥmad, al-Nasāʾī, Ibn Khuzayma, and Ibn Ḥibbān (6:270).

3. This is further confirmed by the statement of ʿUrwa that "ʿĀ'isha would say that the Messenger of Allah ﷺ did not pray *ḍuḥā* but she herself prayed it, and she would say that the Messenger of Allah ﷺ left out many good deeds lest people took them as their regular practice, then they would be imposed as *farḍ*."[411] The Ulema explained that this fear no longer applied after the time of the Prophet ﷺ and it should be prayed on a regular basis as long as people pray it individually and understand its status as that of desirability, not obligation.

4. This is further confirmed by the authentic report of Abū Saʿīd al-Khudrī in al-Tirmidhī (*ḥasan gharīb*) and Aḥmad: "The Messenger of Allah ﷺ used to pray *ḍuḥā* to the point that we said he shall never leave it, and he used to leave it to the point that we said: he never prays it."

5. This is further confirmed by Ibn ʿUmar's reply when asked about *ṣalāt al-ḍuḥā*: "It is an innovation and what a fine innovation it is!" (*bidʿatun wa-niʿmati al-bidʿatu hiya*).[412] Another reply to the same question by Ibn ʿUmar: "At the time ʿUthmān was killed no one considered it desirable [in the Religion] (*mā aḥadun yastaḥibbuhā*), and the people did not innovate anything that is dearer to me than that prayer."[413] Both reports mean: *ṣalāt al-ḍuḥā* as prayed on a regular basis in the Mosque in congregation.

[411] Narrated by al-Bukhārī, Muslim, Abū Dāwūd, Mālik, Aḥmad, and others.

[412] Narrated from al-Ḥakam ibn al-Aʿraj by Ibn Abī Shayba (2:172) with a sound chain according to Ibn Ḥajar in *Fatḥ al-Bārī* (1959 ed. 3:52) and from Mujāhid by Ibn al-Jaʿd in his *Musnad* (p. 314) and al-Ṭabarānī in *al-Muʿjam al-Kabīr* (12:424).

[413] Narrated from Sālim ibn ʿAbd Allah ibn ʿUmar by ʿAbd al-Razzāq with a sound chain according to Ibn Ḥajar in *Fatḥ al-Bārī* (1959 ed. 3:52).

6. In exact illustration of the above understanding there is a report from Masrūq that Ibn Mas'ūd prayed *fajr* as *imām* then left, and people would wait for sunrise then get up and pray *ṣalāt al-ḍuḥā*. When news of this reached Ibn Mas'ūd he said: "You shall not impose upon the servants of Allah what He Himself did not impose upon them! If you must pray it, pray it in your houses." Ibn Baṭṭāl said: "And the *madhhab* of Ibn Mijlaz and the *Salaf* was the observance of strict privacy for it lest the public mistake it for an obligation." It is also narrated that 'Ā'isha prayed *ṣalāt al-ḍuḥā* in the strictest privacy.[414]

7. 'Umar said, as in Ibn Abī Shayba: "Servants of Allah! Pray the *ḍuḥā* prayer." It is unthinkable that after this instruction from the Commander of the Faithful, one of the Rightly-Guided Caliphs, and one of the foremost people of knowledge among the senior Companions, his son should declare it a *bid'a* in absolute terms.

Ṣalāt al-Āwwābīn between *Maghrib and 'Ishā?*

What about the appellation *Ṣalāt al-Āwwābīn* for the *nafl* prayers offered between *maghrib* and *'ishā*? The evidence for this appellation is as follows:

1. A *mursal* ḥadīth is narrated from the *Tābi'ī* Muḥammad ibn al-Munkadir, from the Prophet ﷺ that the latter said: "Whoever prays between *maghrib* and *'ishā*, [let him know that] this is *ṣalāt al-awwābīn*."[415]

[414] All in *Ṭarḥ al-Tathrīb* (3:63-64).

[415] Narrated by Ibn al-Mubārak in *al-Zuhd wal-Raqā'iq* (p. 445 §1259) and Ibn Naṣr in *Qiyām al-Layl* as stated respectively by al-'Irāqī in *Takhrīj Aḥādith al-Iḥyā'* and al-Ghumārī in *al-Mudāwī* (6:346 §8804). Ibn Kathīr cites it in *Ikhtiṣār 'Ulūm al-Ḥadīth* (p. 48) and al-Suyūṭī declares it *ḍa'īf* in *al-Jāmi' al-Ṣaghīr* (§8804).

2. A *mawqūf* report from ʿAbd Allah ibn ʿUmar states: "*ṣalāt al-awwābīn* is [during] the gap between *maghrib* and ʿ*ishā*, until the time people spring to *ṣalāt*."[416] The same is attributed to ʿAbd Allah ibn ʿAmr ibn al-ʿĀṣ.[417]

3. A *marfūʿ* ḥadīth from Ibn ʿUmar, from the Prophet ﷺ but found only in the sixth-century *Tārīkh Jurjān* (1:74) states: "For whoever follows up [with worship] between *maghrib* and ʿ*ishā* shall be built in Paradise two palaces at one hundred years' distance one from another, with enough trees to cover the people of both East and West in fruit: it is called *ṣalāt al-awwābīn* and it is verily the heedlessness of the heedless [to leave it]. And truly there are supplications that are answered only between *maghrib* and ʿ*ishā*." The same is attributed *maqṭūʿ* to Ibn al-Munkadir and Abū Ḥāzim.[418]

4. Abū Nuʿaym narrated with his chain from the *Tābiʿī* ʿAṭā' al-Khurāsānī that he named the *nawāfil* prayers between *maghrib* and ʿ*ishā*: *ṣalāt al-awwābīn*.[419]

5. It is said that Imām Jaʿfar al-Ṣādiq applied its name to both the morning and the evening on the basis of the verses {*Lo! We subdued the hills to hymn the praises (of their Lord) with him at nightfall and sunrise, And the birds assembled; all were turning (awwābun) unto Him*} (38:18-19).

[416] Narrated by Ibn Abī Shayba (2:14 §5922).
[417] Narrated by Ibn al-Mubārak in *al-Zuhd* (p. 445) and al-Qurṭubī in his *Tafsīr* (14:101).
[418] In al-Bayhaqī's *al-Sunan al-Kubrā* (3:19) and *Shuʿab al-Īmān* (3:133).
[419] In *Ḥilyat al-Awliyā'* (1985 ed. 5:200). Ibn al-Jawzī also cites it in *Ṣifat al-Ṣafwa* (4:152).

There is no stronger evidence for this appellation nor is it applied to the *maghrib*-to-*ʿishā nafl* other than in the very late books of *Fiqh*.[420]

There is no question that unlimited *nafl* after *maghrib* is recommended in the Sunna and the commentaries of Qur'ān all refer to it in explanation of the verse {*They forsake their beds to cry unto their Lord in fear and hope*} (32:16), its best number being six *rakʿas* according to the evidence listed in the relevant sections of *Ṭarḥ al-Tathrīb*, *Nayl al-Awṭār*, and elsewhere.[421]

In conclusion, the appellation *awwābīn* is firmly established for the *ḍuḥā* prayer but less so for the post-*maghrib nafl* although there is sufficient evidence to silence those who call the latter appellation an innovation. "Nor is Ibn al-Munkadir's report contradicted by its use in the *Ṣaḥīḥ* [for *ṣalāt al-ḍuḥā*] since there is no objection to calling both prayers by the name *ṣalāt al-awwābīn*."[422] Furthermore, the sense of Oft-Returning is perfectly applicable in the evening *nawāfil* prayers and the analogy with the morning ones is clear enough since both prayers take place at the extremities of the day, both vary from two to several *rakʿas*, both are non-*rawātib* Sunnas, and both carry immense rewards. Al-Nawawī in *al-Maqāṣid* said none of the people of *Wilāya* reached high levels except by adhering firmly to these two prayers. And Allah knows best.

[420]Such as al-Bajūrī's *Ḥāshiya* in Shāfiʿī *Fiqh* (1:135) and Ibn ʿĀbidīn in his *Ḥāshiya* (2:12-13) although the latter does not name it as such but only states: "And six *rakʿas* after *Maghrib* so that he will be recorded among the oft-returning (*li-yuktab min al-awwabīn*)."

[421]Cf. ʿAbd al-Qādir ʿĪsā Dyāb's *al-Mīzān al-ʿAdl* (p. 352-353).

[422]Al-Shawkānī, *Nayl al-Awṭār* (3:66).

Saying "*Sayyidinā* Muḥammad" in *Tashahhud*

In the introduction to his commentary on Imām al-Jazūlī's manual of invocations of blessings on the Prophet ﷺ titled *al-Dalālāt al-Wāḍiḥāt Sharḥ Dalā'il al-Khayrāt*, Qāḍī Yūsuf al-Nabhānī gave a wealth of historical and legal details on the etiquette of invoking blessings on the Prophet ﷺ. In the course of his presentation he recapitulates his detailed examination – which he first presented in the introduction to his *Sa'ādat al-Dārayn* – of the preferability of adding the title *Sayyidinā* ("our Master") to the name of the Prophet ﷺ in *tashahhud*. This is the position preferred by the late Shāfi'ī authorities in particular, such as Ibn 'Abd al-Salām, al-Isnawī, al-Maḥallī, al-Suyūṭī, al-Fayrūzābādī, al-Ramlī, al-Sakhāwī, al-Haytamī, and others. It is also the preferred position of some of the contemporary Ḥanafī Ulema of Syria such as Dr. Sāmir al-Naṣṣ and the two ḥadīth Masters Nūr al-Dīn 'Itr and his teacher Shaykh 'Abd Allah Sirāj al-Dīn among others.

Shaykh Nūr al-Dīn 'Itr said:

> The Four Schools are in agreement over the permissibility of saying *Sayyidinā Muḥammad* inside prayer, a fortiori outside it. The difference of opinion is between the Ḥanafīs who said that it is preferable not to say *Sayyidinā* in *tashahhud*, and the Shāfi'īs who consider it necessary out of respect. The Ḥanafīs have a rule: strict obedience is better than respect (*al-imtithāl khayrun min al-adab*). The proof of the Shāfi'īs is that the Prophet ﷺ only omitted it out of humbleness but he did say, "I am the Master of human beings on the Day of Resurrection and this is no vain boast.... Ādam and all those after him are nowhere but under my flag, and I will be the first one to rise from the earth – this is no vain boast!"[423] Therefore we stick to

[423] See note 427 below.

this proof! As for the statement that this is a *bid'a*: **this statement itself** is a *bid'a*. None of the past Imāms of Islam ever said such a thing. Rather, the ḥadīth we just mentioned is firmly established as authentic. Our teacher, the ḥadīth Master of these lands, the *Muḥaddith* Shaykh 'Abd Allah Sirāj al-Dīn – who follows the Ḥanafī *madhhab* – chose this position and declared it in one of his public classes before all of us. He said it is better to say *Sayyidinā Muḥammad*, and he chose the Shāfi'ī *madhhab* in the matter out of respect.[424]

Other proofs for giving precedence to respect (*adab*) over obedience (*ṭā'a*) in *tashahhud* are:

1. The refusal of Abū Bakr to pray as *imām* in front of the Prophet ﷺ although the latter ordered him. After the prayer, the Prophet ﷺ asked him: "Abū Bakr, what prevented you from standing firm when I ordered you to?" Abū Bakr excused himself with his famous statement: "*Mā kāna li-Ibni Abī Quḥāfata an yataqaddama bayna yaday Rasūlillāh* – It was not fitting for the son of Abū Quḥāfa to stand ahead of the Messenger of Allah." The Prophet ﷺ approved of him.[425]

2. The statement of Ibn Mas'ūd: "When you invoke blessings on your Prophet, invoke blessings in the best possible way (*idhā ṣallaytum fa-aḥsinū al-ṣalāta 'alā nabiyyikum*) for – you do not know – this might be shown to him. Therefore, say: 'O Allah! Grant your *ṣalāt*, mercy, and blessings upon the Master of Messengers (*Sayyid al-Mursalīn*), the Imām of the Godfearing, and the Seal of Prophets, Muḥammad your servant and Messenger, the Imām of goodness and leader of goodness and Messenger of Mercy! O Allah! Raise him to a glorious station

[424] 'Itr, lesson on his *I'lām al-Anām Sharḥ Bulūgh al-Marām*, Jāmi' al-Shamsiyya, Damascus, Ramaḍān 1422.

[425] Narrated from Sahl ibn Sa'd al-Sā'idī by al-Bukhārī, Muslim, Mālik, Abū Dāwūd, al-Nasā'ī, and Aḥmad.

for which the first and the last of creatures will yearn! O Allah! Grant mercy to Muḥammad and to the House of Muḥammad as You granted mercy to Ibrāhīm and to the House of Ibrāhīm! Truly, You are the Lord of glory and praise! O Allah! Bless Muḥammad and the House of Muḥammad as You blessed Ibrāhīm and the House of Ibrāhīm! Truly, You are the Lord of glory and praise!'"[426]

The proofs for calling the Prophet ﷺ *sayyid* are in the verses {*lordly* (*sayyidan*), *chaste, a Prophet of the righteous*} (3:39) and {*they met her lord and master* (*sayyidahā*) *at the door*} (12:42) as well as in the following Prophetic narrations:

a) "I am the Master (*sayyid*) of human beings";[427]

b) "This son of mine [al-Ḥasan] is a leader of men (*sayyid*)";[428]

c) "Get up to meet your chief (*qūmū ilā sayyidikum*) [Saʿd ibn Muʿādh]";[429] this ḥadīth is also narrated as "*qūmu li-sayyidi-kum*" which means the same thing.[430]

[426] See note 184.

[427] Narrated from: Abū Hurayra by al-Bukhārī, Muslim, al-Tirmidhī (*ḥasan ṣaḥīḥ*), Abū Dāwūd, Aḥmad, al-Nasā'ī in *al-Sunan al-Kubrā* (6:378), Ibn Abī Shayba (6:307, 6:317, 7:257), Ibn Saʿd (1:20), Ibn Ḥibbān (14:381), al-Bayhaqī in *al-Sunan al-Kubra* (9:4); Ḥudhayfa by al-Ḥākim (4:617) and al-Ṭabarānī in *al-Awsaṭ* cf. al-Haythamī (10:377) and others; Abū Saʿīd al-Khudrī by al-Tirmidhī (*ḥasan ṣaḥīḥ*), Ibn Mājah, and Aḥmad; Anas by Aḥmad and al-Dārimī; Ibn ʿAbbās by Aḥmad; ʿUbāda ibn al-Ṣāmit by al-Ḥākim (1990 ed. 1:83 *ṣaḥīḥ*); Ibn Masʿūd by Ibn Ḥibbān (14:398); ʿAbd Allah ibn Salām by al-Ṭabarānī and Abū Yaʿlā cf. al-Haythamī (8:253) and al-Maqdisī's *al-Aḥādīth al-Mukhtāra* (9:455); and Jābir ibn ʿAbd Allah by al-Ḥākim (1990 ed. 2:660 *ṣaḥīḥ al-isnād*) and al-Ṭabarānī in *al-Awsaṭ* cf. al-Haythamī (10:376); etc.

[428] Narrated from Abū Bakrah by al-Bukhārī, al-Tirmidhī, al-Nasā'ī, Abū Dāwūd, and Aḥmad.

[429] Narrated from Abū Saʿīd al-Khudrī by al-Bukharī, Muslim, Abū Dāwūd, al-Nasā'ī, and Aḥmad.

[430] Cf. al-Ṭaḥāwī, *Mushkil al-Āthār* (2:38), Ibn Kathīr, *Bidāya* (4:122), and al-Zabīdī, *Itḥāf al-Sādat al-Muttaqīn* (7:142).

d) Sahl ibn Ḥunayf said "My liege-lord!" (*yā sayyidī*) when he asked the Prophet ﷺ a certain question.[431]

e) Mālik and Sufyān gave the *fatwā* that one should not say *Yā Sayyidī* in *du'ā'*, but rather *Yā Rabbī*.[432]

Many more proofs are adduced in the monograph by our teacher Shaykh Muḥammad 'Iṣām ibn al-Sayyid Yūsuf 'Arār al-Ḥasanī al-Dimashqī entitled *al-Uns wal-Isti'nās bi-Dhikri Lafẓ al-Siyādati fil-Adhān wal-Iqāmati wa-bayn al-Nās* (Damascus: Dār al-Thaqāfa lil-Jamī', 2004).

[431] Narrated from Sahl ibn Ḥunayf by Abū Dāwūd, Aḥmad, al-Nasā'ī in *al-Kubrā* (6:72 §10086, 6:256 §10873) and *'Amal al-Yawm wal-Layla* (p. 252 §257, p. 564 §1034), al-Ṭaḥāwī in *Sharḥ Ma'ānī al-Āthār* (4:329), al-Ṭabarānī in *al-Kabīr* (6:93 §5615), and al-Ḥākim (1990 ed. 4:458 *isnād ṣaḥīḥ*).

[432] Cited by Ibn Rajab in his *Jāmi' al-'Ulum wal-Ḥikam* (Dār al-Ma'rifa ed. p. 107).

Proofs for Visitation of the Graves by Women

The most correct position is that the dispensation** (rukhṣa) **for the visitation of graves is firmly established for women.

– Ibn ʿĀbidīn[433]

In his *Advice to our Brothers the Scholars of Najd*, Sayyid Yūsuf al-Rifāʿī states, addressing present-day Wahhābīs: "You forbid women from visiting the noble *Baqīʿ* with no agreed-upon, clear and explicit proof from the Law!" The following is a demonstration of the permissibility of visits to *al-Baqīʿ* according to the principles of Sacred Law and the textual proofs of the Sunna.

First of all, the Prophet ﷺ commanded us to visit him even after his lifetime and he himself visited the graves as shown by several ḥadīths:

1. "Whoever visits my grave, my intercession becomes guaranteed for him."[434]

2. At the time the Messenger of Allah ﷺ sent Muʿādh ibn Jabal to Yemen, the Messenger of Allah ﷺ went out with him to give him his last recommendations. Muʿādh was mounted while the Messenger of Allah ﷺ was walking by Muʿādh's mount. When he finished he said: "Muʿādh! It may be that (*ʿasā an*) you shall not meet me again after this year of my life. Perhaps you will (*laʿallaka*) pass by my mosque here, and my grave [*i.e.* to visit me]?" Hearing this, Muʿādh wept uninterruptedly at the thought of parting with the Messenger of Allah ﷺ. Then he [the Prophet] turned and, facing Madīna, said: "Those closest to me are those who guard themselves from Allah (*al-muttaqūn*), whoever they are and wherever they are."

433 Ibn ʿĀbidīn, *Ḥāshiya* (1386/1966 ed. 2:242).

434 See http://mac.abc.se/home/onesr/d/wvmg_e.pdf and our translation of Ibn Jahbal's *Refutation of Ibn Taymiyya*, forthcoming at AQSA Publications *in shā Allah.*

Another version adds: "Do not weep, Mu'ādh! Weeping [uncontrollably] is from Shaytan."[435]

3. The Prophet ﷺ insisted that such visits to his grave should not be only on the occasion of *Ḥajj* when he said: "Do not take my grave as an '*Īd* and do not turn your houses into graves for indeed your *ṣalāt* reaches me." (See the next section for a detailed study on this ḥadīth.)

4. The Prophet ﷺ used to visit the graveyard of the martyrs of Uḥud punctually at the end of every year (*'alā ra'si kulli ḥawl*) together with Abū Bakr, 'Umar, and 'Uthmān.[436]

5. Al-Bayhaqī and others narrated that the Prophet ﷺ said: "Whoever visits the grave of his parents or the grave of one of them every Jumu'a, he will be forgiven and be recorded among the pious sons" (*man zāra qabra abawayhi aw aḥadihimā fi kulli Jumu'a, ghufira lahu wa-kutiba barran*).[437] And he ﷺ is without the shadow of a doubt the most pious of all pious sons.

[435]Both versions are narrated by Imām Aḥmad with two sound chains as stated by al-Haythamī, al-Bazzār (7:91), al-Ṭabarānī in *al-Kabīr* (20:121) and *Musnad al-Shāmiyyīn* (2:102), Ibn Abī 'Āṣim in *al-Āḥād wal-Mathānī* (3:420) and *al-Sunna*, Ibn Ḥibbān (2:414), and al-Bayhaqī in *al-Sunan al-Kubrā* (10:86).

[436]Narrated *mursal* from Muḥammad ibn Ibrāhīm in al-Ṭabarī's *Tafsīr* (13:142) cf. Ibn Kathīr's (2:512) and al-Wāqidī in the *Siyar* as cited by Ibn Kathīr in *al-Bidāya*.

[437]Narrated from Abū Hurayra by al-Ṭabarānī in *al-Awsaṭ* (6:175 §6114), *al-Ṣaghīr* (2:160 §955), and *al-Kabīr* with a weak chain because of 'Abd al-Karīm Abū Umayya cf. al-Haythamī (3:59-60); Ibn Abī al-Dunyā in *Makārim al-Akhlāq* (p. 83) and al-Bayhaqī in *Shu'ab al-Īmān* (6:201 §7901) with an incomplete *mu'ḍal* chain in addition to the fact that both their and al-Ṭabarānī's chain contain Muḥammad ibn al-Nu'mān who is unknown while his shaykh Yaḥyā ibn al-'Alā' al-Bajalī al-Rāzī is discarded as stated by al-'Irāqī cf. al-Munāwī (6:141). Cited by al-Ḥakīm al-Tirmidhī in *Nawādir al-Uṣūl* (*Aṣl* 15) and al-Suyūṭī in *al-Lum'a fī Khaṣā'iṣ al-Jum'a* (p. 109 §193).

6. Also, al-Bazzār narrates that the Prophet ﷺ visited the Jannat al-Maʿlā graveyard in Makka, where his dear wife Sayyida Khadīja was buried and he called the whole place a blessed graveyard: "*Niʿma al-maqbaratu hādhihi*."[438]

As for to the visitation of graves by women, those who object to such visitation adduce chiefly three ḥadīths as their proof, two of these being the weak-chained narrations, (a) "Allah curses the women who visit the graves" (*laʿana Allahu zāʾirāt al-qubūr*)[439] and (b) "Allah curses the women who visit the graves and take them for places of worship and candles,"[440] and the third one being, (c) "Allah curses the women who frequently visit the graves" (*laʿana Allahu zawwārāt al-qubūr*).[441]

[438]Narrated from Ibn ʿAbbās by Aḥmad, al-Bukhārī in *al-Tārīkh al-Kabīr* (1:284), ʿAbd al-Razzāq (3:579), Ibn Abī Ḥātim in his *ʿIlal* (2:270), and al-Ṭabarānī in *al-Kabīr* (11:137) with a strong chain cf. al-Haythamī (3:297-298) and Ibn Ḥajar in *Taʿjīl al-Manfaʿa*.

[439]Narrated from Abū Hurayra by Ibn Ḥibbān (7:452 §3178) with a weak chain because of ʿUmar ibn Abī Salama ibn ʿAbd al-Raḥmān al-Zuhrī who is weak as stated by al-Arnaʾūṭ and Maʿrūf in *Taḥrīr al-Taqrīb* (3:74 §4910). Also narrated from Ḥassān ibn Thābit from the Prophet ﷺ by Ibn Abī Shayba (3:31) with a weak chain because of ʿAbd al-Raḥmān ibn Bahmān who is unknown as a narrator (*majhūl*). The ḥadīth itself is "fair due to witness and corroborating chains and versions" (*ḥasan li-ghayrih*) as stated by al-Arnaʾūṭ in the *Musnad* (5:128 n. 2).

[440]Narrated from Ibn ʿAbbās by al-Tirmidhī (*ḥasan*), Abū Dāwūd, al-Nasāʾī in *al-Sunan* and *al-Sunan al-Kubrā* (1:657 §2174), Aḥmad, Ibn Abī Shayba (2:151, 3:30), al-Ṭaḥāwī in *Sharḥ Mushkil al-Āthār* (12:178-179 §4741-4742), al-Baghawī in *Sharḥ al-Sunna* (2:416-417 §510), Ibn Ḥibbān (7:452-454 §3179-3180), al-Ḥākim (1990 ed. 1:530) who indicated its weakness, al-Bayhaqī in *al-Sunan al-Kubrā* (4:78 §6992), Ibn al-Jaʿd in his *Musnad* (p. 224), al-Ṭabarānī in *al-Kabīr* (12:148), and al-Haythamī in *Mawārid al-Ẓamʾān* (p. 200), all with the same weak chain containing Abū Ṣāliḥ Mawlā Umm Hāniʾ who is weak as stated by Ibn Ḥajar in al-Mundhirī's *al-Targhīb* (1997 ed. 4:190) and al-Arnaʾūṭ in *Ṣaḥīḥ Ibn Ḥibbān* and the *Musnad* (5:128 §2984). However, the ḥadīth itself is acceptable since al-Tirmidhī and al-Baghawī declared it "fair"; while Ibn al-Sakan included it among the sound (*ṣaḥīḥ*) narrations as stated by Ibn al-Mulaqqin in *Tuḥfat al-Muḥtāj* (2:31).

[441]Narrated from Abū Hurayra by al-Tirmidhī (*ḥasan ṣaḥīḥ*), Ibn Mājah, and Aḥmad; from Ibn ʿAbbās by Ibn Mājah with a weak chain because of Abū Ṣāliḥ;

As indicated by Sayyid al-Rifāʿī, the above narrations do not constitute "agreed-upon, clear and explicit proof from the Law" for the prohibition of women visiting graves in Islam. Accordingly, the majority of the Ulema concur that women are permitted to visit the graves if there is no danger of temptation and sin.[442] This is established by the following proofs:

7. The Prophet ﷺ said: "I forbade you to visit the graves but [now] do visit them!"[443] There is no proof for restricting this absolute permission to men alone.

8. ʿĀ'isha said: "The Prophet ﷺ forbade the visitation of graves, then permitted it, and I think he said: 'For, truly, they remind you of the hereafter.'"[444] ʿĀ'isha's practice and further comments confirm that she understood this Prophetic permission as absolute.

and from Ḥassān ibn Thābit by Ibn Mājah and Aḥmad with a weak chain because of ʿAbd al-Raḥmān ibn Bahmān. Note: Ibn Mājah's versions have *zuwwārāt.*

442 As stated by Ibn Ḥajar in *Fatḥ al-Bārī* (1959 ed. 3:148), al-Shawkānī in *Nayl al-Awṭār* (chapters on burial and the rulings pertaining to graves), al-Mubārakfūrī in *Tuḥfat al-Aḥwadhī* (4:139), and others.

443 Narrated as part of a longer ḥadīth: from Burayda by Muslim, al-Tirmidhī (*ḥasan ṣaḥīḥ*), Abū Dāwūd, al-Nasā'ī, ʿAbd al-Razzāq (3:569), and others; from Abū Saʿīd al-Khudrī by Aḥmad with a chain of sound narrators as stated by al-Haythamī (3:58), Mālik, al-Ḥākim (1990 ed. 1:530) who declared it sound by Muslim's criterion, al-Bayhaqī in *al-Sunan al-Kubrā* (4:77 §6984), and al-Bazzār with a chain of sound narrators as stated by al-Haythamī (3:58); from Ibn Masʿūd by Ibn Mājah, al-Dāraquṭnī in his *Sunan* (4:259), ʿAbd al-Razzāq (3:572-573), Ibn Ḥibbān (3:261), al-Ḥākim (1990 ed. 1:531), and al-Bayhaqī in *al-Sunan al-Kubrā* (4:77 §6983) all with weak chains according to al-Arna'ūṭ; from Anas by Aḥmad and al-Bazzār with chains containing al-Ḥārith ibn Nabhān who is weak according to al-Haythamī (4:27), al-Ḥākim (1990 ed. 1:531-532), and al-Bayhaqī in *al-Sunan al-Kubrā* (4:77 §6984).

444 Narrated by al-Bazzār with a chain of trustworthy narrators as stated by al-Haythamī (3:58).

9. ʿĀʾisha ﷺ came to Makka after her brother's death saying, "Where is the grave of my brother?" Then she came to the grave and prayed over him, a month after his death.[445] Another version states that Ibn Abī Mulayka said: "ʿĀʾisha's brother died six miles away from Makka, so we carried him until we reached Makka and buried him there. ʿĀʾisha came to us after that and reproached us for doing so. Then she said: 'Where is the grave of my brother?' We showed it to her and she alighted from her howdah and prayed at his grave."[446]

10. When ʿAbd Allah ibn Abī Mulayka saw ʿĀʾisha ﷺ visiting the grave of her brother ʿAbd al-Raḥmān he said to her: "Did not the Prophet ﷺ forbid this [visitation of graves]?" She replied: "Yes, he had forbidden it. Then he ordered us to visit them."[447] Ibn ʿAbd al-Barr mentions that Imām Aḥmad adduces this report as proof that women are permitted to visit the graves.[448]

The wording and verb tenses used by the Prophet ﷺ and the Companions in the above narrations show that these narrations unambiguously abrogate the narrations that express prohibition, as pointed out by Ibn al-Ṣalāḥ in the chapter on *al-nāsikh wal-mansūkh* of his *ʿUlūm al-Ḥadīth*. This was confirmed before him by al-Ḥākim who narrated the ḥadīth: "Allah curses the women who frequently visit the graves" then said: "Those narrations pertaining to the prohibition of visiting graves are abrogated, the abrogator being the ḥadīth of ʿAlqama ibn Marthad, from Sulaymān ibn Burayda, from his father, from the Prophet ﷺ: 'I forbade you to visit the graves but [now] do visit them!'"[449]

445 Narrated from Ibn Abī Mulayka by al-Bayhaqī in *al-Sunan al-Kubrā* (4:49).
446 Narrated by ʿAbd al-Razzāq (3:518) and Ibn ʿAbd al-Barr in *al-Tamhīd* (6:261).
447 Narrated by Abū Yaʿlā (8:284) with a sound chain, al-Ḥākim (1990 ed. 1:532), al-Bayhaqī in *al-Sunan al-Kubrā* (4:78 §6993), and Ibn ʿAbd al-Barr, *al-Tamhīd* (3:233).
448 Ibn ʿAbd al-Barr, *al-Tamhīd* (3:234).
449 Al-Ḥākim (1990 ed. 1:530). Cf. note 443.

11. Due to her strictness and, perhaps, in acknowledgement of Ibn Abī Mulayka's remark, ʿĀ'isha ﵂ disliked to visit the grave of her brother as is evident from her remark in al-Tirmidhī's report of her visitation to ʿAbd al-Raḥmān: "If I had been present at the time of your death I would have never visited you [now]."[450] Yet this is another proof that she did not understand the Prophet's ﷺ prohibition as absolute – were it not abrogated – since she did allow herself to visit her brother despite it.

12. The Prophet ﷺ passed by a woman who was weeping next to a grave and said: "Fear Allah and be steadfast!" She replied: "Leave me alone! You were not afflicted with my affliction" – without recognizing him. Then she was told this was the Prophet ﷺ. She came to see him and, not finding anyone at the door she [entered directly and] said, "I did not recognize you!" He said: "Steadfastness is only at the first shock."[451] If women were prohibited from visiting graves, the Prophet ﷺ would have prohibited her in the first place.

13. ʿĀ'isha ﵂ asked: "What should I say, Messenger of Allah [at al-Baqīʿ]?" He replied: "Say: 'Greetings to you, people of the abodes among the men and women believers! May Allah grant mercy to those of you and us who went ahead and those who tarried back! Truly we shall – if Allah wills – join up with you.'"[452]

Al-Bayhaqī, Ibn Ḥajar and al-Nawawī said that the above narrations show that it is permitted for women to visit the graves in confirmation of ʿĀ'isha's visitation of her brother, as the Prophet ﷺ only admonished the mourning woman to be steadfast without forbidding her from visiting the grave, and he

[450] Narrated from ʿAbd Allah ibn Abī Mulayka by al-Tirmidhī.
[451] Narrated from Anas in all the Six Books.
[452] Narrated as part of a longer ḥadīth by Muslim and al-Nasā'ī.

gave instructions to ʿĀʾisha ﷺ on what to say when visiting the graves.[453]

14. The Prophet ﷺ said: "I had forbidden you to visit graves but Muḥammad has been permitted to visit the grave of his mother, so visit them, for truly, they remind you of the hereafter."[454]

15. Another version states: "I had forbidden you to visit graves but do visit them for they truly remind one of the hereafter."[455]

16. Another version states: "Whoever wants to visit graves [may], truly they remind you of the hereafter."[456]

17. Another version states: "I had forbidden you to visit graves but do visit them, for they help to renounce the world and they remind you of the hereafter."[457]

18. Another version states: "I forbade you to visit graves then it appeared to me that they soften the heart, bring tears to the eyes, and remind one of the hereafter. Therefore, visit them, but do not say reprehensible things!"[458]

19. It is established the Prophet ﷺ placed a rock on top of ʿUthmān ibn Maẓʿūn's ﷺ grave saying: "With it I shall designate the grave of my [milk-]brother and later bury in it whoever dies among my relatives."[459] The complete report states that the

[453] Al-Bayhaqī, *al-Sunan al-Kubrā* (4:78), Ibn Ḥajar, *Fatḥ al-Bārī* (1959 ed. 3:184); al-Nawawī, *Sharḥ Ṣaḥīḥ Muslim* (7:41-42).
[454] Narrated from Burayda by al-Tirmidhī (*ḥasan ṣaḥīḥ*).
[455] Part of a longer ḥadīth narrated from Burayda by Aḥmad.
[456] Part of a longer ḥadīth narrated from Burayda by al-Nasāʾī.
[457] Narrated from Ibn Masʿūd by Ibn Mājah.
[458] Part of a longer ḥadīth narrated from Anas by Aḥmad.
[459] Narrated from an unnamed Companion by Abū Dāwūd and al-Bayhaqī in *al-Sunan al-Kubra* (3:412) with fair chains cf. Ibn Ḥajar, *Talkhīṣ al-Ḥabīr* (2:134); Ibn al-Mulaqqin, *Tuḥfat al-Muḥtāj* (2:29), and al-Arnaʾūṭ's edition of Ibn al-Qayyim's *Zād al-Maʿād* (1:506).

Prophet ﷺ asked a man to place a rock on top of Ibn Maẓʿūn's grave; when he was unable to move it, he ﷺ rolled up his sleeves and helped him and the whiteness of his arms was visible. Ibn Maẓʿūn was the first of the *Muhājirūn* buried in Baqīʿ al-Gharqad. Ibrāhīm, the Prophet's ﷺ son, was buried next to him.

The proof for the visitation of women in the above narrations is that the positive effects of remembering the hereafter, weeping, and softening the heart are not exclusively limited to men but extend to women as well. Therefore women are also addressed by these narrations which are to be taken in the most general, inclusive sense. This is confirmed by the practice of Fāṭima ؑ the daughter of the Prophet ﷺ as shown in the following two narrations:

20. Our liege-lord Jaʿfar al-Ṣādiq narrated with his chain from al-Ḥasan ibn ʿAlī that Fāṭima the daughter of the Prophet ﷺ – may Allah be well-pleased with all of them! – used to visit the grave of her uncle Ḥamza ibn ʿAbd al-Muṭṭalib every Jumuʿa[460] and she used to pray and weep there.[461] Another version adds that she had marked the grave with a rock in order to recognize it.[462] Another version states that she used to tend the grave and repair any damage it had incurred.[463]

---

[460] Narrated to here from Jaʿfar ibn Muḥammad, from his father, without mention of al-Ḥasan by ʿAbd al-Razzāq (3:572) with a broken (*munqaṭiʿ*) chain.

[461] Narrated by al-Ḥākim (1990 ed. 1:533, 3:30) who declared its chain sound, al-Bayhaqī, *al-Sunan al-Kubrā* (4:78), and Ibn ʿAbd al-Barr in *al-Tamhīd* (3:234) although al-Dhahabī condemns it strenuously while al-Bayhaqī alludes to its weakness.

[462] Al-Athram and Ibn ʿAbd al-Barr narrated it as mentioned by al-Qurṭubī in his *Tafsīr* (10:381); also ʿAbd al-Razzāq (3:574) with a very weak chain because of al-Aṣbagh ibn Nubāta, who is discarded (*matrūk*) as a narrator.

[463] Al-Ḥakīm al-Tirmidhī in *Nawādir al-Uṣūl* (*Aṣl* 15).

21. The women wept over Ruqayya ◉ when she died, so ʿUmar tried to forbid them but the Messenger of Allah ◉ said, "Wait, ʿUmar!" Then he said: "[Women,] beware of the devil's croaking! As long as it comes from the eye and the heart, it is coming from mercy; and as long as it comes from the tongue and the hand,[464] it is coming from Satan." Whereupon, Fāṭima began to weep over the grave of Ruqayya and the Prophet ◉ was wiping her tears from her face with his hand – or, the narrator said, his sleeve.[465]

In the Ḥanafī School, it is permitted for women to visit graves as long as they are properly dressed and ensure that there is no undue intermixing with non-*maḥram* men and that they do not behave inappropriately, such as wailing. The *Fatāwā Hindiyya* (5:350), one of the foremost references for *fatwā* in the School, says: "The Scholars differed about women visiting graves. Al-Sarakhsī said that the soundest position is that it is not wrong." Al-Sarakhsī states in *al-Mabsūṭ* (24:10): "The soundest opinion in our School is that the dispensation (to visit graves) is present for both men and women, because it has been related that ʿĀʾisha ◉ used to visit the grave of the Messenger of Allah ◉ at all times, and that when she went on *Ḥajj* she visited the grave of her brother ʿAbd al-Raḥmān ◉." This is confirmed by Ibn Nujaym in *al-Baḥr al-Rāʾiq*. Ibn ʿĀbidīn said in his supercommentary on this work, *Minḥat al-Khāliq Ḥāshiyat al-Baḥr al-Rāʾiq* (2:210), that al-Ramlī said: "As for women, if they visit graves to renew their sorrows, or to cry and wail, as is the customary practice of many,

---

[464] A reference to imprecations and slapping of the cheeks still exhibited today by mourning Arab-Christian women, other non-Muslims, and, sadly, many Muslims.

[465] Narrated from Ibn ʿAbbās by Aḥmad, al-Ṭayālisī (2:351) and al-Bayhaqī in *al-Sunan al-Kubrā* (4:70 §6946) with a chain containing ʿAlī ibn Zayd ibn Judʿān (cf. n. 108). Al-Bayhaqī considers this ḥadīth sound as it is confirmed by established narrations. It is partly narrated – but with an identical chain – by al-Ḥākim (3:190=1990 ed. 3:210) where al-Dhahabī said: "Its chain is passable (*ṣāliḥ*)," however, in his *Mīzān* (3:129) he grades the report "disclaimed" (*munkar*) due to the mention of Fāṭima's presence at the burial.

it is not allowed for them to visit graves. This is how the Prophetic ḥadīth 'Allah has cursed women who visit graves,' is understood. However, if they visit for contemplation, compassion, and seeking *baraka* by visiting the graves of the righteous, then it is not wrong if they are elderly. It is disliked if they are young [*i.e.* there is fear of *fitna* from their attending]. Among that which shows that women's visiting graves is not unlawful is the ḥadīth narrated by Anas 🙵 that the Prophet 🙵 passed by a woman who was crying by a grave. He said, 'Fear Allah and be patient.' The permissibility is implied, said the *Fuqahā'*, because he did not forbid her from visiting the grave; had it been unlawful, it would have been obligatory for the Prophet 🙵 to forbid her."[466]

Even if we should consider the first two of the three ḥadīths adduced by the objectors (a and b) authentic as a handful of scholars did, they do not form proof of prohibition for two reasons. First, they are abrogated according to the correct view as demonstrated. Second, they elucidate one another and are elucidated by the third ḥadīth adduced (c), in the sense that the curse does not concern women who visit the graves in absolute terms, but only those women who both (1) visit excessively and (2) commit certain reprehensible acts during visitation as stated by al-Tirmidhī, al-Baghawī, al-Ṭaḥāwī, al-Qurṭubī, and others.[467] This qualified prohibition is confirmed by the fact that the soundest version of the prohibition ḥadīth states, "Allah curses the women who *frequently* visit the graves," in which case the prohibition is patently restrictive, concerning only a specific type of women visitors and not all of them.

---

[466] This paragraph from Shaykh Farāz Rabbānī with slight editing.

[467] Cf. al-Tirmidhī in his *Sunan* after narrating the ḥadīth of *zawwārāt* from Abū Hurayra; al-Ṭaḥāwī in *Sharḥ Mushkil al-Āthār* (12:179-186); al-Baghawī in *Sharḥ al-Sunna* (2:417, 5:464); and al-Qurṭubī in his *Tafsīr* (20:170), as cited by al-Shawkānī in *Nayl al-Awṭār* (chapters on burial and the rulings pertaining to graves).

Another confirmation is that this qualified prohibition extends to men as well, as stated in the ḥadīth of the Prophet ﷺ: "Allah curse the Jews and Christians! They took the graves of their Prophets as places of worship."[468] This men-inclusive qualified prohibition is further confirmed by the version stating: "I forbade you from visiting the graves and now [allow you to] visit them, but do not utter words that make your Lord angry!"[469]

The gist of this documentation is not that Muslim women today are indifferently permitted to visit graves, since temptation and sin abound in our time and there is poor observance of the etiquette of Sacred Law shown by either Muslim men or women who visit graves. To say the least, as al-Bayhaqī said: "If women keep themselves clear from following funeral processions, going out to cemetaries, and visiting graves, it would be healthier for their Religion – and from Allah comes success."[470] Al-Ḥakīm al-Tirmidhī expounded it in *Aṣl* 15 of his *Nawādir al-Uṣūl*.

Yet, the negative situation of contemporary Muslim visitors to city and country cemetaries hardly applies to the women pilgrims who visit al-Baqīʿ and the Prophet ﷺ in Madīna, where the effusion of emotion is counter-balanced by the natural decorum of Madīna al-Munawwara. Therefore, their status there should be that of allowance together with male Muslims rather than prohibition as confirmed by the *fatwā* of the Ulema and contrary to the claims of a handful of Wahhābī dissenters such as the late ʿAbd al-ʿAzīz ibn Baz, Muḥammad ibn Ibrāhīm ibn ʿAbd al-Laṭīf, Ḥammād al-Anṣārī and his student Bakr Abū Zayd, Abū Bakr al-Jazā'irī, and other claimants of religious jurisdiction over the Two Sanctuaries and the Islamic-book market.

[468] Narrated from ʿĀ'isha by al-Bukhārī and Muslim.
[469] Narrated from Abū Saʿīd by al-Bazzār with a chain of sound narrators as stated by al-Haythamī (3:58); from Ibn ʿAbbās by al-Azdī in his *Musnad* (p. 194); and from Anas by Aḥmad, Abū Yaʿlā (6:372), and Ibn Abī Shayba (3:29).
[470] Al-Bayhaqī, *al-Sunan al-Kubrā* (4:78).

As for the absolute prohibition, including the Mosque and al-Baqīʿ in Madīna, insisted upon by the Saudi Bakr Abū Zayd in his epistle titled *Juzʾ fī Ziyārat al-Nisāʾ lil-Qubūr*[471] and his odd claims that (a) the narrations prohibiting women from following the funeral bier apply to prove the prohibition of visitation and (b) *zawwārāt* is incorrect and must be read *zuwwārāt* in the sense of female visitors, without the sense of frequency:[472] such claims stem from an unreasonable, stubborn rejection of the evidence and a blind following of the familiar founts of originality and nonconformity – Ibn Taymiyya and Ibn al-Qayyim. But truth is more deserving of being followed than famous figures.

The Book *Morals and Manners in Islam*

A book by the title *Morals and Manners in Islam: A Guide to Islamic Ādāb* (Leicester: The Islamic Foundation, 1986, reprinted 1989 and 1991) by Marwān Ibrāhīm al-Kaysī contains the following errors with regard to the visitation of cemetaries and their architecture:

1. The author states [p. 171]: "There are two main purposes for a Muslim to visit a cemetary: to pray for the dead, and to remind himself of the Hereafter." He omitted a third purpose: to obtain *baraka* or blessing, and a fourth is to supplicate for one's needs at places of particular blessing, especially through the visitation of the Prophet ﷺ and the *Awliyāʾ* such as the Companions, etc. There is Consensus in Islam that travel to visit the Prophet ﷺ is a desirable act of worship (*qurba*) as stipulated in Qāḍi ʿIyāḍ's *al-Shifāʾ* and it is authentically related from Imām al-Shāfiʿī that he used to pray next to Imām Abū Ḥanīfa's grave in Baghdād in order to ask for the fulfillment of his needs there.[473]

[471] In his *al-Ajzāʾ al-Ḥadīthiyya* (p. 107-141).

[472] Even his fellow Wahhābī, al-Muʿallimī, reads it *zawwārāt* and defines it as "those who frequently visit" in his *ʿImārat al-Qubur* (p. 156)!

2. On the same page the author says: "Nothing is to be said over the grave other than ['Peace be upon the Muslim and faithful inhabitants of the abodes. May God show mercy to those of us who go before and those who go after and God willing, we will meet you'], except to pray for the dead." Further down [p. 179] he claims: "It is an innovation to admonish the dead person after his death." This is all incorrect, as it is desirable (*mustaḥabb*) or Sunna to give *talqīn* or instruction to the dead after burial, even according to Shaykh Muḥammad ibn 'Abd al-Wahhāb in his *Aḥkām Tammanī al-Mawt*. There is extensive evidence for this as presented in the *Encyclopedia of Islamic Doctrine* and *The Reliance of the Traveller* (p. 921-924 w32.1-2). The fact that a person is dead and buried does not mean he cannot hear the living. It is a salient feature of modernists that they deny many beliefs and practices connected with *ghayb* and the invisible.

3. The author also claims [p. 171]: "It is forbidden to touch any grave with the intention of gaining a blessing from it." This is also incorrect and the correct ruling is that it is disliked, although some – such as Imām Aḥmad ibn Ḥanbal – declared there was no harm in touching or even kissing the Prophet's ﷺ grave. Al-Dhahabī even labeled as *Khawārij* those who would dispute this ruling.[474]

4. The author claims [p. 184]: "Upright tombstones on the grave itself are forbidden." If by the upright tombstones are meant the grave's signposts (*shāhidān*) then this claim is utterly rejected and disproved by age-old Islamic practice from East to West.

[473] Narrated by al-Khaṭīb in *Tārīkh Baghdād* (1:123) and Ibn Abī al-Wafā' in *Ṭabaqāt al-Ḥanafiyya* (p. 519).

[474] See the chapter on Imām Aḥmad, section on *Tabarruk*, in our *Four Imāms*.

5. On the same page he states: "No form of construction should be erected on graves... Graves must not be plastered with gypsum." The truth is there is difference of opinion on this subject and two reasons were mentioned for the permissibility of building up the grave or plastering it with gypsum: to protect it from collapse generally speaking, and to keep it in the public view if it is the grave of a Shaykh, a Scholar, or someone from the family of the Prophet ﷺ as mentioned in Ibn ʿĀbidīn's *Ḥāshiya* (1:601). Shaykh Ismāʿīl Ḥaqqī said in his Qur'ānic commentary *Rūḥ al-Bayān* under the verse {*The mosques of Allah may only be built and maintained by those who believe in Allah and the Day of Judgment, perform the prayers and give zakāt, and are afraid of none other than Allah and they are those who are guided*} (9:18):

> Shaykh ʿAbd al-Ghanī al-Nābulusī said in *Kashf al-Nūr ʿan Aṣḥāb al-Qubūr* ("The Unveiling of Light from the Occupants of the Graves"), to paraphrase him, that a good innovation that agrees with the objectives of the Sacred Law is called a sunna. Thus, building domes over the graves of Scholars, friends of Allah (*awliyā*) and the righteous and placing covers, turbans and cloth over them is permissible if the objective therein is to create reverence in the eyes of ordinary people so that they will not disdain the occupant of that grave.

If the above were not the case, or if it were not in conformity with the Sunna, then ponder the statement of our Mother ʿĀ'isha in Abū Dāwūd: "When the Negus died, we were told [*i.e.*, by the Prophet ﷺ] that a light would be seen perpetually at his grave."

We already mentioned that the Prophet ﷺ placed a large boulder on top of ʿUthmān ibn Maẓʿūn's grave to mark it, saying: "By this I shall know where the grave of my brother ʿUthmān is and add to it my relatives." Abū Dawūd and others narrated it.

A stronger proof than any non-*mutawātir* text is the universal practice of the *Umma* from the earliest centuries in building up tombs over the graves of those celebrated for their piety so that they would find them easily. Hence, in the time of the *khilāfa* of our liege-lord ʿUmar ibn al-Khaṭṭāb ☙, a mud-brick wall was built around the grave of the Holy Prophet ☙. After this, in the time of Walīd ibn ʿAbd al-Malik, our liege-lord ʿAbd Allah ibn al-Zubayr ☙ strengthened this wall in the presence of the Companions and inserted solid bricks, as mentioned in *Khulāṣat al-Wafā* of al-Samhūdī. Fāṭima ☙ had also marked the grave of her uncle Ḥamza ☙ with a rock and used to visit it every Jumuʿa as already shown.

Imām al-Shawkānī admitted that the *Salaf* built up the graves high. Of the ḥadīth of our liege-lord ʿAlī ☙ ordering the destruction of tombs in the *Ṣaḥīḥayn*, *Sunan*, and *Musnad* with various wordings, Ibn al-Jawzī in al-*Taḥqīq* said: "This [ḥadīth] is understood to refer to the elevated graves they used to build with high and beautiful structures." Al-Zaylaʿī mentioned it in *Naṣb al-Rāya*.

Imām al-Nawawī in his *Sharḥ Ṣaḥīḥ Muslim* said: "The Sunna is that the grave not be raised up a lot above the earth['s surface], nor rounded, but that it be raised up approximately a hand-span (*shibr*) and flattened, and this is the *madhhab* of al-Shāfiʿī and those [of the other schools] who agreed with him, while al-Qāḍī ʿIyāḍ related that most of the Ulema prefer it to be rounded [in the shape of a mound], and this is the *madhhab* of Mālik."

Al-Shawkānī in *Nayl al-Awṭār* added to this that it is *ḥarām* to build them up high and he claimed that the fact that the *Salaf* and *Khalaf* built them up high is no proof that it is not *ḥarām*. Al-ʿAẓīm Ābādī approved him whole-heartedly in *ʿAwn al-Maʿbūd*. But al-Ṣanʿānī in *Subul al-Salām* said: "The vast majority hold that the prohibition of building up and plastering graves is one of preference (*tanzīh*) [*i.e.*, not strictness (*taḥrīm*)]."

Indeed, there is nothing wrong in making prominent the graves of the *Awliyā*, as stipulated by Shaykh ʿAbd al-Ghanī al-Nābulusī and others.[475] Dāwūd ibn Ṣāliḥ said: "[The governor of Madīna] Marwān [ibn al-Ḥakam] one day saw a man placing his face on top of the grave of the Prophet. He said: "Do you know what you are doing?" When he came near him, he realized it was Abū Ayyūb al-Anṣārī. The latter said: "Yes; I came to the Prophet, not to a stone."[476] The use of the word "stone" in this ḥadīth, if authentic, indicates that the Prophet's ﷺ grave was built up with stone already in the time of Abū Ayyūb al-Anṣārī ☙.

May Allah enlighten our understandings, our hearts, and our graves with His kindness and forgiveness! *Wa-ṣallā Allahu ʿalā Sayyidinā Muḥammadin wa-ʿalā Ālihi wa-Ṣaḥbihi wa-Sallam.*

---

[475] See Ustādha Umm Sahl's article "Domes over the Graves of the *Awliya*" at http://www.masud.co.uk under miscellany.

[476] Narrated by Aḥmad (38:558 §23585) and al-Ḥākim (4:515=1990 ed. 4:560 *ṣaḥīḥ*) cf. Shaykh al-Islām al-Subkī in *Shifāʾ al-Siqām* (p. 126) and Majd al-Dīn ibn Taymiyya in *al-Muntaqā* (2:261f.). See the excerpts from the latter cited in *al-Nūr al-Lāmiʿ fī Maʾthūr al-Mawlid al-Nabawī al-Jāmiʿ* (p. 67-73) by the contemporary Moroccan Shaykh Mūḥtāyin al-Ḥājj ʿAbd Allah al-Fārisī.

The Ḥadīth: "Do Not Make My Grave an *ʿĪd*"

The Holy Prophet ﷺ said: "Do not take my house as an *ʿĪd* and do not make your houses into graves, but send *ṣalawāt* upon me, for indeed your *ṣalāt* reaches me."[477]

The established wording is: "Do not take my **grave** as an *ʿĪd* and do not turn your houses into graves, but send *ṣalawāt* upon me, for indeed your *ṣalāt* reaches me."[478]

Note on the *Fiqh* of the Ḥadīth

Note that Imām Abū Dāwūd narrated this ḥadīth in the chapter titled "Visitation of the Graves" which is the last chapter of the book titled "Rituals of *Ḥajj*" in his *Sunan* and, in order to leave no doubt as to the command of visiting the grave of the Prophet ﷺ, the very next narration is about the Prophet's ﷺ visitation of the graves of the *Shuhadāʾ* of Uḥud. In other words, Abū Dāwūd's understanding of the ḥadīth is that the Prophet ﷺ insisted that the visit to his grave should not be only on the occasion of *Ḥajj*. His commentator, al-ʿAẓīm Ābādī, not only ignores this under-

[477] Abū Yaʿlā (12:131 §6761) and ʿAbd al-Razzāq (3:71 §4839) narrate it in this wording, both of them with *mursal* chains and Abū Yaʿlā's version adding: "and your *salām*".

[478] Narrated from Abu Hurayra by Abū Dāwūd (ʿAbd al-Bāqī ed. 2:83 §2042) Aḥmad (2:367), al-Ṭabarānī in his *Awsaṭ* (8:81-82 §8030), and al-Bayhaqī in *Shuʿab al-Īmān* (3:491 §4162). Imām al-Nawawī said it is *ṣaḥīḥ* as per Ibn Kathīr in his *Tafsīr* (3:516) even though al-Haythamī (2:247) considers the above chain weak because it contains ʿAbdAllah ibn Nafiʿ al-Ṣāʾigh, since it is confirmed by another narration from our liege-lord al-Ḥasan ibn ʿAlī ibn Abī Ṭālib by Ibn Abī Shayba (3:30 §11818), also with a *mursal Ahl al-Bayt* chain from al-Ḥasan al-Muthannā by ʿAbd al-Razzāq (3:577 §6726) which al-Dhahabī cites in his *Siyar* (see below), and with a *munkar Ahl al-Bayt* chain by al-Bazzār (2:147-148 §509) cf. Ibn Ḥajar, *Lisān al-Mīzān* (under Jaʿfar ibn Ibrāhīm al-Jaʿfarī) who mentions yet other chains, among them that narrated by Abū Yaʿlā as well as in the precious monographs on the *ṣalāt* on the Prophet ﷺ by Ibn Abī ʿĀṣim and the Qāḍī Ismāʿīl al-Mālikī.

standing but goes to the opposite extreme of the meaning in his *'Awn al-Ma'būd* to claim that "In the ḥadīth there is an indication that it is forbidden to travel to visit the Prophet ﷺ"! The reason for this is that this self-proclaimed non-*muqallid* imitated Ibn Taymiyya's very same claim in his epistle *al-Tawassul wal-Wasīla* reproduced in *Majmū' al-Fatāwā* (1:238), in which the latter truly innovated – for, as Imām al-Lacknawī said, "no one in Islam ever said such a thing before Ibn Taymiyya," – a claim which the first one to reject was his own student, al-Dhahabī (see below).

Al-Sakhāwī on the meaning of the Ḥadīth

The translation of the word "*'Īd*" as "place to gather as for visitation" or even simply "place" is inaccurate. For example, "*'Īd al-Aḍḥā*" and "*'Īd al-Fiṭr*" have never been translated as the "place of sacrifice" and the "place of breaking fast." The translation of any word in the ḥadīth should be as literal as possible, and additional or explanatory meanings be placed in brackets, not the other way around. The literal meaning of "*'Īd*" is "anniversary festival," because "*'Īd*" denotes two things:

- a time that returns (=*'āda*) annually;
- a time one observes with festive activities (=*'ayyada*).

A further meaning connoted is that of gathering, and only then does *'Īd* begin to have the connotation of "place" which the above mistranslation arbitrarily gave as the primary meaning. Thus, to begin with, the ḥadīth should be literally translated:

"Do not make my grave an anniversary festival."

Since this rendering mixes two unmixable classes of words, namely the grave – a solid object – and the anniversary festival – a time – it becomes clear that the final meaning is:

"Do not make the visit to my grave an anniversary festival."

This is understood in the sense of an insistence on the part of the Prophet ﷺ that the believers should visit him frequently and at all times, rather than visit him sparsely, which one might falsely understand from the misinterpretations of Ibn Taymiyya and those who imitate him, which superimpose on the ḥadīth the exact reverse of its intended meaning!

"Visit me often and at all times" is the explanation preferred by Ḥāfiẓ al-Sakhāwī the student of Imām al-Ḥadīth Ibn Ḥajar in his chapter entitled "On the meaning of the ḥadīth: Do not make my grave an *'Īd*" in his masterpiece *al-Qawl al-Badī' fīl-Ṣalāt 'alā al-Ḥabīb al-Shafī'* (Beirut 1987/1407) p. 159-160:

> The author of *Silāḥ al-Mu'min* [the *Muḥaddith* Taqī al-Dīn Abū al-Fatḥ Muḥammad ibn Muḥammad ibn 'Alī al-'Asqalānī *thumma* al-Miṣrī, known as Ibn al-Shāfi'ī (677-745)] said: "It is probable that the intent (*murād*) of the Prophet's saying: 'Do not make my grave an *'Īd*' is emphasis and encouragement (*al-ḥathth*) on the frequency of visiting him and not treating his visit like an anniversary festival which does not occur in the year other than at two times."

This meaning is also reported from the *Ḥāfiẓ* of Egypt 'Abd al-'Aẓīm al-Mundhirī the author of *al-Targhīb wal-Tarhīb.*

Al-Sakhāwī continues:

> This meaning is supported by his saying: "Do not make your houses graves," that is, "do not abandon prayer in your houses

and thus turn them into places similar to the graves where one does not pray." There is no agreement on this. It seems that the Prophet ﷺ was pointing to what he said in the other ḥadīth concerning the prohibition of taking his grave as a place of prostration (*masjid*), or else that his intent was from the perspective of gathering. We have already seen something to that effect in the ḥadīths of this chapter. One of the commentators of the *Maṣābīḥ* [al-Baghawī's *Maṣābīḥ al-Sunna*] said: "The Prophet's saying is an abridged form of the sense: 'Do not make the visit to my grave an anniversary festival,' and its meaning is the prohibition of (formally) gathering for the purpose of his visit the way people gather together to celebrate '*Īd*. The Jews and Christians used to gather for the visit of their prophets' graves and busy themselves with entertainment and music, so the Prophet ﷺ forbade his Community from doing that." It was also said that it is probable the Prophet's prohibition was intended to prevent hardship (*raf' al-mashaqqa*) for his Community, and also because it was disliked that they commit excess in overly honoring his grave. I say: The emphasis and encouragement on visiting his noble grave is mentioned in numerous ḥadīths. It would suffice to show this if there was only the ḥadīth whereby the truthful and God-confirmed Prophet ﷺ promises that his intercession, among other things, becomes guaranteed for whoever visits him; and the Imāms are in complete agreement, from the time directly after his passing until our own, that this is among the best acts of drawing near to Allah. Shaykh al-Islam (Taqī al-Dīn) al-Subkī said in his book *Shifā' al-Siqām*: "A large number of Imāms have inferred from the ḥadīth 'No one greets me except Allah has returned my soul to me so that I can return his *salām*' [Abū Dāwūd with a sound chain in the same chapter of his *Sunan* as the ḥadīth under discussion] the legal desirability (*istiḥbāb*) of visiting the grave of the Prophet ﷺ." I say: This is a sound inference because when the visitor greets the Prophet ﷺ his reply is given from near, and this is a much sought-after benefit which Allah has made easily available for us to return again and again to the very beginning of that blessing.

Al-Dhahabī on the meaning of the Ḥadīth

Al-Dhahabī says in his biographical masterpiece *Siyar Aʿlām al-Nubalāʾ*:

> [The *Tābiʿī*] al-Ḥasan ibn al-Ḥasan ibn ʿAlī relates that he saw a man standing in front of the house which contains the grave of the Prophet ﷺ, invoking Allah's blessings upon him, whereupon he said to the man: "Do not do that, for the Messenger of Allah ﷺ said: 'Do not make (the visit to) my grave an anniversary festival (*ʿīd*), nor turn your houses into graves. Invoke blessings upon me wherever you are, for your invocation reaches me.'" This [particular] report is missing the Companion-link (*mursal*) and what al-Ḥasan adduces in his *fatwā* is worthless as a proof, because one who stands before the Blessed Chamber (*ḥujra*) in all humility and submission, invoking blessings upon his Prophet ﷺ – O how blessed that one is! For he has made his visitation excellent and beautified it with humbleness and love, and he has performed more worship than the one who invoked blessings on the Prophet ﷺ from his own land or in his prayer. The reason is that the one who performs visitation has both the reward of visiting him and that of invoking blessings upon him, while those who invoke blessings upon him from all over the world only have the reward of invoking blessings upon him, and upon whoever invokes blessings once, Allah sends ten blessings. However, the person who visits the Prophet ﷺ and does not observe

> decorum in his visitation, or prostrates to the grave, or does something outside the Law, such a person has done both good and bad. He must be taught gently. Allah is forgiving and merciful. By Allah! The Muslim is not moved to distraction and lamentation and kissing the walls and weeping much, except because **he is a lover of Allah and of His Prophet. His love is the standard and the distinguishing mark between the people of Paradise and the people of Hellfire.** The visit to his grave is among the best of the acts by which one draws near to Allah. As for travelling to visit the graves of Prophets and saints, even if we should concede that there is no authorization for it due to the general sense of the Prophet's ﷺ saying: "Mounts are not saddled except to go to three mosques," nevertheless, saddling the mounts to go visit the Prophet ﷺ is intrinsic to saddling them to go visit his mosque – which is sanctioned by the Law without contest – for there is no access to his Chamber except after entering his mosque. Therefore, let his visitor begin by greeting the Mosque, then turn to greet the Master of the Mosque. May Allah grant us this, and also to you. *Āmīn*![479]

Shaykh Shu'ayb al-Arna'ūṭ comments: "The author meant by this excursus to refute his shaykh, Ibn Taymiyya."

[479] Al-Dhahabī, *Siyar* (Risāla ed. 4:484-485).

Rajab and Mid-Shaʿbān Supererogatory Prayers

When Shaykh al-Islam al-ʿIzz Ibn ʿAbd al-Salām declared invalid in 637 the practice of congregational prayer for the nights of mid-Shaʿbān (*ṣalāt niṣf Shaʿbān=laylat al-barāʾa*) and the first Jumuʿa of Rajab (*ṣalāt al-raghāʾib=laylat al-raghāʾib*), the ḥadīth Master Ibn al-Ṣalāḥ responded with a dissenting *fatwā*, whereupon Ibn ʿAbd al-Salām published an epistle titled *al-Targhīb ʿan Ṣalāt al-Raghāʾib al-Mawḍūʿa wa-Bayānu mā fīhā min Mukhālafat al-Sunan al-Mashrūʿa* ("The Dissuasion from the Fabricated 'Prayer of Dear Wishes' and Exposition of its Contraventions of the Lawful Prophetic Sunnas"). Ibn al-Ṣalāḥ responded with a refutation, which Ibn ʿAbd al-Salām followed up with a counter-refutation.[480]

Ibn al-Ṣalāḥ's argument was that such prayers cannot be declared prohibited on the mere basis that the ḥadīth adduced for them is weak, since their practice, even as innovations, is supported in general terms by the Qur'ānic and Sunna command to pray in such texts as,

{*O you who believe! Bow down and prostrate yourselves, and worship your Lord, and do good, that perhaps you may prosper*} (22:77);

"Prayer is goodness at your disposal;"[481] and "Prayer is a light."[482]

Ibn ʿAbd al-Salam argued that the two prayers contradict specific teachings of the Prophet ﷺ such as (1) the strong encouragement to pray all supererogatory prayers – other than the specific occasions of the Two Feasts, *tarāwīḥ*, eclipses, and great needs such as supplication for rain – alone and in one's house;[483] and (2) the

[480] These texts were published under the title *Musājala ʿIlmiyya bayn al-Imāmayn al-Jalīlayn al-ʿIzz ibn ʿAbd al-Salām wa-Ibn al-Ṣalāḥ*, eds. Muḥammad Nāṣir al-Albānī and Zuhayr al-Shāwīsh (Beirut: al-Maktab al-Islāmī, 1961 and 1985).
[481] *"Al-ṣalātu khayrun mawḍūʿun"*, see note 195.
[482] *"Al-ṣalātu nūrun"*, see note 197.

prohibition of singling out the night of Jumu'a for supererogatory prayers and its day for fasting.[484] Ibn al-Ṣalāḥ countered that this encouragement was general and did not make up specific evidence against the performance of a communal supererogatory prayer, as illustrated by Ibn 'Abbās' *tahajjud* behind the Prophet ﷺ[485] and his leading the midmorning prayer with Anas, Umm Sulaym, and Umm Ḥarām.[486]

Like Ibn 'Abd al-Salām, al-Nawawī strenuously rejects the validity of *ṣalāt al-raghā'ib*, calling it a "repulsive" (*qabīḥa*), "thoroughly abominable" (*munkaratun ashadda inkārin*), and "invalid" (*bāṭila*) innovation which only the foolish put into practice.[487] He rejects the ruling of his Damascene colleague Ibn al-Ṣalāḥ without naming him:

> One should not be misled by a certain Imām who was confused about the ruling pertaining to them [*ṣalāt al-raghā'ib* and the voluntary congregational prayer of the night of mid-Sha'bān], on which he authored some pages in which he argues for their desirability (*istiḥbābihimā*) for, surely, he is mistaken in that. The Shaykh and Imām Abū Muḥammad 'Abd al-Raḥmān ibn Ismā'īl al-Maqdisī authored an invaluable book establishing that they are null and invalid, and he did well and excelled – may Allah have mercy on him![488]

[483] In al-Bukhārī and Muslim: "The best prayer after the prescribed prayers is that prayed alone in one's house."

[484] Narrated from Abū Hurayra by Muslim.

[485] Narrated from Ibn 'Abbās by al-Bukhārī and Muslim.

[486] Narrated from Anas by Abū Dāwūd. Cf. Ibn 'Umar's reply when asked about *ṣalāt al-ḍuḥā*: "It is an innovation and what a fine innovation it is!" (*bid'atun wa ni'mati al-bid'atu hiya*) and "No one considered it desirable [in the Religion] (*mā aḥadun yastaḥibbuhā*), and the people did not innovate anything that is dearer to me than that prayer." Both reports are cited in the section on *ṣalāt al-ḍuḥā* and mean: *ṣalāt al-ḍuḥā* as prayed in congregation on a regular basis in the Mosque.

[487] Al-Nawawī, *Fatāwā* (p. 59-60).

[488] Al-Nawawī, *al-Majmū' Sharḥ al-Muhadhdhab* (3:549).

Al-Dhahabī praises Ibn al-Ṣalāḥ except when it comes to this issue: "He was peerless in his time but there is one matter in which he departed from his principles and went astray, that is, *ṣalāt al-raghā'ib*: he declared it valid and defended it although its ḥadīth is unquestionably false (*bāṭil*)."[489]

Concerning the night of mid-Sha'bān Ibn Taymiyya wrote:

> [Some] said there is no difference between this and other nights of the year. However, the opinion of many of the people of learning and that of the majority of our [Ḥanbalī] colleagues and other than them is that it is a night of superior merit, and this is what is indicated by the words of Aḥmad [ibn Ḥanbal], in view of the many ḥadīths transmitted about it and in light of what confirms this in the words and deeds transmitted from the early generations (*al-āthār al-salafiyya*). Some of its merits have been narrated in the books of ḥadīth of the types *Musnad* and *Sunan*. This holds true even if other things have been forged concerning it.[490]

Similarly, al-Suyūṭī said:

> "As for the night of mid-Sha'bān, it has great merit and it is desirable (*mustaḥabb*) to spend part of it in [supererogatory] worship. However, this must be done alone, not in congregation."[491]

So the authorities agree on the desirability of extra supererogatory worship prayed individually on the night of mid-Sha'bān. This position is based on the following evidence:

[489] Al-Dhahabī, *Siyar* (Risāla ed. 23:143).

[490] Ibn Taymiyya, *Iqtiḍā' al-Ṣirāṭ al-Mustaqīm* (1369/1950 ed. p. 302).

[491] Al-Suyūṭī, *Ḥaqīqat al-Sunna wal-Bid'a aw al-Amr bil-Ittibā' wal-Nahī 'an al-Ibtidā'* (1405/ 1985 ed. p. 58). See evidence for the merit of extra worship in the night of mid-Sha'bān in the *Encyclopedia of Islamic Doctrine* (6:99-103).

1. "Allah looks at His creation on the night of mid-Shaʿbān and He forgives all His creation except for the idolater and the one bent on hatred."[492]

2. "The night of mid-Shaʿbān, let all of you spend in prayer and its day in fasting, for Allah descends to the nearest heaven during that night beginning with sunset and says: 'Is there no one asking forgiveness that I may forgive them? Is there no one asking sustenance that I may grant them sustenance? Is there no one under duress that I may relieve them? Is there not such-and-such, is there not such-and-such, and so forth until until dawn rises.'"[493]

3. "Allah Most High descends to the nearest heaven on the night of mid-Shaʿbān and He forgives to more people than the number of hairs on the hides of the sheep of the tribes of Kalb."[494]

4. "Allah looks upon His creatures on the night of mid-Shaʿbān and He forgives all His servants except two: one intent on hatred, and the homicide."[495]

5. "Truly Allah the Glorious and Majestic look at His servants on the night of mid-Shaʿbān. He forgives those who ask forgiveness, He bestows mercy on those who ask mercy, and He gives respite to the people of envy and hatred who linger in their state."[496]

[492]Narrated by Ibn Ḥibbān (12:481 §5665) with a sound chain according to al-Arna'ūṭ and by al-Ṭabarānī with a chain of sound narrators according to al-Haythamī.

[493]Narrated from ʿAlī by Aḥmad and Ibn Mājah with a chain containing Ibn Abī Sabra who is very weak, but it is strengthened by the next ḥadīths.

[494]Narrated from ʿĀ'isha by Aḥmad, Ibn Mājah, and al-Tirmidhī who said that he had heard al-Bukhārī grading this ḥadīth as weak because some of the sub-narrators did not narrate directly from each other.

[495]Narrated from ʿAbd Allah ibn ʿAmr by al-Tirmidhī, Aḥmad, and al-Bazzār with a chain he graded "fair" (*ḥasan*) through the great *Tābiʿī* jurist al-Qāsim ibn Muḥammad ibn Abī Bakr al-Ṣiddīq.

[496]Narrated from ʿĀ'isha by al-Bayhaqī in *Shuʿab al-Īmān* (3:382 §3835) where he comments: "This ḥadīth is missing the Companion in its chain, and is a good

Shaykh ʿAbd al-Qādir al-Gīlānī recommended the following modality in his *Ghunya*:

> As for the ritual prayer traditional for the night of mid-Shaʿbān, it consists of one hundred cycles, including one thousand repetitions of *Qul Huwa Allahu Aḥad* (that is to say, ten recitations in each *rakʿa*). This prayer is called *Ṣalāt al-Khayr*, and its blessings are many and varied. Our righteous predecessors used to gather to perform it in congregation. It contains much merit and rich reward. It is reported of al-Ḥasan [al-Baṣrī], may Allah be well-pleased with him, that he said: "Thirty of the Companions of the Messenger of Allah ﷺ related to me that Allah will look seventy times upon one who performs this prayer on this night, and with each glance He will fulfill seventy of that person's needs, the least of them being forgiveness."

Also among those who wrote on the immense merits of the night of mid-Shaʿbān are al-Haytamī, ʿAbd al-Ra'ūf al-Munāwī, Mullā ʿAlī al-Qārī, al-Sanhūrī al-Mālikī, Nūr al-Dīn al-Bayrūtī, al-Kawtharī, al-Ghumārī, and Muḥammad Ḥasanayn Makhlūf.

Unlike the night of mid-Shaʿbān, there is no evidence in the Law for the merit or lawfulness of a specific voluntary prayer – even individually, let alone in congregation – for the night of the first Jumuʿa of Rajab. As for the long report that describes the modality of the prayer specific to that night, naming it *ṣalāt al-raghā'ib* and beginning with the words "Rajab is the month of Allah, Shaʿbān is my month, and Ramaḍān is the month of my Community," it was forged by Ibn Jahḍam al-Hamadhānī the author of *Bahjat al-Asrār* according to the ḥadīth Masters.[497]

ḥadīth (*hādhā mursal jayyid*). It is probable that al-ʿAlā' ibn al-Ḥārith took it from Makḥūl, and Allah knows best."

[497]Cf. Ibn Ḥajar al-ʿAsqalānī, *Tabyīn al-ʿAjab fīmā Warada fī Rajab*; Ibn ʿAbd al-Salām, *Fatāwā*; Ibn al-Jawzī, *al-Mawḍūʿāt*; al-Dhahabī, *Tartīb al-Mawḍūʿāt*; al-Suyūṭī, *al-La'ālī' al-Maṣnūʿa*; al-Ṣāghānī, *al-Mawḍūʿāt*; Ibn ʿArrāq, *Tanzīh al-*

Al-Qārī said in *al-Asrār al-Marfū'a*: "Abū al-Fatḥ ibn Abī al-Fawāris cited it in his *Amālī* as narrated *mursal* from al-Ḥasan [al-Baṣrī]. Thus did al-Suyūṭī mention it in *al-Jāmi' al-Ṣaghīr*."

Al-Ḥasan actually said that the month of al-Muḥarram was the best of the four sacred months and this is Imām al-Nawawī's position also, not the month of Rajab, while Ibn Rajab said in *Laṭā'if al-Ma'ārif* that it is more apparent that Dhū al-Ḥijja is the best. But in *Ṣaḥīḥ Muslim*, the *Sunan*, and the *Musnad*, from Abū Hurayra and 'Alī: The Prophet ﷺ said: "The best fast after Ramaḍān is that of the month of Allah, al-Muḥarram." If it is asked why then did 'Ā'isha relate that he ﷺ never fasted any month [other than Ramaḍān] more than Sha'bān, the answer is in her own narration also, that "he ﷺ used to fast three days of every month but he sometimes delayed this until he made it up in Sha'bān." Yes, one of the many names of Rajab in *Jāhiliyya* was "the month of Allah" (*shahrullāh*) as per *Laṭā'if al-Ma'ārif*; this is even related from the Prophet ﷺ through very weak chains (by al-Bayhaqī in the *Shu'ab* and al-Daylamī in *al-Firdaws*) and without the other two clauses of the above narration. Even so, Ibn Ḥajar and al-Fattanī included the latter report among the forgeries. There is also the narration: "Sha'bān is my month and Ramaḍān is the month of Allah."[498]

Sharī'a al-Marfū'a; Ibn al-Qayyim, *Naqd al-Manqūl* and *al-Manār al-Munīf*; al-Fattanī, *Tadhkirat al-Mawḍū'āt*; al-Shawkānī, *al-Fawā'id al-Majmū'a*; al-Ḥūt, *Asnā al-Maṭālib*, and al-Ṭarābulusī, *al-Kashf al-Ilāhī*.

[498]Narrated from 'Ā'isha by al-Daylamī in *Musnad al-Firdaws* with a very weak chain because of al-Ḥasan ibn Yaḥya al-Khushanī who is discarded (*matrūk*) as a narrator, and Ibn 'Asākir in reverse order. There is also the narration: "Ramaḍān is the month of my *Umma*, if one of them gets sick they [should] visit him, and if a Muslim fasts without lying or backbiting, and his breakfasting is pure [*i.e. ḥalāl*], and he hurries [to mosques] in the night hours, safeguarding his obligations, he shall come out of his sins just like the snake comes out of its skin." Narrated by Abū al-Shaykh as stated by al-Mundhirī in *al-Targhīb*.

The Prophet ﷺ connected the word *raghā'ib* not to the month of Rajab or its first Jumuʿa, but rather to the pre-*fajr* Sunna and the *ḍuḥā* prayers:

"Do not leave the two *rakʿas* that come before *ṣalāt al-fajr* for in those two [*rakʿas*] are your dearest wishes (*fīhimā al-raghā'ib*)."[499]

"You must pray the two *rakʿas* of *ḍuḥā* for in them are your dearest wishes (*fīhimā al-raghā'ib*)."[500]

At any rate, the fact that there exists disagreement among the scholars about the permissibility of a practice in Islam is enough cause to preclude absolute prohibition of that practice.

Imām Sufyān al-Thawrī said: "When you see someone do something over which there is difference of opinion, and you hold a divergent view, do not forbid him!"[501]

Al-Nawawī himself stated: "The scholars only condemn that which musters Consensus; as for what does not muster unanimous consensus, there is no [permission to pass] condemnation, as every *mujtahid* is correct according to one of the two views on the issue."[502]

[499] A fair (*ḥasan*) ḥadīth narrated from Ibn ʿUmar by al-Ṭabarānī in *al-Kabīr* (12:407-408 §13502) and *al-Awsaṭ* (3:216 §2959), al-Khaṭīb in *Tārīkh Baghdād* (1:240-241 and 12:393), al-Zaylaʿī in *Naṣb al-Rāya* (2:161), from Abū Hurayra by Ibn ʿAsākir (67:337), from Anas by al-Ḥārith in his *Musnad* (1:327 §212) and al-Dhahabī with his chain in the *Siyar* (Fikr ed. 14:349=Risāla ed. 19:370), and *mawqūf* from Ibn ʿUmar by Abū Yūsuf in *al-Āthār* (p. 64) and Ibn ʿAsākir (11:95) cf. al-Haythamī (2:217-218), al-Suyūṭī, *al-Jāmiʿ al-Ṣaghīr* (§2794, §5565, §9761), al-Munāwī (3:78), al-Ghumārī, *al-Mudāwī* (6:547 §9761), and al-Aḥdab, *Zawā'id* (1:258-261 §57 *ḥasan li-ghayrih*).

[500] Narrated from Anas by al-Khaṭīb in his *Tārīkh* (11:124) with a very weak chain because of ʿAbd al-Ḥakam al-Qasmalī cf. al-Suyūṭī, *al-Jāmiʿ al-Ṣaghīr* (§5566) and al-Aḥdab, *Zawā'id* (7:579-580).

[501] Narrated by al-Khaṭīb in *al-Faqīh wal-Mutafaqqih* (Beirut ed. 2:69).

[502] Al-Nawawī, *Sharḥ Ṣaḥīḥ Muslim*, Chapter entitled *al-Amru bil-Maʿrūf wal-Nahī ʿan al-Munkar*, Ḥadīth of the Prophet ﷺ: "Whoever of you sees wrongdoing, let

This rule was mentioned by al-Suyūṭī and Ibn Taymiyya with the wording *lā yunkaru al-mukhtalafu fīhi, innamā yunkaru al-mujma'u 'alayh.*[503]

him change it with his hand; if he cannot, then with his tongue; if he cannot, then with his heart, and that is the weakest belief." Narrated from Abū Sa'īd al-Khudrī by Muslim.

[503] Al-Suyūṭī, *al-Ashbāh wal-Naẓā'ir* (p. 292); Ibn Taymiyya, *al-Fatāwā al-Kubrā* (2:33). The evidence supporting the merit of extra worship on the night of mid-Sha'bān was listed in the *Encyclopedia of Islamic Doctrine.*

Epilogue

An Innovation of Misguidance: Unenlightened Feminism

The people shall always be in a good state as long as they take their knowledge from their elders, their trusted ones, and their people of knowledge. When they start taking it from their boys and their reprobates, they shall be destroyed. – ʿAbd Allah ibn Masʿūd[504]

Shaykh Wahbī Sulaymān Ghāwjī listed, at the end of his monograph on the excellent innovation, *Kalimatun ʿIlmiyyatun Hādiyatun fil-Bidʿati wa-Aḥkāmihā*, several innovations of misguidance which plague the Religion in our time. Among them:

1. The separation of religion from state.

2. The confinement of Islam to certain matters (for example family law) and the exclusion of its jurisdiction over other matters (for example criminal penalties).

3. The belief as well as the expression of "the banquet of Islam" *(māʾidat al-Islām)* as if Islam were optional for consumption or abandonment.

4. Applying to the Muslims the Divine and Prophetic texts that pertain to the disbelievers.

5. Giving in to the temptation of mentioning the defects of the Ulema in a way that resembles slander and actual calumny more than it resembles pure and sincere advice, as may be found even

[504]Narrated from Saʿīd ibn Wahb by Abū ʿUbayd and Yaʿqūb ibn Shayba as cited by Ibn Ḥajar, *Fatḥ* (13:291), Ibn al-Mubārak, *al-Zuhd* (p. 281), Maʿmar ibn Rāshid (*ṣaḥīḥ*) in his *Jāmiʿ* (in ʿAbd al-Razzāq 11:246), al-Ṭabarānī, *al-Kabīr* (9:114 §8589-8592) and *al-Awsaṭ* through narrators declared trustworthy accord-ing to al-Haythamī (1:135), al-Khaṭīb chainless in *al-Faqīh wal-Mutafaqqih* (2:79), Ibn ʿAbd al-Barr, *Jāmiʿ Bayān al-ʿIlm* (1:158, 2:159), and Abū Khaythama in *al-ʿIlm* (§155). Al-Bayhaqī cites it in the chapter entitled "The Common Person's Imitation of the Learned One" in his *Madkhal ilā al-Sunan al-Kubrā* (1:237-247).

in some of the classics of old such as Ibn ʿAbd al-Barr's *Intiqā'* and al-Khaṭīb al-Baghdādī's *Tārīkh Baghdād.*

6. Connecting other than Allah Most High to a situation out of ignorance, such as saying, "Were it not for this money I had saved, or this medicine, or this surgeon, or had I been driving instead of walking, I would have died, or I would not have survived this economic depression, or this or that...." In reality all is in the Hand of Allah Most High beyond our calculations and expectations. Weak or nonexistent belief in *Qadar* is the wont of materialists as well as Christians and Jews.

7. Changing the formulas of *tawassul* to sound as if one if asking other than Allah Most, a typical error of the visitors of the *Awliyā'* sometimes accompanied by other errors such as tying votive threads to the grave, a blatantly unislamic practice. Forbidding *tawassul* is also an innovation of misguidance.

8. Literalist interpretation of the texts that bear on the Divine Attributes that connote anthropomorphism.

9. The consideration of the three Abrahamic dispensations – Judaism, Christianity, and Islam – as a single Religion or that all religions lead to truth and salvation after the masonic philosophy of Jamāl al-Dīn Asad Ābādī al-Afghānī and his student Muḥammad ʿAbduh. This is actually believed by so-called Perennialists and other free-thinking self-proclaimed Sufis.

We may add to this list one of the ugliest innovations of misguidance to date, which issued from actual Ulema from a major school of the Indo-Pakistani region, consisting in attributing something they called "the possibility of lies" *(imkān-e-kadhib)* to Allah Most High. To Him we belong and to Him is our return!

We conclude this book with an overview of a classic contemporary innovation of misguidance, from which we seek refuge in Allah Most High!

In March, 2005 the so-called American "Progressive Muslims" movement orchestrated a Friday prayer at the Synod House of the Cathedral of Saint John the Divine in New York City with male and female congregants led by a woman named Amīna Wadūd, presented by her advertisers as a "professor of Islamic studies at Virginia Commonwealth University" and "the author of the groundbreaking book *Qur'ān and Woman: Rereading the Sacred Text from a Woman's Perspective*."[505] Their boast that Wadūd is "the first woman to lead men in prayers" shows a studious, unprincipled ignorance of the defining role of past practice in the understanding of misguided innovation. A sister movement, the "Muslim Women's League," did boast a precedent in Ghazālat al-Shabībiyya.[506] This dajjālic character was the mother of the lawless Khārijī Shabīb ibn Yazīd ibn Nu'aym al-Shaybānī (d. 77) who had placed her on the *minbar* of al-Kūfa to give *khuṭba* after he had stormed it at the head of an army of eight hundred men and two hundred arm-bearing women – until, after two years of bloody rampage and civil unrest, al-Ḥajjāj destroyed them and their followers.[507]

The "Progressives" and their friends have resolved their inability to prove the licitness of their behavior within Islam by flouting the system from outside with a *J'accuse!* of chauvinism and male sexism that begins with our liege-lords Abū Hurayra and Abū Bakrah al-Thaqafī and trudges through centuries of sexist Qur'anic exegesis, sexist jurisprudence, and sexist ḥadīth

[505] http://www.muslimwakeup.com/events/archives/2005/03/friday_prayer_l.php.

[506] http://www.mwlusa.org/publications/essays/polirights.html as of June, 2005, *ditto* http://www.mwlusa.org/publications/positionpapers/politics.html.

[507] Cf. 'Abd al-Qāhir al-Baghdādī, *al-Farq bayn al-Firaq* ('Aṣriyya ed. p. 78-80=Āfāq ed. p. 89-92) and his *Milal wal-Niḥal* (p. 74-76).

transmission down to our times. Only in this way can they "break the interpretive monopoly," that is, pick and choose from the Qur'ān and Ḥadīth in a vacuum, free at last from the annoying guidelines and preconditions of scholarly exertion in Islam such as ethics, knowledge of Arabic, a firm grasp of the texts, and a living familiarity with our legal and intellectual history.

The anti-method of the "Progressives" contains the seeds of their own demise: the very claim that it is legitimate for anybody to claim authority makes it all the more possible to reject the claimant's authority in turn and start perpetually newer, "more progressive" trends from where the previous trend left off, often disowning it as the early Khārijites did of one another. The "Progressives," for example, have invented a *ḥijāb*-less prayer for themselves as their New York congregation displayed. One day their female leader might actually make this state of undress the law and frown upon its lingering use by female congregants still possessed of a (male chauvinistic) sense of shame. Later, American "Progressive" illuminati will insist that the Fātiḥa be recited in English inside prayer (perhaps allowing Swahili during Kwanzaa), free from racist Arabocentric strictures.

In the end, a Muslim might pray in short shorts behind his sing-songy female imām with the non-Arab accent, after she has graced the congregants with a *khuṭba* about "God, praise Her." She is *ḥijāb*-less "because {*Lā ikrāha fīl-Dīn*}" and shakes hands indiscriminately with men, none of whom minds that she wears "Opium" to the prayer. Another congregant prays with malt liquor on her breath. The man next to her prays in a *junub* state but he is not *junub* according to a Ẓāhirī position if there was no ejaculation. He married his granddaughter, which is licit according to a Khārijī view – temporarily and without witnesses, of course. Their self-imagined Sufis are fond of name-dropping "Ibn ʿArabī" – whom they rank slightly above René Guénon – to spin any given ruling of the Qur'ān and Sunna into their idea of the *Dīn*. Whoever suggests the necessity of taking religious knowledge from those who are knowledgeable in the Religion they consider a rigid and possibly pro-terrorist conservative. They all pay their religion-neutral non-mosque hall rent with interest earnings "because interest is not *ribā*" but do not consider that *zakāt* is due on paper money, thus saving a bundle which they can invest in Halliburton or Annhauser-Bush stocks so they can live the good life.

All of the above types can still holler that they are Muslims, that they are followers of the Prophet Muḥammad ﷺ, though not of his command to hold fast to his Way and that of his Rightly-Guided companions by biting on it with their very jaws.

One of the arguments for banning formal prayer from U.S. public schools is that others would then have their chance to pray their own way too, including Satanists. Each of the horrendous "prayer of the future" scenarios we have extrapolated is based on an aberrant *fiqh*-arguable position in the books to illustrate that when you subordinate worship to a (wo)man-made discourse on equality and democracy you open a very risky door. A skillful enough academic with a moral mission such as Khālid Abūl Fadl (who has boasted of praying behind his wife long before the New York travesty) or Ṭāriq Ramaḍān can resuscitate each and every one of those heresies and sell them to U.S. and other shoppers as a new and improved, updated, politically correct Islam.

Defenders of the "Progressives" dismiss this historically-based model of the Pandoran dynamics of unbridled revisionism as a *reductio ad absurdum*. They evade the fundamental issue of the lawlessness of innovation and instead shed crocodile tears for "the very real social problems of which this controversy is but one symptom." In their misty eyes, enough misbehavior by bad Muslim men provides justification to tamper with the roots of the Religion and radically revise the very contents of the Qur'ān and the Sunna. They applaud the very novelties which our Prophet ﷺ decried as "newfangled matters neither you nor your forefathers ever heard of before." In their hurry to emulate the former followers of Moses and Jesus, they would have the Muslims also disappear into the lizard-hole of ex-believers who "liberated" themselves into irreligion.

Sadly for the "Progressives," our Prayer is not a platform for pluralism. Valid concerns about family and gender issues no more suddenly make the modalities of Muslim worship negotiable than did, say, the valid concerns of non-Arabs against Arabocentrism in the time of al-Jāḥiẓ or in Iran or Kemalist Turkey. One should not have to tamper with *Ṣalāt* in the process of inveighing against the sins of male pride or sexism. We need not run out of options other than throwing out the baby with the bath water; surely the *Umma* has more imagination and more resources than to tamper with its Pillars. Surely our Prophet ﷺ taught us enough about Allah for us to worship Allah for His sake and to know better than to use the Sacred as tools for something ulterior. Precaution and common sense (if not knowledge of our Principles) dictate that we not mix the religion with post-20th century -isms and liberation theologies; and that we insure at least the formal Divine acceptance of our worship and that of our families through adherence to the "path of the Believers" that the Qur'ān makes the precondition for such acceptance.

Nor is blank permission the basic principle *(aṣl)* in matters of worship. In worship, as in the creed, the *aṣl* is *ḥurma* [categorical prohibition] because matters of worship are Divinely ordained. (In sexual intercourse also the *aṣl* is *ḥurma* and becomes permission only through the contract of marriage.) Hence the Prophet ﷺ did not say "Pray as you see fit" but "Pray as you see me pray" and he stressed Prayer as the central pillar upon which rests the tent of one's Islam and the first thing for which one shall be brought to account on the Day of Judgment. A concerned Muslim could never advise any son or daughter or brother or sister except with the strictest precaution toward it.

For those who still believe there is such a thing as sunna and *bid'a*, not only the multiplicity but the slavish catering of new sects to political and social fads and the unfailing minorityism of old and new sects are all, ultimately, a testimony to the established middle path and a reinforcement of orthodoxy.

A Feminist *Mubtadi'a*: Amīna Wadūd

In a brief article dated May 2002 and published on the internet, "'Ā'isha's Legacy: the struggle for women's rights in Islam," Amīna Wadūd revealed the most simplistic scholarship imaginable, apparently assuming that none of her intended public would challenge her entirely novel presentation of history, law, and hermeneutics. This is who the *New Internationalist* website blurb enthroned as our "foremost Muslim feminist scholar" whose article "will introduce readers to Islamic feminism."[508]

In that article, Wadūd does a tap dance around the exclusivity of the Qur'ān as a source of Law in Islam except when it comes to illustrating proto-feminist themes, such as praising our Mother 'Ā'isha "from whom," Wadūd says, "the Prophet [ﷺ] said we should learn 'half our religion'" (a forgery according to Ibn Ḥajar, Ibn Kathīr, al-Mizzī, al-Dhahabī, al-Qārī, *et alia*). Wadūd chooses to dismiss Ḥadīth in her main argumentation and when she invokes it to make a point – in violation of her own principles – she invokes the weakest possible kind. This kind of contradiction is all-too-typical of Orientalists and their Muslim competitors-in-revisionism; they pit the Qur'ān against Ḥadīth then quote ḥadīthic sources right and left if it suits them.

Wadūd should not have invoked only the Qur'an but also Ḥadīth for the main issues she raises, and then only the strong and authentic ḥadīths. For example, the ḥadīth of the creation of woman from a rib which is in *Ṣaḥīḥ al-Bukhārī* and *Ṣaḥīḥ Muslim*.[509] This is not to say that Eve "is a flawed female helpmate extracted from him [Ādam] as an afterthought or utility"! Those are Wadūd's own inflammatory words. However, the rib is the protection of the heart and Woman represents the protection of

[508] http://www.newint.org/issue345/legacy.htm. *New Internationalist* (vol. 345, May, 2002).
[509] From Abū Hurayra cf. Abū Dharr in al-Dārimī and Samura ibn Jundub in Aḥmad.

Man rather than the reverse; but for such protection to take place, man must protect woman in the first place. This is because if any harm reaches the rib (woman) then the heart (man) is left unprotected. The Prophet ﷺ said in that very same ḥadīth: "Therefore, treat women kindly." Unfortunately, this hadith does not find favor as feminist evidence in feminist discourse.

Similarly "Qur'ān-only" feminists ignore the fact that it is in the ḥadīth that one will find the strongest and most explicit excoriation of wife-beating and that it is from the Qur'ān that Muslim wife-beaters usually fish out their idea of a justification.

These flaws are no accident but underlie a pattern of shoddy thinking – the coarsest, shallowest type of historical revisionism. Wadūd says: "During the Abbasid period, when Islam's foundations were developed, leading scholars and thinkers were exclusively male. They had no experience with revelation first hand, had not known the Prophet directly and were sometimes influenced by intellectual and moral cultures antithetical to Islam." The marvelous jump from profiling the early Ulema as male non-Companions to actually accusing them of being "sometimes influenced by cultures antithetical to Islam" is mind-boggling. Surely, even the worst of Abbasid culture had more immunity to unislamic trends than 21st-century American Muslim culture can dream of achieving! But this pseudo-historicism is only a veneer. All Wadūd wants is for readers to hear "excusively male" and conclude that the formative period of Muslim culture needs rewriting. However, in the process of her gender assassination she commits blunder after blunder:

1. Leading scholars and thinkers were not exclusively, but predominantly, male during the Abbasid period as in any other period, and even then, so what? If those Abbasid Scholars had been predominantly women, is it to say that they would have been inherently more honest and qualified?

2. No one has "experience with revelation first hand" except Prophets unless she means direct contact with one that had experience with revelation first hand, *i.e.* the Companions, a predominantly male group. Wadūd predictably would have another problem with the fact that the Prophets themselves are an exclusively male category.

3. Every student knows that the Ulema of Islam by and large kept fiercely aloof from politics, let alone "intellectual and moral cultures antithetical to Islam." To say that they were adversely misguided as a whole is baseless calumny of the first order, not to mention that it tears to shreds the notion of the *Umma*'s infallibility and vitually shouts at our Creator: "You have misled us!"

Wadūd goes on to claim: "In particular, they [the male scholars] moved away from the Qur'an's ethical codes for female autonomy to advocate instead women's subservience, silence and seclusion. If women's agency was taken into consideration it was with regard to service to men, family and community." This mock trial is the desired caricature of male conspiracy which unenlightened feminists propose. It is not only simplistic but invidious to scholarly history and dishonest to the *Umma* past and present.

Wadūd is the academic face of a fanatically revisionist Islam intent on rewriting not only *fiqh* and *tafsīr* but the Qur'ān itself. After she founded the woman group "Sisters in Islam" in Kuala Lumpur in the early nineties, her teaching contract at the International Islamic University of Malaysia was not renewed. Nevertheless, the seeds were planted and an August, 1994 *Economist* editorial entitled "In the Name of Eve" openly promoted "Sisters in Islam" and their idea of women's "equality that Koran, give or take a verse or two, gives them in principle."

A strong scholarship on the place of woman in Islamic intellectual history should refute such fraudulent endeavors with facts and keep quack feminism out of Islam. This is not to say that issues of domestic violence, sexual abuse, or hasty *ḥudūd* justice taking place in the midst of Muslim society should not be addressed. They should be addressed, exposed, excoriated; but not at the expense of the entire Islamic tradition. As one student of knowledge wrote, "until practicing Muslims who strive to adhere to *Sharīʿa*, who study, who would otherwise be labeled as 'conservatives' stand up and say something, Muslim women's issues will continue to be the domain of non-Muslim feminists and the establishment who brush them off with [the remark], 'That's cultural, not Islam,' and then launch into the Lecture on the Ideal Status of Muslim Women versus the Reality of Western Women."

Countless generations of Muslim women played an integral role in transmitting the Religion of Islam from the Prophet Muḥammad – upon him and them blessings and peace – and his successors including its texts and practice from the earliest centuries down to our time. But in her "first Friday sermon by a woman" according to a *Guardian* article dated Saturday, March 19, 2005 Amina Wadūd is quoted as saying, "Women were not allowed to (have) input in the basic paradigms of what it means to be a Muslim."

An instance of Wadūd's "input in the basic paradigm" is her reference to our Creator as "He," "She," "It." The article went on, "Particularly controversial was Wadūd's periodic substitution of the Arabic word for God, Allah, with the pronouns, he, she and it, arguing that God's omnipresence defied gender definition." In her slightly outdated, post-Vatican II apostasy *(ilḥād)* of the Divine Name, it appears Wadūd follows the lead of Pīr Wilāyat Khān and his syncretist, perennialist, New Age "Sufi Order of the West."

More relevantly, she is reviving its scandalousness by trying to inject it into the mainstream and disturb not just a happy few but as many as possible. The sociologist of American Islam, Yvonne Haddad, is quoted in the same article as saying, " People in America think they are going to be the vanguards of change, but for Arab Muslims in the Middle East, American Muslims continue to be viewed on the margins of the faith." (Haddad seems to think that American Muslims are viewed more favorably by non-Arab Muslims than by Arabs.)

In an interview entitled "Dr. Amina Wadūd Leads the Ummah in a Historical Prayer"[510] Wadūd is quoted as saying: "The end conclusion was that the principle of Ijtehad will be used to discontinue slavery even when the Quran did not advocate for its immediate end." While it is true the Qur'ān did not literally command the immediate end of slavery it certainly advocated for its immediate end by equating the freeing of slaves with salvation and worship in many verses. Our teacher Nūr al-Dīn 'Itr gave this golden rule for self-hating Muslims over the issue of slavery in Islam: "Not a single book of jurisprudence or its principles contains a chapter entitled 'slavery' in all Islam but they all have a chapter entitled 'emancipation.'"[511]

Wadūd also said, "The Quran worked to eradicate the previously negative practices toward women, and moved forward to justice. We must realize that this was done fourteen centuries ago. At that time, it was not even possible to imagine women with spiritual equality." The contrary is true: it is precisely in our time that we are hard-pressed to see women or men of high spiritual rank while it was frequent fourteen centuries ago to see women with spiritual superiority, let alone imagine women of spiritual equality. The Prophet ﷺ made glowing references to his first wife Khadīja, his youngest wife 'Ā'isha, his daughter Fāṭima, various

[510] http://naseeb.com/naseebvibes/prose-detail.php?aid=3631 as of 19 March 2005.
[511] Class communication.

women of the *Muhājirūn* and *Anṣār*, and the women of former times such as Āsia the wife of Pharaoh, the most truthful Virgin Mary, and others.

Wadūd then says, "We are members of our current History. We make History, we imagine our future." The belief that "we make History" is the core of qadarism [absolute free will] which Wadūd here expresses more explicitly while it remains implicit in most of her statements about history, empowerment, and change. The belief in *qadar* which the Prophet, upon him blessings and peace, taught is that it is Allah Who makes history and that its end has already been written while we remain (contrary to the heresy of fatalism and determinism) fully responsible for our actions.

"Leading ṣalāt (prayer) is representative of the devotion to ritual as well as the capability of participation for women," Wadūd says. However, contrary to what Islam views as the abrogated dispensations of Judaism and Catholicism, Islam does not accept any change in its creed and worship. Leading *Ṣalāt* is an integral aspect *(hay'a)* of a Divinely-ordained pillar of worship, not a platform for the "participation" of a gender or this or that interest group. The Prophet ﷺ described this pillar as the central pillar of the Religion, announced it will be the first item of reckoning in the last Judgment, and warned us in his very last breath not to jeopardize it.

Wadūd continues, "Within the framework of intellectual development, common sense is always considered inferior and insufficient to ḥadīth or *fiqh*." It is one of the more intellectually lazy and deceitful assumptions that the Islamic disciplines are somehow dissociated from basic common sense. In reality, intelligence is the soul of ḥadīth and *fiqh* and they are, of all the human discourses we know, its greatest proponents.[512]

[512] As the Prophet ﷺ said in his mass-transmitted saying, "For whomever Allah desires immense good He grants them superlative understanding of the Religion."

Then Wadūd puts forward her grandly irresponsible idea that each man and each woman is his or her own Imām: "The final analysis is that each human is responsible for being a Khilafa [*sic*] who must act like an agent responsible to obey Allah, according to their best understanding of interpretations from experts as well as for discussing alternatives brought about by real life experience." Behind the gibberish read: "no leader, just me and myself." Wadūd is casting off the shackles of {*ask the people of the remembrance*} (16:43), {*above every learned one there is one more learned*} (12:76), {*obey those in authority among you*} (4:59), and {*hold fast to the rope of Allah and do not separate*} (3:103) as so many male constraints, substituting instead the idols of subjectivism and empiricism.

A person is responsible for his or her own actions and is duty-bound to follow the Divine dispensation whether or not they understand its expert interpretations or have "discussed" so-called alternatives on empirical bases. To follow a School of Law is precisely the safest and most Qur'ānic and Sunna-based way of assuming such a responsibility. It is simply not for each of the two billion Muslims on the planet to manufacture his or her own dissent under the pretext of individual responsibility, "according to their best understanding of interpretations from experts as well as for discussing alternatives brought about by real life experience!" *Khilāfa* is not a fluid honorific that gets to be used as a pretext to dissolve a Muslim's categorical obligations into meaningless relativism that re-emerges into such forms as we see nowadays in free-wheeling, nihilistic pseudo-*jihād*.

Wadūd goes on to massacre exegesis and legal precedent through shallow misreadings of the Qur'ān and early history. She claims, "The second caliph of Islam, Hazrat Omar did not collect the booty as referenced in the Quran. This booty taking was a common practice at the time when the Quran was taken more literally." In fact, our liege-lords Abū Bakr, 'Umar, 'Uthman, and 'Alī all collected the booty and distributed it in the same way with respect to both the letter and the spirit of the Qur'ān. That there was some discontentment in no way indicates a less literal understanding of the Qur'ān than in the time of the Prophet ﷺ. There is no difference in the basic Qur'ānic distribution of the spoils of war, according to the four Rightly-Guided Caliphs and the four Imāms of jurisprudence, from the time of Abū Bakr to that of 'Alī ﵁.

Wadūd protests, "The interpretation that I should shut up and sit down was not the method that I would use to live Islam. I cannot be an agent or a khilafa [*sic*] unless I am honest about what is in my heart." Feminists who use the straw man of male silencing of women only reveal their ignorance of Islamic history, which shows anything but demure silent women. The woman who stood and corrected her *khalīfa* (our liege-lord 'Umar) in the midst of his Jumu'a sermon clearly did not "shut up and sit down." However, she was speaking from both knowledge and a sense of justice, not justice alone uninformed by knowledge. Hence, 'Umar vindicated her. Moreover, all the while, she never at any point left the Qur'anic confines of {*obey those of you who are in authority*}. She practiced *naṣīḥa* with the greater courage: within the system, not by trying to stab the system in the back with intimations of subversion and distrust from a mediatized hiding-place. That woman won the palm of honesty here and hereafter and she would have taken to her heels at the mere idea of her being her own *khalīfa*.

"VIBES: 'Is it true that pre-Islamic women were braver and more outgoing than those in the post-Islam era?' Wadūd: 'No, I don't aspire to this view. Take the Prophet's wife, Khadija. She was unable to manage her own business without a male representative.'" How so? That our Mother Khadīja relied on male employees does not automatically show she did not manage her own business without a male representative.

Wadūd openly admits using Divine worship for ulterior ends: "The fact is that a mixed congregational prayer is in no way a precedence of sorts, but simply **a public announcement that should lead to positive feelings**. I realize that this single act won't transform the community, but is symbolic of the possibilities within Islam." To intentionally use prayer as a public announcement is the soul of what the Prophet, upon him blessings and peace, decried as self-display *(riyā')* and the minor polytheism *(al-shirk al-aṣghar)*.

The *Umma* has always been uplifted by what is symbolic of the ideal within Islam, not by exploring the possibilities of chaos that are the undoing of human beings and societies. The *Dhikr* Allah Most High guarantees to protect includes the truthful meaning, not just the letter of the Qur'ān. The *taḥrīf* or tampering the Qur'ān castigates refers to the meaning of the Pentateuch before its letter. The importation of this *taḥrīf* into Islam is being promoted before our eyes as we speak. The first step to that *taḥrīf* is to divorce the Qur'an from its hermeneutics, the Sunna. The final stage is that she "did not agree with the Qur'ān" itself as Wadūd is quoted as saying by Nazim Baksh in a *Q-News* article titled "Waking up to Progressive Muslims."[513]

O Allah! Protect us from knowledge which is of no benefit and from knowledge that will become a proof against us in the Next World! *Āmīn. Wal-ḥamdu lillāhi Rabb al-'ālamīn.*

[513]http://www.ihyafoundation.com/index.php?page=nazim_baksh/15. Also available at http://www.q-news.com/ProgressiveMuslims.pdf.

Indexes

Index of Qur'ānic Verses

2:117 137
2:156 64
2:166 44
2:181 99
2:201 155
2:251 38
3:39 182
3:53 155
3:103 227
3:159 117
3:173 116
4:59 27, 28, 69, 118, 227, 228
4:83 28
4:115 58, 67
5:6 57
5:118 98
6:44 116
9:18 197
9:92 60
10:89 144
12:42 182
12:76 227
14:36 98
15:24 163
16:16 41
16:43 227
17:25 167, 171
18:10 155
20:15 117
20:114 99
21:2 132
21:7 27
21:98 117
22:77 94, 206
24:36 168
24:54 54
27:23 116
32:16 179
33:21 22
33:33 163
38:18 168
38:18-19 178
39:16 99
40:70-71 99
41:26 159
45:21 98
46:9 12
46:25 116
52:27 99
53:37 174
53:39 116
54:46 99
57:27 127
59:7 36
65:2-3 99
82:6 99
93:5 99
110:1 25
112 82

Index of Narrations

A truly beautiful woman used to pray behind the Prophet… 162
Abū Bakr and ʿUmar, the two leaders of rightful guidance (ʿAlī), 47
Abū Bakr came and drew a large bucket or two… (dream) 34, 69
Abū Bakr, what prevented you from standing firm… 181
Abū al-Dardā' would study the Qur'ān with a group… 158
Abū Hurayra used to recite *qunūt* in the Dawn prayer, 156
Abū ʿUbayda ibn al-Jarrāḥ is the trustee of this Community, 32
Ādam and all those after him are under my flag… 180
After the coming out of Ya'jūj and Ma'jūj, ʿĪsā shall supplicate, 150
After me your affairs will be ruled by… 62
After that, there will be kingship, 37, 65
[The] age of the world is like a little rain water on a mountain plateau, 28
ʿĀ'isha used to visit the grave of the Messenger at all times… 192
ʿAlī is the best in judgment among us (ʿUmar), 39
ʿAlī ordering the destruction of tombs, 198
Allah ﷻ curse the Jews and Christians! They took the graves… 194
Allah ﷻ curses the women who frequently visit the graves, 186, 188, 193
Allah ﷻ curses the women who visit the graves, 186
Allah ﷻ has angels roaming the roads to find the people of *dhikr*… 152
Allah ﷻ has engraved truth on the tongue of ʿUmar and his heart, 36, 67
Allah ﷻ has made it obligatory to obey them, (Ibn ʿAbbās and others), 27
Allah ﷻ is greater and truly great! (unnamed Companion), 81
Allah ﷻ is most modest and noble… 150
Allah ﷻ looked into the hearts of creatures… (Ibn Masʿūd), 52
Allah ﷻ ordained for you the fast of Ramaḍān… 127
Allah ﷻ sent forth Muḥammad and we knew nothing… (Ibn ʿUmar), 56
Allah ﷻ shall not make my Community ever concur on error, 53
Allah ﷻ, truly, prevented the elephants from entering Makka, 86
Allah ﷻ will give kingship to whomever He will, 34
ʿAmmār is filled with belief to his marrow, 63

Among your best days is the day of Jumuʿa, 120
[The] ankles of the Holy Prophet were swollen... 94
As long as they take their knowledge from... (Ibn Masʿūd), 29, 214
Al-Awwābīn are those who pray *ṣalāt al-ḍuḥā* (ʿAwn al-ʿUqaylī), 167
Al-Awwābīn are those who remember their sins (Ibn ʿUmayr), 167
Bashshirū wa-lā tunaffirū, 12
Be glad, for Allah has forgiven you, 145
Bear patiently, Family of Yāsir, your tryst is in Paradise, 63
[The] best fast after Ramaḍān is that of the month of Allah... 211
[The] best in judgment is ʿAlī, 39
[The] best of this Community after its Prophet are... (ʿAlī), 48
[The] best place for a woman's *ṣalāt* is in the privacy of her house, 165
[The] best prayer after the prescribed prayer is that prayed alone...207
[The] best women are those who do not see men... (Fāṭima), 165
Beware of the devil's croaking! 192
Beware of newfangled matters... 60
Bidʿa is of two kinds... (al-Shāfiʿī), 13
Bilāl! Tell me about the deed... 80
[The] boy from Daws asked for it before you, 145
Bury the dirt you see in the Mosque... 173
[The] Caliphs (*al-khulafā'*) are five... (al-Shāfiʿī), 59
Come close together, all of you, 147
[The] Companions were the purest of heart... (al-Ḥasan), 58
{*Consult with them*} That is: in some of the affairs (Ibn ʿAbbās), 117
Continue what you were doing, 145
Dhikr-beads
  Abū Hurayra, 101
  Al-Ḥasan, 101
  Ibn Ḥajar, 101
  ʿIkrima, 101
  ʿUmar al-Mālikī, 101
Did any of you see anything in his dream? 34, 66

Do not forbid the bondswomen of Allah from the mosques, 160, 161
Do not leave the two *rak'as* that come before *ṣalāt al-fajr*... 212
Do not leave your house tomorrow morning... 147
Do not make your houses graves, 202
Do not take my grave as an *'Īd*... 185, 200-204
Do not take my house as an *'Īd*... 200
Do not weep, I have completed the Qur'ān... ('Abd Allah ibn Idrīs), 112
Do not weep, Mu'ādh! 185
[The] doorsill and the walls of the house began to say *Āmīn*, 147
Du'ā is *'ibāda* itself, 155
Each of you shall be in a good state as long as...(Ibn Mas'ūd), 28, 29
[The] earth does not consume the bodies of Prophets, 119
Every human being shall be consumed by the earth but... 119
Every innovation is misguidance, 15, 76, 114, 125, 134, 139
Every misguidance is in the Fire, 114
Every newfangled matter is an innovation... 60, 114-115, 140
Every religion has its knights... (Yazīd ibn Zuray'), 23
Except the mastic tree (*al-idhkhir*) (al-'Abbās), 86
Fasting all year
- Abū Bakr ibn 'Ayyāsh, 112
- Abū Ḥanīfa, 96
- Abū al-Ḥārith al-Madanī, 112
- Abū Ṭalḥa, 96, 97
- 'Ā'isha, 96, 97
- Baqī ibn Makhlad, 113
- Ibn Ma'mar, 97
- Ibn 'Umar, 95-97
- Manṣūr Abū 'Attāb al-Sulamī, 96, 111
- Muṣ'ab ibn Thābit, 110
- al-Nawawī, 96
- Sa'd ibn Ibrāhīm ibn 'Abd al-Raḥmān al-Zuhrī, 96, 108
- Sa'īd ibn al-Musayyab, 96, 104

Fasting all year
al-Shāfiʿī, 96, 97
Shuʿba, 96, 110
Thābit al-Bunānī, 96, 105
al-Tustarī, 96, 109
ʿUmar, 95-97
ʿUthmān, 95, 96
Wakīʿ, 96, 112
Fāṭima had also marked the grave of her uncle Ḥamza with a rock… 198
Fāṭima used to visit the grave of her uncle Ḥamza… 191
Fāṭima was the first to use the casket (Ibn ʿAbd al-Barr), 93
Fear Allah and be patient, 193
Fear Allah and be steadfast! 189
[The] first innovation was satiety (ʿĀ'isha), 71
[The] first to initiate studies in the mosque of Damascus is Hishām, 158
Follow ʿAmmār's guidance, 45, 62, 64
Follow the largest mass… 53
Follow us [Companions] or you shall go astray (ʿImrān), 55
[The] foot of ʿAbd Allah shall weigh more heavily than Uḥud… 64
Get up to meet your chief [Sa'd ibn Muʿādh], 182
Give glad tidings and do not repel people (*bashshirū wa-lā tunaffirū*), 12
Go, for verily Allah shall empower your tongue and guide your heart, 39
Go to Abū Bakr! 33
Greetings to you, people of the abodes among the believers! 189
[A] group does not gather in one of the Houses of Allah reciting… 158
Groves of Paradise: the gatherings of *dhikr*, 151-152
Had there been a Prophet after me, verily it would have been ʿUmar, 36
Had they entered it they would not have come out… 118
[The] Hand of Allah is with the *Jamāʿa*, 53
Hang back! You may not walk in the middle of the road… 164
Al-Ḥanīfiyyat al-Samḥa, 12
Al-Ḥasan may reconcile two great factions, 38

He has asked Allah ﷻ by His greatest name... 85
He [Allah ﷻ] made them the ministers of His Prophet...(Ibn Mas'ūd), 52
He must conclude it with *Āmīn*, 143
He used to pray two *rak'as* before going out... (Ibn Rawāḥa's widow), 91
He ['Uthmān] used to spend the whole night praying, 95
He [Ibn 'Umar] would spend the night praying until morning, 95
Hold fast to 'Ammār's covenant, 63
Hold fast to the covenant of Ibn Umm 'Abd [Ibn Mas'ūd], 45, 64
How could we do something the Prophet did not do? (Abū Bakr and Zayd), 87
How did you know it [the *Fātiḥa*] was among the words that heal? 84
How will you [Mu'ādh] pass judgment if a judgment is asked of you? 50
Hunger is the secret of Allah ﷻ on His earth (Sahl al-Tustarī), 109
Al-Ḥusayn has beaten us *i.e.* with martyrdom, 149
I am astonished at eyes that sleep at night (Umm al-Ṣahbā'), 105
I am the first of the kings (Mu'āwiya), 37
I am going to invoke Allah ﷻ, therefore say *Āmīn* ('Umar), 148
I am happy that my Community have whatever Ibn Mas'ūd... 32, 46
I am the Master (*sayyid*) of human beings... 180, 182
I am nearer to every believer than his own soul... 114
I am not a Prophet nor do I receive revelation... ('Alī), 48
I am the patron/protecting friend (*walī*) of the believers, 114
I am a trustee for my Companions... 40
I came to the Prophet, not to a stone (Abū Ayyūb al-Anṣārī), 199
I exhort you to hear and obey even if your leader is... 60
I forbade you from visiting the graves and now [allow you to], but... 194
I forbade you to visit the graves but [now] do visit them! 187-190
I had forbidden you to visit graves but do visit them... 190
I had forbidden you to visit graves but Muḥammad has been... 190
I interpreted the black [sheep] to refer to the Arabs... 35
I make *tasbīḥ* every day according to my ransom (Abū Hurayra), 101
I neither lie nor was ever called a liar! (al-Ḥasan), 23

I never raised *adhān* except I prayed two *rak'as* (Bilāl), 80
I never saw any strong master of his people... better than 'Umar, 35
I never saw anyone do such accomplished work as he ['Umar] did 34, 69
I never saw the Prophet pray *ṣalāt al-ḍuḥā* ('Ā'isha), 174
I recommend to you my Companions, then those... after them, 40
I remember the past of this world as a cool spring... (Ibn Mas'ūd), 28
I saw a flock of black sheep and dirt-white sheep... 35
I saw the gates of heaven open because of those words, 81
I saw myself drawing water from a well... 34, 69
I saw a tremendous throng that...blocked up the entire firmament, 55
I searched for *ṣalāt al-ḍuḥā* in the Qur'ān... (Ibn 'Abbās), 167
I shall make free women of you again ('Umar), 160
I was given three things... 150
I would not leave the eight *rak'as* of *ṣalāt al-ḍuḥā*... ('Ā'isha), 175
I would prefer serving one Muslim who is in need... ('Āmir), 58
Ibn 'Abbās' *tahajjud* behind the Prophet, 207
Ibn Mas'ūd and his mother were part of *Ahl al-Bayt* (Abū Mūsā), 46
Ibn Mas'ūd instituted a Sunna for you, so follow that Sunna, 46, 121
Ibn 'Umar and Ibn al-Zubayr supplicating [together], 149
Ibn 'Umar used to supplicate together with al-Qāṣṣ, 149
If a case comes before you which you cannot defer... (Ibn Mas'ūd), 50
If the Companions made *wuḍū'* to the wrists... (Ibrāhīm al-Nakha'ī), 57
If the Emigrants are satisfied, you [Helpers] are but followers (Abū Bakr), 43
If the judge (*al-ḥākim*) rules by exerting his mind... 115
If the Messenger had seen what the women of our time do ('Ā'isha), 162
If one of you says *Āmīn* and the angels in the heaven say *Āmīn*...148
If people obey Abū Bakr and 'Umar they... follow the right direction, 33
If something comes up that is not in the Book... (Ibn Mas'ūd), 49
If 'Umar and 'Alī concur on something: that is authority (Wakī'), 69
If the woman reaches the age of puberty... 163
If you see the groves of Paradise, graze in them, 151

If your women ask permission to go out to *ṣalāt*, do not forbid them! 160
[The] imām is a shield from behind which the people fight, 156
[An] Imām of right guidance forbade it… (Ibn Sīrīn), 57, 66
[An] imām who makes his *du'ā* particular to himself has betrayed… 155
Imitate their [the Companions'] manners and their ways (al-Ḥasan), 58
Imitation is for the Companions of the Messenger (Aḥmad), 43
In the morning every single joint of yours must pay a *ṣadaqa*… 173
In nations long before you were people… 36
Innovated matters are of two kinds… (al-Shāfi'ī), 129
Innovation is two types… (al-Shāfi'ī), 129
Innovations are of two kinds (al-Shāfi'ī), 128
Is it righteousness? 163
Is there any stranger among you? 145
[The] *isnād* is the believer's weapon (Sufyān), 23
[The] *isnād* is an integral part of the Religion… (Ibn al-Mubārak), 23
[The] Israelites divided into seventy-one sects… 54
It [Sūrat al-Ikhlāṣ] equals a third of the Qur'ān, 83
It [*ṣalāt al-ḍuḥā*] is a *bid'a* (Ibn'Umar), 174
It is guaranteed. It is guaranteed. It is guaranteed. 45
It is an innovation and what a fine innovation it is (Ibn'Umar), 92, 128, 176, 207
It was an opinion I consider true…
  'Alī, 48
  'Umar ibn 'Abd al-'Azīz, 57
It was not fitting for the son of Abū Quḥāfa to stand ahead… 181
It would be best if they left it [*ṣalāt al-ḍuḥā*] until the sun… ('Alī,), 167
[The] Jews do not envy you for anything as much as… ('Ā'isha), 146
Keep away Mālik's white hair from the Fire (Mālik ibn Dīnār), 106
Khubayb was the first to inaugurate the two *rak'as*… (Abū Hurayra), 91
[The] killer's extended family is responsible for the indemnity, 51
Kissing of the Prophet's hand, 120
Know that the best of your good deeds is prayer, 94

Labbayka wa-sa'dayka wal-khayru bi-yadayk (Ibn 'Umar), 88
Last night as [I dreamed] I was hoisting up [water from a well]… 34
[The] lawful is clear and the unlawful is clear… 49
Leave what seems dubious to you for what does not… 49
Let each of you look carefully from whom he takes his Religion, 23
Let no one say: 'I am afraid, I am afraid [to judge], (Ibn Mas'ūd), 49
Let us restrict this door to women only, 164
Mankind makes up one portion and I and my Companions… 24, 25, 45
[The] *Maqām* was attached to the House… ('Ā'isha), 88
May Allah hear whoever praises Him! 80
May you perish the day 'Uthmān is killed! 33
[The] Messenger ﷺ and those in authority after him instituted ways… ('Umar ibn 'Abd al-'Azīz) 57, 67
[The] Messenger ﷺ did not pray *ḍuḥā* but she ['Ā'isha] prayed it, 176
[The] Messenger ﷺ prayed among us then turned to face us… 60
[The] Messenger ﷺ raised his hands in supplication, 146
[The] Messenger ﷺ used to pray *ḍuḥā* in four *rak'as*, 172
[The] Messenger ﷺ used to pray *ḍuḥā* to the point that we said … 176
[The] Messenger ﷺ was among us while the Qur'ān was revealed (Jābir), 56
[The] most compassionate of my Community… is Abū Bakr, 39
[The] most truthful of all speech is the Book of Allah… 114
Mounts are not saddled except to go to three mosques, 205
Mu'ādh instituted a Sunna for you, so follow it exactly, 46, 121
Mu'ādh! It may be that you shall not meet me again… 184
Mūsā supplicated while Hārūn said *Āmīn*, 144, 150
My beloved instructed me never to leave three things…
  Anas, 171
  Abū al-Dardā', 175
  Abū Hurayra, 171, 175
My Community, my Community! 98
My Community shall divide into seventy-three sects, 24, 40

My Community shall never concur on error, 53
My Companions are like the stars… 41, 44
My Companions are trustees for my Community, 24, 40
My liege-lord! (*yā sayyidī*) (Sahl ibn Ḥunayf), 183
[The] most beloved Religion of all to Allah, 12
[The] Natural, Easy Religion, 12
Nawāfil prayers between *maghrib* and *ʿishā*: *ṣalāt al-awwābīn* (ʿAṭā'), 178
Never speak over matters in which you have no Imām (Aḥmad), 44
New matters shall arise after me… 68
Niʿma al-maqbaratu hādhihi, 186
No blessing has ever descended but through Muḥammad (al-Shāfiʿī), 12
No group assembles, one of them supplicating… 143-144
No group assembles in one of the Houses of Allah, reciting… 157
No harm should be done nor reciprocated, 51
No obedience is due to creatures in disobedience of Allah, 118
No obedience is due to whoever does not obey Allah, 61
No one greets me except Allah has returned my soul to me… 203
No one in Makka prayed more than him [Abū Ḥanīfa]… 107
No people gather for the remembrance of Allah except… 152
No people gather while some of them make invocation… 155
None enters Hellfire who prays before sunrise and before sunset, 120
None is assiduous in keeping *ṣalāt al-ḍuḥā* except… 171
None was ever born in Islam purer than Abū Bakr then ʿUmar, (ʿAlī) 48
[The] number of *rakʿas* in the congregational *tarāwīḥ* is twenty (Rightly-Guided Caliphs), 126
O Allah! The Fire made all sleep leave me (Shaddād ibn Aws), 100
O Allah, I ask You by the fact that I testify… (unnamed Companion), 85
O Allah, if You ever granted to anyone prayer in the grave (Thābit), 105
O Allah! Our Lord and the Lord of everything! 154
O Allah, save me from the Fire! (Ṣila), 105
Obedience is only in good matters, 61, 118
Ostracism of Kaʿb ibn Mālik and others for fifty days, 120

Our Lord! To You belongs all praise... (Rifā'a), 81
Pass judgment according to what is in the Book of Allah
Ibn Mas'ūd, 49
'Umar, 47
People did not innovate anything dearer to me... (Ibn 'Umar), 128, 176, 207
[The] people of *Fiqh* and Religion... (Ibn 'Abbās and others), 27
People shall be in a good state as long as... (Ibn Mas'ūd *et al.*), 29, 214
People used to ask the Messenger about the good... (Hudhayfa), 53
People who were communicated to although they were not prophets, 36
People whom Allah chose for His Prophet's company...
(Ibn Mas'ūd), 52, 58
Praise to Allah Who has graced the messenger of the Messenger... 51
Pray as you have seen me pray, 82, 219
Prayer in their own homes is better for them, 161
Prayer is better than sleep (Bilāl), 85
Prayer is goodness at your disposal, 94, 206
Prayer is a light, 94, 206
Praying all night
Abū Bakr ibn 'Ayyāsh, 112
Aḥmad, 111
Abū al-Ḥārith al-Madanī, 112
Ibrāhīm ibn Ad-ham, 110
Shaddād ibn Aws, 100
Ṣila, 105
Thābit al-Bunānī, 105
Prohibition of singling out the night of Jumu'a and its day, 207
[The] Prophet ﷺ banged the pulpit with his staff during *khuṭba*... 102
[The] Prophet ﷺ did not cease to make *qunūt*... 156
[The] Prophet ﷺ forbade the shunning of one Muslim by another... 120
[The] Prophet ﷺ forbade the visitation of graves, then permitted it... 187
[The] Prophet ﷺ passed by Prophets followed by their nations... 55
[The] Prophet ﷺ placed a rock on 'Uthmān ibn Maẓ'ūn's grave, 190, 197

[The] Prophet ﷺ prayed it [*al-ḍuḥā*] the morning he entered Makka, 168
[The] Prophet ﷺ said *Āmīn* to our supplication, 145
[The] Prophet ﷺ said: "O Allah! Our Lord" after every prayer, 154
[The] Prophet ﷺ used to defer his departure so ladies leave first, 164
[The] Prophet ﷺ used to fast three days of every month but… 211
[The] Prophet ﷺ used to visit the graveyard of the martyrs… 185
[The] Prophet ﷺ would not pray *ḍuḥā* except returning from a trip, 175
[The] Prophet's ﷺ praise of women, 225-226
Pursuing the highest *isnād* is part of the Religion (Aḥmad), 23
[The] Qur'ān was revealed and the Messenger instituted *Sunan*… ('Imrān ibn Ḥuṣayn), 55
Raise your hands and say *Lā ilāha illAllah*, 145
Raising Hands with *Takbīr* in the *Qunūt* of *Witr*
- 'Alī, 102
- al-Barā', 102
- Ibn 'Abbās, 102
- Ibn Mas'ūd, 102
- Ibn 'Umar, 102
- 'Umar, 102

Rajab is the month of Allah, Sha'bān is my month, and Ramaḍān… 209
Ramaḍān is the month of my *Umma*… 211
Recite [pl.] the Qur'ān and ask Allah with it… 151
Reciting a single verse over and over inside Prayer
- The Prophet ﷺ, 98
- Abū Ḥanīfa, 99
- 'Ā'isha and Asmā', 99
- al-Ḍaḥḥāk, 99
- Ibn Mas'ūd, 99
- Sa'īd ibn Jubayr, 99

Religion does not disappear except… (al-Awzā'ī), 23
Religion is ease, 12
Religion is nothing but imitation itself (Aḥmad), 43

Remembering your good qualities and forgetting bad ones is delusion (Bilāl ibn Sa'd al-Ash'arī), 103
Remit them to Abū Bakr! 33
Remit them to 'Umar! 33
Remit them to 'Uthmān! 33
Rise forgiven, your evil deeds have been changed into good deeds! 151
[A] ruling is one of two kinds (Mālik), 59
Safīna alighted on a desert island after a shipwreck… 65
Al-Salāmu 'alaynā min Rabbinā (Ibn Mas'ūd), 88
Ṣalāt al-awwābīn is between *maghrib* and *'ishā*… (Ibn 'Umar), 178
Ṣalāt al-awwābīn when the young camels' hoofs burn from the heat, 170
Ṣalāt al-ḍuḥā, 166-177
Ṣalāt al-ḍuḥā is in the Book of Allah… (Ibn 'Abbās), 168
[The] *Sawād al-A'ẓam*… 54
Seawater is pure and purifying, 51
Servants of Allah! Pray the *ḍuḥā* prayer ('Umar), 177
Serving a Muslim in need for one hour is better than…58
Sha'bān is my month and Ramaḍān is the month of Allah, 211
Al-Shāfi'ī used to pray next to Imām Abū Ḥanīfa's grave… 195
Shaking hands (Ash'arīs), 87
[The] simile of the people of learning on the earth… stars in the sky, 44
Something we have used at the beginning… (al-Ḥasan), 101
Standing in prayer in Ramaḍān is an innovation (Abū Umāma), 127
[The] stars are trustees for the heaven… 40
[The] staunchest in the Religion of Allah is 'Umar, 39
Steadfastness is only at the first shock, 189
Stick to whatever 'Umar innovates, 68
[The] straight path is that upon which 'Umar was… (Ibn Mas'ūd), 69
Successorship after me shall last for thirty years… 37, 65
Successorship of prophethood, 34-38
[The] *Sunan* have been instituted for you… ('Umar), 47
Sunna and *Jamā'a* are defined by… (Abū Ḥanīfa), 25

[The] Sunna is the commentary of the Qur'ān (Aḥmad), 20
[The] Sunna consists in reports from the Messenger (Aḥmad), 20
[The] Sunna in Islam is more rare and precious... (Ibn ʿAyyāsh), 19
[The] supplicant and the one who says *Āmīn* are partners in reward, 150
Take for your leaders the two that come after me, 32, 36, 62, 65
Take half your religion from the fair little one [ʿĀ'isha], 219
Tamīm al-Dārī was the first *qāṣṣ* in Islam, 92
Tamīm was the first to install lighting in mosques, 98
Tamīm would recite the entire Qur'ān in a single *rakʿa*, 98
Tell him Allah ﷻ loves him, 82
There are three hundred and sixty joints in a human being... 173
There is no emigration after victory but... 25
There is no harm in touching or kissing the Prophet's grave (Aḥmad), 196
There shall be Prophethood among you then... successorship, 34-38, 65
There will be kingship and tyranny, 66
There will be Prophethood among you for as long as Allah wishes... 65
They [Ibn Masʿūd's legs] shall be heavier in the Balance than Uḥud, 64
[Truly] this black seed is a cure for every disease except death, 120
This is the most difficult question... ever put to me (Ibn Masʿūd), 49
This is the night of bowing (Uways al-Qaranī), 104
This is Ṭayba [Madīna]! This is Ṭayba! This is Ṭayba! 102
[Truly] this knowledge is our religion, 23
This man [ʿUthmān] shall follow right guidance... 39
This matter shall not be terminated until... twelve Caliphs, 38
This son of mine – al-Ḥasan – is a leader among men... 38, 182
This was not done before! (Ubay), 92
Those closest to me are those who guard themselves from Allah ﷻ... 184
Those that obey Allah ﷻ and teach others... (Ibn ʿAbbās and others), 27
Those who are in command (Abū Hurayra), 27
Those whom people look at and take (knowledge) from (ʿUmar), 43
Three types of persons give *fatwas*... (Ḥudhayfa ibn al-Yamān), 55
Today a man came to me asking... (Ibn Masʿūd), 28

Today you are none other than a ship (*Safīna*), 65
Tomorrow shall come to you a people more sensitive in their hearts, 87
Tomorrow we meet our beloved ones… (Ash'arīs), 87
Treat women kindly, 222
[The most] truthful in his modesty is 'Uthmān, 39
Twelve Caliphs, all of them from Quraysh… 38
Ubay is the most proficient in the Qur'ānic readings, 39
'Umar banned loiterers from the Mosque after the last prayer… 160
'Umar came and the bucket turned into a huge pail… 34, 35, 69
[Truly] 'Umar followed the straightest way ('Alī), 37
'Umar is among those in authority ('Ikrima), 69
'Umar patrolled the mosque after '*ishā*', 148
'Umar was the first to gather the people… ('Urwa), 126
[Truly] 'Umar was a wise leader ('Alī), 68
'Umar would pray '*ishā* then enter his house and not cease praying… 95
'Uthmān had men and women all pray behind a single *imām*…161
'Uthmān introduced the second *adhān*, 92
'Uthmān prevented the female *jamā'a* from budging until… 164
[The] way to Allah is closed except… (al-Junayd), 22
We have fled to the Messenger of Allah to get away from the fire… 118
We shall make you glad concerning your Community (ḥadīth *qudsī*), 99
What a fine innovation it [the *ḍuḥā* prayer] is! (Ibn 'Umar), 128, 176
What a fine innovation this is! ('Umar), 92, 125, 129-133
What if it is not in the Sunna…? 50
What is the best trait in women? 165
What the Messenger and his Two Companions instituted… 35, 68
Whatever Ibn Mas'ūd narrates to you, believe it! 32, 63
Whatever the Muslims consider right… (Ibn Mas'ūd), 46, 121
When certain narrators used lies, we used history… (Sufyān), 23
When I supplicate, you all say *Āmīn*, 151
When the Negus died, we were told a light would be seen at his grave, 197
When the shadows lean and the souls go forth… 171

When the verse {*When comes the Help of Allah*} was revealed..., 25
When they start taking [knowledge] from their boys...
(Ibn Mas'ūd), 29, 214
When you hear the Imām say: *wa-lā al-ḍallīn*, say: *Āmīn*, 156
When you see disagreement, you must stay with the largest mass, 53
When you invoke blessings on your Prophet, invoke in the best way, 181
When you visit a sick person or a dead one... 147
Whenever Ibn 'Abbās was asked about something... (Ibn Abī Yazīd), 50
Where is the grave of my brother? ('Ā'isha), 188
Whoever begins something good then others practice it... 122-123
Whoever dissents from them [the *Jamā'a*] departs to Hell, 53
Whoever fasts all his life, the Fire shall straiten him for this much, 96
Whoever fasts all his life has neither fasted nor broken his fast, 96
Whoever fights 'Ammār, Allah fights him, 63
Whoever gets up when the sun is before his eyes... 170
Whoever innovates a good Sunna... 139
Whoever innovates an innovation of misguidance... 125, 139
Whoever innovates in this Matter of ours... 124
Whoever innovates something new or abets someone who does... 125
Whoever institutes a good practice...75-76, 121-124, 134
Whoever missed something of his regular nightly devotion... 167
Whoever of you lives shall live to see great divisions... 60
Whoever of you must sing, let him sing such things ('Umar), 100
Whoever of you sees wrongdoing, let him change it... 213
Whoever prays between *maghrib* and *'ishā*... 177
Whoever prays the *fajr* prayer then sits in his place until sunrise... 169
Whoever regularly prays the two *rak'as* of *ḍuḥā*... 173
Whoever says the Qur'ān is created is an innovator (Ibn 'Ulayya), 128
Whoever visits my grave, my intercession becomes guaranteed... 184, 203
Whoever wants to visit graves... 190
Whoever wishes to follow the Sunna... (Ibn Mas'ūd and Ibn 'Umar), 52
Whoever you [Companions] commend, Paradise is guaranteed... 45

With these two *rak'as* you [Bilāl] entered Paradise, 80
Woman is created from a rib... 221
Woman is nakedness... 163
[The] worst of all matters are newfangled matters... 114
Write it for Abū Shāh! 86
Yā Muḥammad! (Khubayb), 91
You [Zayd] are my freedman, 74
You ['Alī] are part of me and I am part of you, 74
You [ﷺ] are sending me to people who are older than me... ('Alī), 39
You [Companions] are the witnesses of Allah ﷻ on earth... 45
You have been left upon the crystal-clear path... ('Umar), 47
You have tried me with the trial of the Prophets... (Fatḥ ibn Sa'īd), 111
You imitate whomever of [the Companions] you like (Aḥmad), 43
You must follow my Sunna and the Sunna of the Rightly-Guided... 30, 32, 60
You must pray the two *rak'as* of *ḍuḥā*... 212
You must stay with the greatest mass, 140
You must stick with the largest mass (Abū Umāma), 54
You [Ja'far] resemble me physically and morally, 74
You shall not impose upon the servants ofAllah ﷻ... (Ibn Mas'ūd), 177
Your affairs will be ruled by men who shall extinguish the Sunna... 62
Your best *ṣalāt* is that prayed in your homes... 175
Your Lord gives, on certain of your days, fragrant gifts... 153
Your Lord said: 'Son of Ādam, pray for Me four *rak'as*...' 169
Your love for it [Sūrat al-Ikhlāṣ] shall cause you to enter Paradise, 82

Bibliography

ʿAbd ibn Ḥumayd. *Musnad.* Eds. Subḥī al-Badrī al-Sāmarrāʾī and Maḥmūd al-Saʿīdī. Cairo: Maktabat al-Sunna, 1988.

ʿAbd al-Khāliq, ʿAbd al-Ghanī. *Ḥujjiyyat al-Sunna.* Herndon, VA: Dār al-Wafāʾ, 1993.

ʿAbd al-Razzāq. *Al-Muṣannaf.* 11 vols. Ed. Ḥabīb al-Raḥmān al-Aʿẓamī. Beirut: al-Maktab al-Islāmī, 1983. With Maʿmar ibn Rāshid al-Azdī's *Kitāb al-Jāmiʿ* as the last two volumes.

———. *Tafsīr al-Qurʾān.* 3 vols. Ed. Muṣṭafā Muslim Muḥammad. Ryad: Maktabat al-Rushd, 1990.

Abū Dāwūd. *Sunan.* 3 vols. Ed. Muḥammad Fuʾād ʿAbd al-Bāqī. Beirut: Dār al-Kutub al-ʿIlmiyya, 1996. See also al-ʿAẓīm Ābādī, *ʿAwn al-Maʿbūd.*

Abū Ghudda, ʿAbd al-Fattāḥ. *Thalāth Rasāʾil fī Faḍl al-Duʿāʾ wa-Rafʿ al-Yadayn fīhi baʿd al-Ṣalawāt al-Maktūba li-Thalāthatin min Kibār al-Fuqahāʾ al-Muḥaddithīn.* Containing his abridgment of al-Tatawī al-Sindī's *al-Tuḥfat al-Marghūba fī Afḍaliyyat al-Duʿāʾ baʿd al-Maktūba*; Aḥmad al-Ghumārī's *al-Minaḥ al-Maṭlūba fī Istiḥbāb Rafʿ al-Yadayn fil-Duʿāʾ baʿd al-Ṣalawāt al-Maktūba*; and Muḥammad ibn ʿAbd al-Raḥmān al-Ahdal's *Sunniyyat Rafʿ al-Yadayn fil-Duʿāʾ baʿd al-Ṣalawāt al-Maktūba.* Aleppo: Maktab al-Manshūrāt al-Islāmiyya, 1997.

Abū Nuʿaym al-Aṣfahānī. [*Al-Muntakhab min*] *Dalāʾil al-Nubuwwa.* 4th ed. Eds. Muḥammad Rawwās Qalʿajī and ʿAbd al-Barr ʿAbbās. Beirut: Dār al-Nafāʾis, 1999.

———. *Dhikr Akhbār Aṣbahān.* 2 vols. Ed. Sven Dedering. Leiden: Brill, 1931-1934.

———. *Ḥilyat al-Awliyāʾ wa-Ṭabaqāt al-Aṣfiyāʾ.* 12 vols. Ed. Muṣṭafā ʿAbd al-Qādir ʿAṭā. Beirut: Dār al-Kutub al-ʿIlmiyya, 1997.

———. *Maʿrifat al-Ṣaḥāba.* 6 vols. Ed. ʿĀdil ibn Yūsuf al-ʿAzāzī. Ryadh: Dār al-Waṭan, 1998.

Abū Shāma. *Al-Bāʿith ʿalā Inkār al-Bidaʿ wal-Ḥawādith.* Ed. Ḥasan Mashhūr Salmān. Ryadh: 1990.

———. *Al-Bāʿith ʿalā Inkār al-Bidaʿ wal-Ḥawādith.* Ed. ʿUthmān Aḥmad ʿAnbar. Cairo: Dār al-Hudā, 1978.

Abū al-Shaykh [Ibn Ḥayyān al-Aṣbahānī]. *Al-Amthāl fil-Ḥadīth al-Nabawī*. Ed. ʿAbd al-ʿAlī ʿAbd al-Majīd Ḥāmid. 2nd ed. Bombay: al-Dār al-Salafiyya, 1988.

Abū Yaʿlā al-Mawṣilī. *Musnad*. 13 vols. Ed. Ḥusayn Salīm Asad. Damascus: Dār al-Ma'mūn līl-Turāth, 1984.

Abū Yūsuf. *Al-Āthār*. Ed. Abū al-Wafā al-Afghānī. Hyderabad al-Dakn: Iḥyā' al-Maʿārif al-ʿUthmāniyya, 1355/1936.

Al-Aḥdab, Khaldūn. *Zawā'id Tārīkh Baghdād ʿalā al-Kutub al-Sitta*. 10 vols. Damascus: Dār al-Qalam, 1996.

Aḥmad ibn Ḥanbal. *Faḍā'il al-Ṣaḥāba*. 2 vols. Ed. Waṣī Allāh Muḥammad ʿAbbās. Beirut: Mu'assasat al-Risāla, 1983.

———. *Al-Musnad*. 20 vols. Ed. Aḥmad Shākir and Ḥamza Aḥmad al-Zayn. Cairo: Dār al-Ḥadīth, 1995.

———. *Al-Musnad*. 50 vols. Ed. Shuʿayb al-Arna'ūṭ. Beirut: Mu'assasat al-Risāla, 2000-2001.

Al-ʿAjlūnī. *Kashf al-Khafā*. 2nd ed. 2 vols. Beirut: Dār Iḥyā' al-Turāth al-ʿArabī, 1932.

Al-Ājurrī. *Al-Sharīʿa*. Ed. ʿAbd al-Razzāq al-Mahdī. Beirut: Dār al-Kitāb al-ʿArabī, 1996.

Al-ʿAlā'ī. *Jāmiʿ al-Taḥṣīl fī Aḥkām al-Marāsīl*. Ed. Ḥamdī ʿAbd al-Majīd al-Salafī. 3rd ed. Beirut: ʿĀlam al-Kutub, 2005.

Al-Arna'ūṭ, Shuʿayb and Bashshār ʿAwwād Maʿrūf. *Taḥrīr Taqrīb al-Tahdhīb*. 4 vols. Beirut: Mu'assasat al-Risāla, 1997.

ʿAwwāma, Muḥammad. *Adab al-Ikhtilāf*. 2nd ed. Beirut: Dār al-Bashā'ir al-Islāmiyya, 1997.

———. *Athar al-Ḥadīth al-Sharīf fī Ikhtilāf al-A'immat al-Fuqahā' RaḍyAllāhu ʿAnhum*. 4th ed. Beirut: Dār al-Bashā'ir al-Islāmiyya, 1997.

Al-ʿAyta, Durriya. *Fiqh al- ʿIbādāt ʿalā al-Madhhab al-Shāfiʿī*. Damascus, 1989.

Al-Azdī, al-Rabīʿ ibn Ḥabīb. *Al-Jāmiʿ al-Ṣaḥīḥ: Musnad al-Imām al-Rabīʿ ibn Ḥabīb al-Azdī*. Beirut: Dār al-Fatḥ and Masqaṭ: Maktabat al-Istiqāma, 1979.

Al-ʿAẓīm Ābādī, Muḥammad Shams al-Ḥaqq. *ʿAwn al-Maʿbūd Sharḥ Sunan Abī Dāwūd*. 14 vols. in 7. Beirut: Dār al-Kutub al-ʿIlmiyya, n.d. Includes Abū Dāwūd's *Sunan* and Ibn al-Qayyim's *Tahdhīb Sunan Abī Dāwūd*.

Al-Baghawī. *Sharḥ al-Sunna*. 8 vols. Eds. Shuʿayb al-Arnaʾūṭ and Zuhayr al-Shāwīsh. Beirut: al-Maktab al-Islāmī, 1971.

Al-Bājūrī. *Ḥāshiya ʿalā Fatḥ al-Qarīb*. 2 vols. Bulāq, 1288/1871.

Bakr Abū Zayd. *Al-Ajzāʾ al-Ḥadīthiyya*. Riyadh: Dār al-ʿĀṣima, 1996.

Al-Bārihbankawī, Muḥammad Ilyās. *Sharḥ Ḥayāt al-Ṣaḥāba lil-Kāndihlawī*. 4 vols. Damascus and Beirut: Dār Ibn Kathīr, 2000.

Al-Bayhaqī. *Al-Asmāʾ wal-Ṣifāt*. 2 vols. Ed. ʿAbd Allāh al-Ḥāshidī. Riyad: Maktabat al-Sawādī, 1993.

———. *Dalāʾil al-Nubuwwa wa-Maʿrifat Aḥwāl Ṣāḥib al-Sharīʿa*. 7 vols. Ed. ʿAbd al-Muʿṭī Qalʿajī. Beirut: Dār al-Kutub al-ʿIlmiyya, 1985.

———. *Faḍāʾil al-Awqāt*. Ed. ʿAdnān ʿAbd al-Raḥmān Mājid al-Qaysī. Makka: Maktabat al-Manāra, 1990.

———. *Al-Iʿtiqād ʿalā Madhhab al-Salaf Ahl al-Sunna wal-Jamāʿa*. Beirut: Dār al-Afāq al-Jadīda, 1981; 2nd ed. Dār al-Kutub al-ʿIlmiyya, 1986.

———. *Al-Madkhal ilā al-Sunan al-Kubrā*. Ed. Muḥammad Ḍiyāʾ al-Raḥmān al-Aʿẓamī. Al-Kuwait: Dār al-Khulafāʾ līl-Kitāb al-Islāmī, 1984. 2nd ed. 2 vols. Riyadh: Maktabat Aḍwāʾ al-Salaf, 1990.

———. *Manāqib al-Shāfiʿī*. 2 vols. Ed. Aḥmad Saqr. Cairo: Dār al-Turāth, n. d.

———. *Maʿrifat al-Sunan wal-Āthār*. 15 vols. Ed. ʿAbd al-Muʿṭī Amīn Qalʿajī. Aleppo and Cairo: Dār al-Waʿī, 1991.

———. *Shuʿab al-Īmān*. 8 vols. Ed. Muḥammad Zaghlūl. Beirut: Dār al-Kutub al-ʿIlmiyya, 1990.

———. *Al-Sunan al-Kubrā*. 10 vols. Ed. Muḥammad ʿAbd al-Qādir ʿAta. Makka: Maktaba Dār al-Baz, 1994.

Al-Bazzār. *Al-Musnad*. [*Al-Baḥr al-Zakhkhār*.] 9 vols. Ed. Maḥfūẓ al-Raḥmān Zayn Allāh. Beirut and Madīna: Muʾassasat ʿUlūm al-Qurʾān & Maktabat al-ʿUlūm wal-Ḥikam, 1989.

———. *Mukhtaṣar al-Musnad*. See Ibn Ḥajar, *Mukhtaṣar Zawāʾid Musnad al-Bazzār*.

Al-Bukhārī. *Al-Adab al-Mufrad*. 3rd ed. Ed. Muḥammad Fuʾād ʿAbd al-Bāqī. Beirut: Dār al-Bashāʾir al-Islāmiyya, 1989.

———. *Al-Kunā: Juzʾ min al-Tārīkh al-Kabīr*. Hyderābād: Dāʾirat al-Maʿārif al-ʿUthmāniyya, 1360/1941. Repr. Beirut: Dār al-Kutub al-ʿIlmiyya, 1983.

———. *Ṣaḥīḥ*. 8 vols. in 3rd Ed. Muḥammad al-Zuhrī al-Ghamrāwī. Bulāq: al-Maṭba'at al-Kubrā al-Amīriyya, 1314/1896. Repr. Cairo: al-Maṭba'at al-Maymūniyya [Muṣṭafā Bābā al-Ḥalabī *et al.*], 1323/1905.

———. *Ṣaḥīḥ*. See Ibn Ḥajar, *Fatḥ al-Bārī*.

———. *Al-Tārīkh al-Kabīr*. 8 vols. Ed. al-Sayyid Hāshim al-Nadwī. Beirut: Dār al-Fikr, n.d.

Al-Būṣīrī. *Miṣbāḥ al-Zujāja fī Zawā'id Ibn Mājah*. 2nd ed. 4 vols. Ed. Muḥammad al-Muntaqā al-Kashnawī. Beirut: Dār al-'Arabiyya, 1983.

Al-Dāraquṭnī. *Al-'Ilal*. 9 vols. Ed. Maḥfūẓ al-Raḥmān Zayn Allāh al-Salafī. Ryad: Dār Tiba, 1985.

———. *Su'ālāt Ḥamza ibn Yūsuf al-Sahmī*. Ed. Muwaffaq ibn 'Abd Allāh ibn 'Abd al-Qādir. Riyadh: Maktabat al-Ma'ārif, 1984.

———. *Sunan*. 4 vols. in 2. Together with Muḥammad Shams al-Ḥaqq al-'Aẓīm Ābādī's *al-Ta'līq al-Mughnī*. Ed. Al-Sayyid 'Abd Allāh Hashim Yamānī al-Madanī. Beirut: Dār al-Ma'rifa, 1966. Repr. Beirut: Dār Ihyā al-Turāth al-'Arabī, 1993.

Al-Dārimī. [*Al-Musnad al-Jāmi'*.] *Fatḥ al-Mannān Sharḥ wa-Taḥqīq Kitāb al-Dārimī al-Musammā bil-Musnad al-Jāmi'*. 10 vols. Ed. Abū 'Āṣim Nabīl Hāshim al-Ghamrī. Makka and Beirut: al-Maktba al-Makkiyya and Dār al-Bashā'ir al-Islāmiyya, 1999.

———. *Musnad* [*Sunan*]. 2 vols. Ed. Fu'ād Aḥmad Zamarlī and Khālid al-Sab' al-'Ilmī. Beirut: Dār al-Kitāb al-'Arabī, 1987.

Al-Daylamī, Shahradār ibn Shīrūyah ibn Shahradār. *Musnad al-Firdaws*. See Ibn Ḥajar, *Tasdīd al-Qaws*.

Al-Daylamī, Shīrūyah ibn Shahradār. *Firdaws al-Akhbār bi-Ma'thūr al-Khiṭāb 'alā Kitāb al-Shihāb*. Ed. Fawwāz Aḥmad al-Zayralī and Muḥammad al-Mu'taṣim Billāh al-Baghdādī. Beirut: Dār al-Kitāb al-'Arabī, 1987.

Al-Dhahabī. *Al-'Ibar fī Khabar Man 'Abar*. 4 vols. Ed. Muḥammad ibn Basiuni Zaghlūl. Beirut: Dār al-Kutub al-'Ilmiyya, n.d. [Uncredited reprint of an earlier edition.]

———. *Manāqib al-Imām Abī Ḥanīfata wa-Ṣaḥibayhi Abī Yūsuf wa-Muḥammad ibn al-Ḥasan*. Beirut: Dār al-Bashā'ir al-Islāmiyya, 1996.

———. *Ma'rifat al-Qurrā' al-Kibār 'alā al-Ṭabaqāt wal-A'ṣār*. 2 vols. Ed. Bashshār 'Awwād Ma'rūf, Shu'ayb al-Arna'ūṭ, and Ṣāliḥ Mahdī 'Abbās. Beirut: Mu'assasat al-Risāla, 1984.

———. *Mīzān al-I'tidāl*. 4 vols. Ed. 'Alī Muḥammad al-Bajawī. Beirut: Dār al-Ma'rifa, 1963.

———. *Mīzān al-I'tidāl*. 8 vols. Eds. 'Alī Muḥammad Mu'awwaḍ and 'Ādil 'Abd al-Mawjūd. Beirut: Dār al-Kutub al-'Ilmiyya, 1995.

———. *Al-Mu'jam al-Mukhtaṣṣ bil-Muḥaddithīn*. Ed. Muḥammad al-Ḥabīb al-Hayla. Ṭā'if: Maktabat al-Ṣiddīq, 1988.

———. *Siyar A'lām al-Nubalā'*. 19 vols. Ed. Muḥibb al-Dīn al-'Amrāwī. Beirut: Dār al-Fikr, 1996.

———. *Siyar A'lām al-Nubalā'*. 23 vols. Ed. Shu'ayb al-Arna'ūṭ and Muḥammad Na'īm al-'Araqsusī. Beirut: Mu'assasat al-Risāla, 1992-1993.

———. *Tadhkirat al-Ḥuffāẓ*. 4 vols. in 2nd Ed. 'Abd al-Raḥmān ibn Yaḥyā al-Mu'allimī. A fifth volume, titled *Dhayl Tadhkirat al-Ḥuffāẓ*, consists in al-Ḥusaynī's *Dhayl Tadhkirat al-Ḥuffāẓ*, Muḥammad ibn Fahd al-Makkī's *Lahẓ al-Alḥāẓ bi-Dhayl Tadhkirat al-Ḥuffāẓ*, and al-Suyūṭī's *Dhayl Ṭabaqāt al-Ḥuffāẓ*. Ed. Muḥammad Zāhid al-Kawtharī. Beirut: Dār Iḥyā' al-Turāth al-'Arabī and Dār al-Kutub al-'Ilmiyya, n.d. Reprint of the 1968 Hyderabad edition.

———. *Tārīkh al-Islām wa-Wafayāt al-Mashāhīr wal-A'lām*. 52 vols. Ed. 'Umar 'Abd al-Salām Tadmurī. Beirut: Dār al-Kitāb al-'Arabī, 1989-2000.

———. *Tartīb al-Mawḍū'āt li-Ibn al-Jawzī*. Ed. Kamāl ibn Basyūnī Zaghlūl. Beirut: Dār al-Kutub al-'Ilmiyya, 1994.

Diyāb, 'Abd al-Qādir 'Īsā. *Al-Mīzān al-'Ādil li-Tamyīz al-Ḥaqq min al-Bāṭil*. 1978. 2nd ed. Ma'arrat al-Nu'mān: Maktabat al-Imām al-Nawawī, 1997.

Al-Dūlābī. *Al-Kunā wal-Asmā'*. 2 vols. in 1. Hyderābād: Dā'irat al-Ma'ārif al-'Uthmāniyya, 1322/1904. Repr. Beirut: Dār al-Kutub al-'Ilmiyya, 1983.

Encyclopedia of Islamic Doctrine. See Kabbani.

Al-Fākihī. *Akhbār Makka fī Qadīm al-Dahr wa-Ḥadīthih*. 6 vols. 2nd ed. Ed. 'Abd al-Mālik 'Abd Allāh Duhaysh. Beirut: Dār Khiḍr, 1994.

Al-Fārisī, Muḥtāyin al-Ḥājj 'Abd Allāh. *Al-Nūr al-Lāmi' fī Ma'thūr al-Mawlid al-Nabawī al-Jāmi'*. Al-Dār al-Bayḍā', 1999.

Ghāwjī al-Albānī, Wahbī Sulaymān. *Kalimatun 'Ilmiyyatun Hādiyatun fil-Bid'ati wa-Aḥkāmihā*. Beirut: Dār al-Imām Muslim, 1991.

Al-Ghazzālī. *Iḥyā' 'Ulūm al-Dīn*. 4 vols. 1374/1929. Repr. Beirut: 'Ālam al-Kutub, n.d.

Al-Ghumārī, 'Abd Allāh ibn Muḥammad ibn al-Ṣiddīq. *Al-Ibtihāj bi-Takhrīj Aḥādīth al-Minhāj*. With al-Bayḍāwī's *Minhāj al-Wuṣūl fī Ma'rifat 'Ilm al-Uṣūl*. Ed. Samīr Ṭaha al-Majdhūb. Beirut: 'Ālam al-Kutub, 1985.

Al-Ghumārī, Aḥmad ibn Muḥammad ibn al-Ṣiddīq. *Al-Mudāwī li-'Ilal al-Jāmi' al-Ṣaghīr wa-Sharḥay al-Munāwī*. 6 vols. Ed. Muṣṭafā Ṣabrī. Cairo al-Maktaba al-Makkiyya, 1996.

———. *Al-Mughīr 'alā al-Aḥādīth al-Mawḍū'a fīl-Jāmi' al-Ṣaghīr*. Cairo: Maktabat al-Qāhira, 1998. Reprint.

Al-Ḥaddād, 'Abd Allāh Maḥfūẓ Muḥammad Ba 'Alawī al-Ḥaḍramī. *Al-Sunna wal-Bid'a*. Damascus and Beirut: Dār al-Qalam and al-Dār al-Shamiyya, 1992.

Ḥaddād, Gibrīl Fouād. *The Four Imāms and Their Schools: Abū Ḥanīfa, Mālik, al-Shāfi'ī, Aḥmad ibn Ḥanbal*. Cambridge: Muslim Academic Trust.

———, trans. Ibn Jahbal al-Kilābī's *Refutation of Him [Ibn Taymiyya] Who Attributes Direction to Allāh*. Introduction by Shaykh Wahbī Sulaymān Ghāwjī al-Albānī. Birmingham: al-Qur'ān wal-Sunna Association.

———. *Mawlid: Celebrating the Birth of the Holy Prophet* ﷺ. Birmingham: al-Qur'ān wal-Sunna Association, 2002

Al-Ḥākim. *Al-Madkhal ilā al-Ṣaḥīḥ*. Ed. Rabī' Hādī al-Madkhalī. Beirut: Mu'assasat al-Risāla, 1984.

———. *Ma'rifat 'Ulūm al-Ḥadīth*, ed. Sayyid Mu'aẓẓam Ḥusayn. Dacca: n.p. 1935. Reprint Beirut: Dār al-Kutub al-'Ilmiyya, 1977.

———. *Al-Mustadrak 'alā al-Ṣaḥīḥayn*. With al-Dhahabī's *Talkhīṣ al-Mustadrak*. 5 vols. Indexes by Yūsuf 'Abd al-Raḥmān al-Mar'ashlī. Beirut: Dār al-Ma'rifa, 1986. Reprint of the 1334/1916 Hyderabad edition.

———. *Al-Mustadrak 'ala al-Ṣaḥīḥayn*. With al-Dhahabī's *Talkhīṣ al-Mustadrak*. 4 vols. Annotations by Muṣṭafā 'Abd al-Qādir 'Aṭā'. Beirut: Dār al-Kutub al-'Ilmiyya, 1990.

Al-Ḥakīm al-Tirmidhī. *Nawādir al-Uṣūl*. Beirut: Dār Sadir, n.d. Repr. of Istanbul ed.

Ḥaqqī, Ismāʿīl al-Bursawī. *Rūḥ al-Bayān*. 4 vols. Āsitāna: al-Maṭbaʿat al-ʿUthmāniyya, 1306/1888.

Al-Ḥārith ibn Abī Usāma. *Musnad*. [*Bughyat al-Bāḥith ʿan Zawāʾid Musnad al-Ḥārith*]. 2 vols. Ed. Ḥusayn Aḥmad Ṣāliḥ al-Bakirī. Madīna: Markaz Khidmat al-Sunna wal-Sīra al-Nabawiyya, 1992.

———. *Musnad*. [*Bughyat al-Bāḥith ʿan Zawāʾid Musnad al-Ḥārith*]. Ed. Musʿad ʿAbd al-Ḥamīd Muḥammad al-Saʿdānī. Beirut: Dār al-Ṭalāʾiʿ, n.d.

Al-Haytamī, Aḥmad (Ibn Ḥajar). *Al-Durr al-Manḍūd fīl-Ṣalāt wal-Salām ʿalā Ṣāḥib al-Maqām al-Maḥmūd* ﷺ. 2nd ed. S.n. Dār al-Madīna al-Munawwara, 1995.

———. *Al-Fatāwā al-Ḥadīthiyya*. Cairo: Muṣṭafā al-Bābā al-Ḥalabī, Repr. 1970, 1989.

———. *Al-Khayrāt al-Ḥisān fī Manāqib Abī Ḥanīfa al-Nuʿmān*. Cairo: Ḥalabī, 1326/1908.

———. *Al-Minhāj al-Qawīm fī Masāʾil al-Taʿlīm*. Ed. Muṣṭafā Saʿīd al-Khinn, Muṣṭafā Dīb al-Bughā, *et al.* 3rd ed. Damascus: Dār al-ʿUlūm al-Insāniyya, 1998.

———. *Al-Tabyīn fī Sharḥ al-Arbaʿīn*. Cairo: ʿĪsā al-Ḥalabī, n.d.

Al-Haythamī, Nūr al-Dīn. *Majmaʿ al-Zawāʾid wa-Manbaʿ al-Fawāʾid*. 10 vols. in 5. Cairo: Maktabat al-Qudsī, 1932-1934. Repr. Beirut: Dār al-Kitāb al-ʿArabī, 1967, 1982, and 1987.

———. *Mawārid al-Ẓamʾān ilā Zawāʾid Ibn Ḥibbān*. Ed. Muḥammad ʿAbd al-Razzāq Ḥamza. Beirut: Dār al-Kutub al-ʿIlmiyya, n.d.

———. *Zawāʾid Musnad al-Ḥārith*, see al-Ḥārith ibn Abī Usāma, *Musnad*.

Al-Ḥimyarī, ʿĪsā ibn Māniʿ. *Al-Bidʿatu al-Ḥasanatu Aṣlun min Uṣūli al-Tashrīʿ*. Beirut, Dār Qurṭuba, 2001.

Ibn ʿAbd al-Barr. *Al-Intiqāʾ fī Faḍāʾil al-Aʾimmati al-Thalāthati al-Fuqahāʾ: Mālik wal-Shāfiʿī wa-Abī Ḥanīfa*. Ed. ʿAbd al-Fattāḥ Abū Ghudda. Beirut: Dār al-Bashāʾir al-Islāmiyya, 1997.

———. *Al-Istīʿab fī Maʿrifat al-Aṣḥāb*. 8 vols. in 4th Ed. ʿAlī Muḥammad al-Bajawī. Beirut: Dār al-Jil, 1992.

———. *Jāmiʿ Bayān al-ʿIlm wa-Faḍlih*. 2 vols. Ed. Abū al-Ashbal al-Zuhayrī. Dammam: Dār Ibn al-Jawzī, 1994.

———. *Al-Tamhīd limā fil-Muwaṭṭa' min al-Ma'ānī wal-Asānīd.* 22 vols. Eds. Muṣṭafā ibn Aḥmad al-'Alawī, Muḥammad 'Abd al-Kabīr al-Bakrī. Morocco: Wizārat 'Umūm al-Awqāf wal-Shu'ūn al-Islāmiyya, 1967-1968.

Ibn 'Abd al-Salām. *Fatāwā.* Ed. 'Abd al-Raḥmān ibn 'Abd al-Fattāḥ. Beirut: Dār al-Ma'rifa, 1986.

———. *Al-Fatāwā al-Mawṣiliyya.* Ed. Iyād Khālid al-Ṭabbā'. Beirut and Damascus: Dār al-Fikr, 1999.

———. *Fatāwā Shaykh al-Islām 'Izz al-Dīn Ibn 'Abd al-Salām.* Ed. Muḥammad Jumu'a Kurdī. Beirut: Mu'assasat al-Risāla, 1996.

———. *Musājala 'Ilmiyya Bayn al-Imāmayn al-Jalīlayn al-'Izz ibn 'Abd al-Salām wa-Ibn al-Salāḥ.* Eds. Muḥammad Nāṣir al-Albānī and Zuhayr al-Shāwīsh. Beirut: al-Maktab al-Islāmī, 1961 and 1985.

———. [*Al-Qawā'id al-Kubrā.*] *Qawā'id al-Aḥkām fī Maṣāliḥ al-Anām.* 2 vols. Dār al-Sharq lil-Ṭibā'a, 1388/1968.

Ibn Abī 'Āṣim. *Al-Āḥād wal-Mathānī fī Faḍā'il al-Ṣaḥāba.* 6 vols. Ed. Bāsim Fayṣal al-Jawābira. Ryad: Dār al-Rāya, 1991.

———. *'Ilal al-Ḥadīth.* 2 vols. Ed. Muḥibb al-Dīn al-Khaṭīb. Beirut: Dār al-Ma'rifa, 1985.

———. *Al-Sunna.* Ed. Nāṣir al-Albānī. Beirut and Damascus: Al-Maktab al-Islāmī, 1993.

Ibn Abī Dāwūd. *Al-Maṣāḥif.* 2 vols. 2nd ed. Ed. Muḥibb al-Dīn 'Abd al-Sabḥān Wā'iẓ. Beirut: Dār al-Bashā'ir al-Islāmiyya, 2003.

Ibn Abī al-Dunyā. *Makārim al-Akhlāq.* Ed. Majdī al-Sayyid Ibrāhīm. Cairo: Maktabat al-Qur'ān, 1990.

Ibn Abī Ḥātim. *Al-Jarḥ wal-Ta'dīl.* 9 vols. Beirut: Dār Iḥyā' al-Turāth al-'Arabī, 1952.

Ibn Abī Shayba. *Al-Muṣannaf.* 7 vols. Ed. Kamāl al-Ḥūt. Ryadh: Maktabat al-Rushd, 1989.

Ibn Abī Ya'lā. *Ṭabaqāt al-Ḥanābila.* 2 vols. Ed. Muḥammad Ḥāmid al-Fiqqī. Cairo: Dār Iḥyā' al-Kutub al-'Arabiyya, n.d.

Ibn Abī Zayd al-Qayrawānī. *Al-Jāmi' fil-Sunan wal-Adab wal-Maghazi wal-Tārīkh.* Ed. M. Abū al-Ajfān and 'Uthmān Baṭṭīkh. Beirut: Mu'assasat al-Risāla; Tunis: al-Maktabat al-'Atīqa, 1982.

———. *Al-Risāla.* With al-'Adawī's *Ḥāshiya 'alā al-Risāla.* 2 vols. Ed. Yūsuf al-Shaykh Muḥammad al-Biqā'ī. Beirut: Dār al-Fikr, 1992.

Ibn ʿAdī. *Al-Kāmil fī Ḍuʿafāʾ al-Rijāl*. 7 vols. Ed. Yaḥyā Mukhtār Ghazawī. Beirut: Dār al-Fikr, 1988.

Ibn ʿAllān. *Al-Futūḥāt al-Rabbāniyya ʿalāl-Adhkār al-Nawawiyya*. 7 vols. in 4. Beirut: Dār al-Fikr, 1978.

Ibn al-ʿArabī, Abū Bakr. *ʿĀriḍat al-Aḥwadhī Sharḥ Sunan al-Tirmidhī*. 13 vols. Beirut, Dār al-Kutub al-ʿIlmiyya, n.d.

———. *Al-ʿAwāṣim min al-Qawāṣim fī Taḥqīq Mawāqif al-Ṣaḥāba baʿda Wafāt al-Nabī* ﷺ. Ed. Muḥibb al-Dīn al-Khaṭīb. Cairo: al-Maṭbaʿat al-Salafiyya, 1952.

Ibn ʿAsākir, Abū al-Qāsim. *Al-Arbaʿīn al-Buldāniyya*. Ed. Muḥammad Muṭīʿ al-Ḥāfiẓ. Beirut and Damascus: Dār al-Fikr, 1992.

———. *Tabyīn Kadhib al-Muftarī fīmā Nasaba ilā al-Imām Abī al-Ḥasan al-Ashʿarī*. Ed. Muḥammad Zāhid al-Kawtharī. Damascus: al-Qudsī, 1347/1929. Repr. Dār al-Fikr, 1979.

———. *Tārīkh Dimashq*. 70 vols. Damascus: Dār al-Fikr, 2000.

Ibn al-Athīr al-Jazarī. *Jāmiʿ al-Uṣūl fī Aḥādīth al-Rasūl*. 2nd ed. 12 vols. Ed. Muḥammad Ḥāmid al-Fiqqī. Beirut: Dār Iḥyāʾ al-Turāth al-ʿArabī, 1980.

———. *Jāmiʿ al-Uṣūl fī Aḥādīth al-Rasūl*. 11 vols. Ed. ʿAbd al-Qādir al-Arnaʾūṭ. Damascus: Ḥalwānī, 1973.

———. *Al-Lubāb fī Tahdhīb al-Ansāb*. 3 vols. Beirut: Dār Ṣādir, 1980.

———. *Al-Nihāya fī Gharīb al-Athar*. 5 vols. Eds. Ṭāhir Aḥmad al-Zāwī and Maḥmūd Muḥammad al-Ṭabbākhī. Beirut: Dār al-Fikr, 1979.

Ibn Ḥajar. *Al-Amāli al-Ḥalabiyya*. Ed. ʿAwwād al-Khalaf. Beirut: Muʾassasat al-Rayyān, 1996.

———. *Al-Dirāya fī Takhrīj Aḥādīth al-Hidāya*. 4 vols. Ed. ʿAbd Allāh Hāshim al-Yamānī. Beirut: Dār al-Maʿrifa, n.d.

———. *Fatḥ al-Bārī Sharḥ Ṣaḥīḥ al-Bukhārī*. 13 vols. Ed. Muḥammad Fuʾād ʿAbd al-Bāqī and Muḥibb al-Dīn al-Khaṭīb. Beirut: Dār al-Maʿrifa, 1959-1960.

———. *Ibidem*. Cairo: al-Maṭbaʿat al-Bahiyya, 1348/1929-1930.

———. *Al-Iṣāba fī Tamyīz al-Ṣaḥāba*. 8 vols in 4. Ed. ʿAlī Muḥammad al-Bijwī. Beirut: Dār al-Jīl, 1992.

———. *Lisān al-Mīzān*. 7 vols. Hyderabad: Dāʾirat al-Maʿārif al-Niẓāmiyya, 1329/1911. Repr. Beirut: Muʾassassat al-Aʿlamī, 1986.

———. *Al-Maṭālib al-ʿĀliya*. 4 vols. Kuwait, 1973.

———. *Mukhtaṣar Zawā'id Musnad al-Bazzār*. 2 vols. Ed. Ṣabrī ʿAbd al-Khāliq Abū Dharr. Beirut: Mu'assasat al-Kutub al-Thaqāfiyya, 1993.

———. *Tabyīn al-ʿAjab bi-mā Warada fī Faḍli Rajab*. Cairo: Maṭbaʿat al-Maʿāhid, 1351/1932.

———. *Tahdhīb al-Tahdhīb*. 14 vols. Hyderabad: Dā'irat al-Maʿārif al-Niẓāmiyya, 1327/1909. Repr. Beirut: Dār al-Fikr, 1984.

———. *Taḥrīr Taqrīb al-Tahdhīb*. 4 vols. By Bashshār ʿAwwād Maʿrūf and Shuʿayb al-Arna'ūṭ. Beirut: Mu'assasat al-Risāla, 1997.

———. *Taʿjīl al-Manfaʿa bi-Zawā'id Rijāl al-A'immat al-Arbaʿa*. Ed. Ikrām Allāh Imdād al-Ḥaqq. Beirut: Dār al-Kitāb al-ʿArabī, n.d.

———. *Talkhīṣ al-Ḥabīr*. 4 vols. Ed. Sayyid ʿAbd Allāh Hāshim al-Yamānī. Madīna, 1964. Repr. 4 vols. in 2, Cairo: Maktabat al-Kulliyāt al-Azhariyya, 1979.

———. *Taqrīb al-Tahdhīb*. Ed. Muḥammad ʿAwwāma. Aleppo: Dār al-Rashid, 1997.

———. *Tasdīd al-Qaws fī Tartīb Musnad al-Firdaws*. Ed. Muṣṭafā Sī Yaʿqūb. Madīna: al-Jāmiʿa al-Islāmiyya, 1986.

Ibn Ḥazm. *Al-Iḥkām fī Uṣūl al-Aḥkām*. 8 vols. Cairo: Dār al-Ḥadīth, 1984.

———. *Al-Muḥallā*. 11 vols. Beirut: Dār al-Āfāq al-Jadīda, n.d.

Ibn Ḥibbān. *Al-Majrūḥīn*. 3 vols. Ed. Maḥmūd Ibrāhīm Zāyid. Aleppo: Dār al-Waʿī, n.d.

———. *Ṣaḥīḥ Ibn Ḥibbān bi-Tartīb Ibn Balbān*. 18 vols. Ed. Shuʿayb al-Arna'ūṭ. Beirut: Mu'assasat al-Risāla, 1993.

———. *Al-Thiqāt*. Also known as *Tārīkh al-Thiqāt*. 9 vols. Ed. Sayyid Sharaf al-Dīn Aḥmad. N.p.: Dār al-Fikr, 1975.

Ibn al-ʿImād. *Shadharāt al-Dhahab fī Akhbār Man Dhahab*. 8 vols. Beirut: Dār Iḥyā' al-Turāth al-ʿArabī, n.d.

Ibn al-Jaʿd. *Musnad*. Ed. ʿĀmir Aḥmad Ḥaydar. Beirut: Mu'assasat Nādir, 1990.

Ibn al-Jawzī. *Gharīb al-Ḥadīth*. 2 vols. Ed. ʿAbd al-Muʿṭī Amīn Qalʿajī. Beirut: Dār al-Kutub al-ʿIlmiyya, 1985.

———. *Al-ʿIlal al-Mutanāhiya fil-Aḥādīth al-Wāhiya*. 2 vols. Ed. Shaykh Khalīl al-Mays. Beirut: Dār al-Kutub al-ʿIlmiyya, 1983.

———. *Manāqib al-Imām Aḥmad*. 2nd ed. Ed. Muḥammad Amīn al-Khanjī al-Kutbī. Beirut: Khanjī wa-Ḥamdān, 1349/1930-1931.

———. *Manāqib ʿUmar ibn al-Khaṭṭāb*. Ed. Zaynab Ibrāhīm al-Qārūṭ. 3rd ed. Beirut: Dār al-Kutub al-ʿIlmiyya, 1987.

———. *Al-Mawḍūʿāt*. 3 vols. Ed. ʿAbd al-Raḥmān Muḥammad ʿUthmān. Madīna: al-Maktabat al-Salafiyya, 1967. See also al-Dhahabī's *Tartīb al-Mawdūʿāt*.

———. *Al-Quṣṣāṣ wal-Mudhakkirīn*. Ed. Muḥammad Basyūnī Zaghlūl. Beirut: Dār al-Kutub al-ʿIlmiyya, 1986.

———. *Ṣayd al-Khāṭir*. Ed. "Board of Editors." Beirut: Dār al-Arqam, <1993?>.

———. *Ṣifat al-Ṣafwa*. 4 vols. 2nd ed. Eds. Maḥmūd Fākhūrī and Muḥammad Rawwās Qalʿajī. Beirut: Dār al-Maʿrifa, 1979.

———. *Al-Taḥqīq fī Aḥādīth al-Khilāf*. 2 vols. Eds. Musʿad ʿAbd al-Ḥamīd al-Saʿdanī and Muḥammad Fāris. Beirut: Dār al-Kutub al-ʿIlmiyya, 1994.

———. *Talbīs Iblīs*. Ed. Sayyid Jumaylī. Beirut: Dār al-Kitāb al-ʿArabī, 1985.

Ibn Kathīr. *Al-Bidāya wal-Nihāya*. 15 vols. Ed. Editing Board of al-Turāth. Beirut: Dār Iḥyā' al-Turāth al-ʿArabī, 1993.

———. *Ibid*. 14 vols. Beirut: Maktabat al-Maʿārif, n.d.

———. *Ikhtiṣār ʿUlūm al-Ḥadīth*. In Aḥmad Shākir, *al-Bāʿith al-Ḥathīth Sharḥ Ikhtiṣār ʿUlūm al-Ḥadīth*. Ed. Badīʿ al-Sayyid Laḥḥām. Damascus. Dār al-Fayḥā', 1994.

———. *Tafsīr al-Qur'ān al-ʿAẓīm*. 4 vols. Beirut: Dār al-Fikr, 1981.

———. *Tuḥfat al-Ṭālib bi-Maʿrifat Aḥādīth Ibn al-Ḥājib*. Ed. ʿAbd al-Ghanī ibn Ḥumayd ibn Maḥmūd al-Kubaysī. Makka: Dār Ḥirā', 1486.

Ibn Khallikān, *Wafayāt al-Aʿyān wa-Anbā' al-Zamān*. 8 vols. Ed. Iḥsān ʿAbbās. Beirut: Dār al-Thaqāfa, 1968.

Ibn Khuzayma. *Al-Ṣaḥīḥ*. 4 vols. Ed. Muḥammad Muṣṭafā al-Aʿẓamī. Beirut: Al-Maktab al-Islāmī, 1970.

Ibn Mājah. *Sunan*. 2 vols. Ed. Muḥammad Fu'ād ʿAbd al-Bāqī. Beirut: Dar al-Fikr, n.d.

Ibn al-Mubārak. *Al-Zuhd*. Ed. Ḥabīb al-Raḥmān al-Aʿẓamī. Beirut: Dār al-Kutub al-ʿIlmiyya, n.d.

Ibn Mufliḥ, Ibrāhīm. *Al-Maqṣad al-Arshad fī Dhikri Aṣḥāb al-Imām Aḥmad*. 3 vols. Ed. ʿAbd al-Raḥmān Sulaymān al-ʿUthaymīn. Riyadh: Maktabat al-Rushd, 1990.

Ibn al-Mulaqqin. *Tuḥfat al-Muḥtāj ilā Adillat al-Minhāj*. 2 vols. Ed. ʿAbd Allāh al-Laḥyānī. Makka: Dār Ḥirā', 1986.

Ibn al-Naqīb al-Miṣrī, Aḥmad. *ʿUmdat al-Sālik. Reliance of the Traveller*. Ed. and trans. Noah Ha Mim Keller. Dubai: Modern Printing Press, 1991.

Ibn Naṣr al-Marwazī. *Al-Sunna*. Ed. Sālim ibn Aḥmad al-Salafī. Beirut: Mu'assasat al-Kutub al-Thaqāfiyya, 1988.

Ibn Qayyim al-Jawziyya. *Iʿlām al-Muwaqqiʿīn ʿan Rabb al-ʿAlamīn*. 3 vols. Eds. Yūsuf Aḥmad al-Bakrī, Shākir Tawfīq al-ʿArūrī. Beirut: Dār Ibn Ḥazm, 1997.

———. *Iʿlām al-Muwaqqiʿīn ʿan Rabb al-ʿĀlamīn*. 4 vols. Ed. Ṭaha ʿAbd al-Ra'ūf Saʿd. Beirut: Dār al-Jīl, 1973.

———. *Jalā' al-Afhām fī Faḍl al-Ṣalāt wal-Salām ʿalā Muḥammadin Khayri al-Anām*. Ed. Muḥyī al-Dīn Mustū. 3rd ed. Beirut and Damascus: Dār al-Kalim al-Ṭayyib and Dār Ibn Kathīr, 1996.

———. *Tahdhīb Sunan Abī Dāwūd*. See al-ʿAẓīm Ābādī.

———. *Zād al-Maʿād fī Hadī Khayr al-ʿIbād*. 6 vols. 30th ed. Eds. ʿAbd al-Qādir al-Arna'ūṭ and Shuʿayb al-Arna'ūṭ. Beirut: Mu'assasat al-Risāla, 1997.

Ibn Qudāma, Muwaffaq al-Dīn. *Al-Mughnī fī Fiqh al-Imām Aḥmad ibn Ḥanbal al-Shaybānī*. 10 vols. Beirut: Dār al-Fikr, 1985; Dār al-Kitāb al-ʿArabī, 1994.

Ibn Rajab. *Dhayl Ṭabaqāt al-Ḥanābila*. 2 vols. Ed. Muḥammad Ḥāmid al-Fiqqī. Cairo: Dār Iḥyā' al-Kutub al-ʿArabiyya, n.d.

———. *Jāmiʿ al-ʿUlūm wal-Ḥikam*. 2 vols. Ed. Wahba al-Zuḥaylī. 2nd ed. Beirut: Dār al-Khayr, 1996.

———. *Jāmiʿ al-ʿUlūm wal-Ḥikam*. Ed. Shuʿayb al-Arna'ūṭ. Beirut: Mu'assasat al-Risāla, 1998[7].

———. *Laṭā'if al-Ma'ārif fīmā li-Mawāsim al-ʿĀm min al-Waẓā'if*. Ed. Yā Sīn Muḥammad al-Sawwās. Damascus and Beirut: 3rd ed. Dār Ibn Kathīr, 1996.

———. *Sharḥ ʿIlal al-Tirmidhī*. 2 vols. Ed. Nūr al-Dīn ʿItr. Damascus: Dār al-Mallāḥ, 1978.

Ibn Saʿd. *Al-Ṭabaqāt al-Kubrā*. 8 vols. Beirut: Dār Sadir, n.d.

Ibn al-Subkī. *Ṭabaqāt al-Shāfiʿiyya al-Kubrā*. 10 vols. Ed. Maḥmūd al-Ṭannāḥī and ʿAbd al-Fattāḥ al-Ḥilw. 2nd. ed. Jiza: Dār Hijr, 1992.

Al-ʿIrāqī, Walī al-Dīn. *Tuḥfat al-Taḥṣīl fī Dhikri Ruwāt al-Marāsīl*. Ed. ʿAbd Allāh Nawwāra. Ryādh: Maktabat al-Rushd, 1999.

Al-ʿIrāqī, Zayn al-Dīn. *Ṭarḥ al-Tathrīb fī Sharḥ al-Taqrīb*. 8 vols. in 4. Ed. Maḥmūd Ḥasan Rabīʿ. Beirut: Dār Iḥyā' al-Turāth al-ʿArabī, 1992. Repr. of the Cairo edition.

Al-Ishbīlī, Abū al-Khayr. *ʿUmdat al-Ṭabīb fī Maʿrifat al-Nabāt*. Ed. Muḥammad al-ʿArabī al-Khaṭṭābī. 2 vols. Beirut: Dār al-Gharb al-Islāmī, 1995.

Ismāʿīl al-Qāḍī al-Mālikī. *Faḍl al-Ṣalāt ʿalā al-Nabī* ﷺ. Ed. Muḥammad Nāṣir al-Albānī. Beirut: al-Maktab al-Islāmī, 1977[3].

ʿItr, Nūr al-Dīn. *Iʿlām al-Anām Sharḥ Bulūgh al-Marām*. 3 vols. Damascus: n.p., 1998-2004.

ʿIyāḍ. *Al-Shifā bi-Taʿrīf Ḥuqūq al-Muṣṭafā*. Ed. ʿAbduh ʿAlī Kawshak. Damascus and Beirut: Maktabat al-Ghazālī and Dār al-Fayḥā', 2000. Abridged by ʿAbd Allāh al-Talīdī, *Itḥāf Ahl al-Wafā' bi-Tahdhīb Kitāb al-Shifā*. Beirut: Dār al-Bashā'ir al-Islāmiyya, 2000. See also al-Qārī's *Sharḥ al-Shifā'*.

———. *Tartīb al-Madārik li-Maʿrifati Aʿlāmi Madhhabi Mālik*. 8 vols. Ed. Saʿīd Aḥmad Aʿrab. Al-Muḥammadiyya (Morocco): Ministry of Awqāf and Religious Affairs of the Kingdom of Maghreb, 1981-1983. Vols. 1-2: 2nd ed.

———. *Tartīb al-Madārik li-Maʿrifati Aʿlāmi Madhhabi Mālik*. 5 vols. in 3. Ed. Aḥmad Bakīr Maḥmūd. Beirut : Maktabat al-Ḥayāt, 1968.

Al-Jaṣṣāṣ. *Aḥkām al-Qur'ān*. 5 vols. Ed. Muḥammad al-Ṣādiq Qamḥāwī. Beirut: Dār Iḥyā' al-Turāth al-ʿArabī, 1985. Reprint.

Al-Jazīrī. *Al-Fiqh ʿalā al-Madhāhib al-Arbaʿa*. 5 vols. Beirut: Dār al-Kutub al-ʿIlmiyya, 1990.

Al-Jurjānī. *Al-Taʿrīfāt*. Ed. Ibrāhīm al-Abyārī. Beirut: Dār al-Kitāb al-ʿArabī, 1985.

Al-Jūzjānī. *Aḥwāl al-Rijāl*. Ed. Subḥī al-Badrī al-Sāmarrā'ī. Beirut: Mu'assasat al-Risāla, 1985.

Kabbānī, Hishām. *Encyclopedia of Islamic Doctrine*. 7 vols. Ed. G.F. Haddad. Mountain View: Al-Sunna Foundation of America, 1998.

Al-Kāndihlawī, Muḥammad Yūsuf. *Ḥayāt al-Ṣaḥāba*. See al-Bārihbankawī.

Al-Kattānī, Muḥammad ibn Ja'far. *Naẓm al-Mutanāthir fīl-Ḥadīth al-Mutawātir*. Ed. Sharaf Ḥijāzī. Cairo: Dār al-Kutub al-Salafiyya, n.d. and Beirut: Dār al-Kutub al-'Ilmiyya, 1980.

Al-Kawtharī. *Maqālāt*. Ryad and Beirut: Dār al-Aḥnāf, 1993.

———. *Maqālāt*. 2nd ed. Cairo: al-Maktabat al-Azhariyya līl-Turāth, 1994.

Al-Khallāl. *Al-Sunna*. 3 vols. Ed. 'Aṭiyya al-Zahrānī. Ryad: Dār al-Rāya, 1990.

Al-Khaṭīb al-Baghdādī. *Al-Faqīh wal-Mutafaqqih*. 2 vols. Ed. 'Ādil al-'Azāzī. Dammām: Dār Ibn al-Jawzī, 1997.

———. *Al-Faqīh wal-Mutafaqqih*. Ed. Ismā'īl al-Anṣārī. Beirut: Dār al-Kutub al-'Ilmiyya, 1980.

———. *Al-Jāmi' li-Akhlāq al-Rāwī wa-Adab al-Sāmi'*. 2 vols. Ed. Muḥammad 'Ajāj al-Khaṭīb. Beirut: Mu'assasat al-Risāla, 1991.

———. *Al-Jāmi' li-Akhlāq al-Rāwī wa-Adab al-Sāmi'*. 2 vols. Ed. Maḥmūd al-Ṭaḥḥān. Ryad: Maktabat al-Ma'ārif, 1983.

———. *Al-Kifāya fī 'Ilm al-Riwāya*. 2nd ed. Ed. Aḥmad 'Umar Hāshim. Beirut: Dār al-Kitāb al-'Arabī, 1986.

———. *Al-Kifāya fī 'Ilm al-Riwāya*. Eds. Abū 'Abd Allāh al-Ṣawraqī and Ibrāhīm Ḥamdī al-Madanī. Madīna: al-Maktabat al-'Ilmiyya, n.d.

———. *Tārīkh Baghdād*. 14 vols. Madīna: al-Maktabat al-Salafiyya, n.d. See also al-Aḥdab, *Zawā'id Tārīkh Baghdād*.

Al-Khazrajī. *Khulāṣat Tadhhīb Tahdhīb al-Kamāl*. With al-Kawkabānī's *Itḥāf al-Khāṣṣa bi-Taṣḥīḥ al-Khulāṣa*. Ed. 'Abd al-Fattāḥ Abū Ghudda. Beirut: Dār al-Bashā'ir al-Islāmiyya, 1996[5]. Reprint of the original 1301/1883 Cairo Bulāq edition.

Al-Kirmānī. *Al-Kawākib al-Darārī fī Sharḥ Ṣaḥīḥ al-Bukhārī*. 25 vols. Cairo: al-Maṭba'at al-Bahiyya al-Miṣriyya, 1933-1962. Repr. 25 v. in 9. Beirut : Dār Iḥyā' al-Turāth al-'Arabī, 1981.

Al-Lacknawī. *Al-Ajwibat al-Fāḍila lil-As'ilat al-'Ashrat al-Kāmila*. Ed. 'Abd al-Fattāḥ Abū Ghudda. Followed by *al-Ta'līqāt al-Ḥāfila 'alā al-Ajwibat al-'Ashra* by Abū Ghudda. 3rd ed. Aleppo: Maktab al-Maṭbū'āt al-Islāmiyya, 1994.

———. *Iqāmat al-Ḥujja 'alā anna al-Ikthār min al-Ta'abbudi Laysa bi-Bid'a*. Ed. 'Abd al-Fattāḥ Abū Ghudda. Aleppo: Maktab al-Maṭbū'āt al-Islāmiyya, 1966. Repr. Beirut, 1992 and 1998.

———. *Tuḥfat al-Akhyār bi-Iḥyā' Sunnati Sayyid al-Abrār* ﷺ with its commentary *Nukhbat al-Anẓār 'alā Tuḥfat al-Akhyār*. Ed. 'Abd al-Fattāḥ Abū Ghudda. Contains the latter's *Bayān Madlūl Lafẓ al-Sunna* and *Bayān Ḥāl Sunan al-Dāraquṭnī*. Aleppo: Maktab al-Maṭbū'āt al-Islāmiyya, 1992.

Al-Lālikā'ī. *Sharḥ Uṣūl I'tiqād Ahl al-Sunna*. 4 vols. Ed. Aḥmad Sa'd Ḥamdān. Ryad: Dār Ṭayba, 1982.

Mālik ibn Anas. *Al-Muwaṭṭa'*. 2 vols. Ed. Muḥammad Fouad 'Abd al-Bāqī. Beirut: Dār al-Kutub al-'Ilmiyya, n.d.

Mamdūḥ, Maḥmūd Sa'īd. *Wuṣūl al-Tahānī bi-Ithbāt Sunniyyat al-Sibḥa wal-Radd 'alā al-Albānī*. 3rd ed. Yemen, Cairo, and Dubai: Dār al-Imām al-Tirmidhī and Maktabat Dār al-Ghannā', 1995.

Al-Maqdisī. *Al-Aḥādīth al-Mukhtāra*. 10 vols. Ed. 'Abd al-Mālik ibn 'Abd Allāh ibn Duhaysh. Makka: Maktabat al-Nahḍat al-Ḥadītha, 1990.

Ma'rūf, Bashshār 'Awwād and Shu'ayb al-Arna'ūṭ. *Taḥrīr Taqrīb al-Tahdhīb*. 4 vols. Beirut: Mu'assasat al-Risāla, 1997.

Al-Mizzī. *Tahdhīb al-Kamāl*. 35 vols. Ed. Bashshār 'Awwād Ma'rūf. Beirut: Mu'assasat al-Risāla, 1980.

Al-Mu'allimī al-Yamānī, 'Abd al-Raḥmān. *'Imārat al-Qubūr*. Makka: al-Maktabat al-Makkiya, 1998.

Al-Mubārakfūrī. *Tuḥfat al-Aḥwadhī bi-Sharḥ Jāmi' al-Tirmidhī*. 10 vols. Beirut: Dār al-Kutub al-'Ilmiyya, 1990. Includes al-Tirmidhī's *Sunan*.

Al-Munāwī. *Fayḍ al-Qadīr Sharḥ al-Jāmi' al-Ṣaghīr*. 6 vols. Cairo: al-Maktabat al-Tijāriyya al-Kubrā, 1356/1937. Repr. Beirut: Dār al Ma'rifa, 1972.

Al-Mundhirī. *Al-Targhīb wal-Tarhīb*. 4 vols. Ed. Ibrāhīm Shams al-Dīn. Beirut: Dār al-Kutub al-'Ilmiyya, 1997.

———. *Al-Targhīb wal-Tarhīb*. 4 vols. Ed. Ibrāhīm Shams al-Dīn. Beirut: Dār al-Kutub al-'Ilmiyya, 1997.

Muslim. *Ṣaḥīḥ*. 5 vols. Ed. M. Fu'ād 'Abd al-Bāqī. Beirut: Dār Iḥyā' al-Turāth al-'Arabī, 1954. Also see al-Nawawī, *Sharḥ Ṣaḥīḥ Muslim*.

Al-Muttaqī al-Hindī. *Kanz al-'Ummāl*. 16 vols. Beirut: Mu'assasat al-Risāla, 1989.

Al-Nabhānī, Yūsuf. *Arbaʿūna Ḥadīthan fī Madḥ al-Sunnati wa-Dhammi al-Bidʿa*. Ed. Bassām ʿAbd al-Wahhāb al-Jābī. Beirut: Dār Ibn Ḥazm, 1995.

———. *Al-Dalālāt al-Wāḍiḥāt Sharḥ Dalā'il al-Khayrāt*. Ed. Bassām ʿAbd al-Wahhāb al-Jābī. Cairo: al-Dār al-Ghannā', 2001.

———. *Ḥujjat Allāh ʿalā al-ʿĀlamīn bi-Muʿjizāt Sayyid al-Mursalīn* ﷺ. N.p.: s.n., 1317/1899.

———. *Nujūm al-Muhtadīn wa-Rujūm al-Muʿtadīn*. Cairo: Muṣṭafā al-Bābī al-Ḥalabī, 1322/1904. Repr. Istanbul: Dār Saʿādat, n.d. With *al-Aḥādīth al-Arbaʿīn fī Wujūbi Ṭāʿat Amīr al-Mu'minīn* and *Khulāṣat al-Bayān fī Baʿḍ Ma'āthir Mawlānā al-Sulṭān ʿAbd al-Ḥamīd Khān wa-Ajdādihi Āli ʿUthmān*. Beirut: al-Maktabat al-Adabiyya, 1312/1894.

———. *Saʿādatu al-Dārayni fīl-Ṣalāti ʿalā Sayyidi al-Kawnayn*. Cairo: 1318/1900.

———. *Shawāhid al-Ḥaqq fīl-Istighātha bi-Sayyid al-Khalq* ρ. N.p.: s.n., 1323/1905.

Al-Nasā'ī. *'Amal al-Yawm wal-Layla*. 2nd ed. Ed. Fārūq Ḥammāda. Beirut: Mu'assasat al-Risāla, 1986.

———. *Sunan*. See al-Suyūṭī, *Sharḥ Sunan al-Nasā'ī*.

———. *Al-Sunan al-Kubrā*. 6 vols. Eds. ʿAbd al-Ghaffār Sulaymān al-Bandārī and Sayyid Kusrawī Ḥasan. Beirut: Dār al-Kutub al-ʿIlmiyya, 1991.

Al-Nawawī. *Etiquette with the Quran*. Trans. Musa Furber. [Chicago:] Starlatch Press, 2003.

———. *Fatāwā*. Ed. Muḥammad al-Ḥajjār. Ḥalab: al-Maṭbaʿat al-ʿArabiyya, 1971.

———. *Khulāṣat al-Aḥkām fī Muhimmāt al-Sunan wa-Qawāʿid al-Islām*. 2 vols. Ed. Ḥusayn Ismāʿīl al-Jamal. Beirut: Mu'assasat al-Risāla, 1997.

———. *Mā Tamassu Ilayhi Ḥājatu al-Qārī li-Ṣaḥīḥ al-Imām al-Bukhārī*. Ed. ʿAlī Ḥasan ʿAbd al-Ḥamīd. Beirut: Dār al-Kutub al-ʿIlmiyya, n.d.

———. *Al-Majmūʿ Sharḥ al-Muhadhdhab*. 18 vols. Ed. Zakariyyā ʿAlī Yūsuf. Cairo: Maṭbaʿat al-ʿĀṣima, 1963-1970.

———. *Al-Maqāṣid fīl-Tawḥīd wal-ʿIbāda wa-Uṣūl al-Taṣawwuf*. Beirut: al-Maṭbaʿat al-Ahliyya, 1324/1906.

———. *Matn al-Arbaʿīn al-Nawawiyya*. Eds. ʿAbd al-Qādir and Maḥmūd al-Arnaʾūṭ. Kuwait: Dār al-ʿUrūba, 1989.

———. *Sharḥ Ṣaḥīḥ Muslim*. 18 vols. Ed. Khalīl al-Mays. Beirut: Dār al-Kutub al-ʿIlmiyya, n.d. Includes Muslim's *Ṣaḥīḥ*.

———. *Sharḥ Ṣaḥīḥ Muslim*. 18 vols. Beirut: Dār Iḥyāʾ al-Turāth al-ʿArabī, 1972.

———. *Tahdhīb al-Asmāʾ wal-Lughāt*. 3 vols. Cairo: Idārat al-Ṭibāʿat al-Munīriyya, [1927?].

———. *Al-Tibyān fī Ādāb Ḥamalat al-Qurʾān*. Ed. ʿAbd al-ʿAzīz ʿIzz al-Dīn al-Sayrawān. Beirut: Dār al-Nafāʾis, 1992[3].

———. *Al-Tibyān fī Ādāb Ḥamalat al-Qurʾān*. Ed. Bashīr Muḥammad ʿUyūn. 2nd ed. Al-Ṭāʾif and Damascus: Maktabat al-Muʾayyad and Maktabat Dār al-Bayān, 1993.

Niẓām al-Mulk. *Majlisān min Amālī Niẓām al-Mulk*. Cairo and Jeddah: Maktabat Ibn Taymiyya and Maktabat al-ʿIlm, 1993.

Nuʿaym ibn Ḥammād al-Marwazī. *Kitāb al-Fitan*. 2 vols. Ed. Samīr Amīn al-Zuhrī. Cairo: Maktabat al-Tawḥīd, 1992.

Al-Qarāfī. *Al-Furūq. Anwār al-Burūq fī Anwāʿ al-Furūq*. 4 vols. Eds. Muḥammad Aḥmad Sirāj, ʿAlī Jumʿa Muḥammad. Cairo: Dār al-Salām, 2001.

———. *Al-Iḥkām fī Tamyīz al-Fatāwā ʿan al-Aḥkām wa-Taṣarrufāt al-Qāḍī wal-Imām*. 2nd ed. Ed. ʿAbd al-Fattāḥ Abū Ghudda. Beirut: Dār al-Bashāʾir al-Islāmiyya, 1995.

Al-Qārī. *Al-Asrār al-Marfūʿa fil-Akhbār al-Mawḍūʿa. (Al-Mawḍūʿāt al-Kubrā)*. 2nd ed. Ed. Muḥammad ibn Luṭfī al-Ṣabbāgh. Beirut and Damascus: al-Maktab al-Islāmī, 1986.

———. *Al-Maṣnūʿ fī Maʿrifat al-Ḥadīth al-Mawḍūʿ*. 5th ed. Ed. ʿAbd al-Fattāḥ Abū Ghudda. Beirut: Dār al-Bashāʾir al-Islāmiyya, 1994.

———. *Sharḥ al-Shifā*. 2 vols. Bulāq: 1275/1858. Repr. Maṭbaʿat al-Ḥajj al-Busnawī, 1285/1868. Repr. Āsitāna [Istanbul]: 1290/1873. Repr. Āsitāna: al-Maṭbaʿat al-ʿUthmāniyya, 1316/1898. Repr. Cairo: 1312/1894. Repr. Beirut: Dār al-Kutub al-ʿIlmiyya, n.d.

———. *Sharḥ Sharḥ Nukhbat al-Fikar*. A supercommentary on Ibn Ḥajar's *Sharḥ Nukhbat al-Fikar*. Ed. Muḥammad and Haytham Nizār Tamīm. Beirut: Dār al-Arqam, n.d.

Al-Qāsimī. *Al-Masḥ 'alā al-Jawrabayn*. Ed. Nāṣir al-Albānī. Beirut: al-Maktab al-Islāmī, 1986[5].

Al-Qasṭallānī. *Masālik al-Ḥunafā ilā Mashāri' al-Ṣalāt 'alā al-Nabī al-Muṣṭafā* ﷺ. Ed. Bassām Bārūd. Abū Dhabī: al-Mujamma' al-Thaqāfī, 2000.

Al-Quḍā'ī. *Musnad al-Shihāb*. 2 vols. Ed. Ḥamdī ibn 'Abd al-Majīd al-Salafī. Beirut: Mu'assasat al-Risāla, 1986.

Al-Qurṭubī. [*Tafsīr*.] *Al-Jāmi' li-Aḥkām al-Qur'ān*. 2nd ed. 20 vols. Ed. Aḥmad 'Abd al-'Alīm al-Bardūnī. Cairo: Dār al-Sha'b and Beirut: Dār Iḥyā' al-Turāth al- 'Arabī, 1952-1953. Reprint.

Al-Qushayrī. *Al-Risāla*. Cairo: Dār al-Ṭibā'a al-'Āmira, 1287/1870. With Zakariyyā al-Anṣārī's commentary in the margins.

———. *Al-Risāla*. Eds. 'Abd al-Halīm Maḥmūd and Maḥmūd ibn al-Sharīf. Cairo: Rida Tawfiq 'Afifi, 1974.

Al-Rāfi'ī. *Al-Tadwīn fī Akhbār Qazwīn*. 4 vols. Ed. 'Azīz Allāh al-'Aṭāridī. Beirut: Dār al-Kutub al-'Ilmiyya, 1987.

Al-Rāmahurmuzī. *Amthāl al-Ḥadīth*. Ed. Aḥmad 'Abd al-Fattāḥ Tamām. Beirut: Mu'assasat al-Kutub al-Thaqāfiyya, 1989.

———. *Al-Muḥaddith al-Fāṣil*. Ed. Muḥammad al-Khaṭīb. Beirut: Dār al-Fikr, 3rd ed. 1984.

Al-Rāzī, Abū Bakr. See al-Jaṣṣāṣ.

Al-Rāzī, Tammām. *Al-Fawā'id*. 2 vols. Ed. Ḥamdī 'Abd al-Majīd al-Salafī. Ryadh: Maktabat al-Rushd, 1992.

Reliance of the Traveller. See Ibn al-Naqīb.

Al-Rifā'ī, Yūsuf ibn al-Sayyid Hāshim. *Adillat Ahl al-Sunna wal-Jamā'a aw al-Radd al-Muḥkam al-Manī' 'alā Munkarāt wa-Shubuhāt Ibn Manī' fī Tahajjumihi 'alā al-Sayyid Muḥammad 'Alawī al-Mālikī al-Makkī*. Kuwait: Dār al-Siyāsa, 1984.

———. *Naṣīḥa li-Ikhwāninā 'Ulamā' Najd*. Damascus: Iqra', 2000. *Advice to Our Brothers the Scholars of Najd*, followed by 'Alawī ibn Aḥmad al-Ḥaddād, *Refutation of the Innovator from Najd* (Introduction). Trans. Gibrīl F. Ḥaddād. Damascus, 2000 and 2002.

Al-Rūyānī. *Musnad*. 2 vols. Ed. Ayman 'Alī Abū Yamānī. Cairo: Mu'assasat Qurṭuba, 1996.

Al-Sakhāwī, Muḥammad ibn ʿAbd al-Raḥmān. *Al-Ajwibat al-Marḍiyya fīmā Suʾila ʿanhu min al-Aḥādīth al-Nabawiyya.* [=*Al-Fatāwā al-Ḥadīthiyya.*] 3 vols. Ed. Muḥammad Isḥāq Muḥammad Ibrāhīm. Ryāḍ: Dār al-Rāya, 1998.

———. *Al-Fatāwā al-Ḥadīthiyya.* Ed. ʿAlī Riḍā ʿAbd Allāh ʿAlī Riḍā. Damascus: Dār al-Maʾmūn, 1995. (First quarter of *al-Ajwibat al-Marḍiyya*.)

———. *Fatḥ al-Mughīth bi-Sharḥ Alfiyyat al-Ḥadīth lil-ʿIrāqī.* 5 vols. Ed. ʿAlī Ḥusayn ʿAlī. Cairo: Maktabat al-Sunna, 1995.

———. *Al-Iʿlān wal-Tawbīkh li-man Dhamma al-Tārīkh.* Beirut: Dār al-Kitāb al-ʿArabī, 1979.

———. *Al-Jawāhir wal-Durar fī Manāqib Shaykh al-Islām Ibn Ḥajar.* Ed. Ḥāmid ʿAbd al-Majīd and Ṭaha al-Zaynī. Cairo: Lajnat Iḥyāʾ al-Turāth al-Islāmī, 1986.

———. *Al-Maqāṣid al-Ḥasana.* Ed. Muḥammad ʿUthmān al-Khisht. Beirut: Dār al-Kitāb al-ʿArabī, 1985.

———. *Al-Maqāṣid al-Ḥasana.* Ed. ʿAbd Allāh Muḥammad al-Ṣiddīq [al-Ghumārī]. Beirut: Dār al-Kutub al-ʿIlmiyya, 1987.

———. *Al-Qawl al-Badīʿ fīl-Ṣalāt ʿalā al-Ḥabīb al-Shafīʿ.* Ed. Muḥammad ʿAwwāma. Beirut: Muʾassasat al-Rayyān, 2002. Unedited: Beirut: Dār al-Kutub al-ʿIlmiyya, 1987.

Al-Ṣanʿānī. *Subul al-Salām Sharḥ Bulūgh al-Marām.* 4th ed. Ed. Muḥammad ʿAbd al-ʿAzīz al-Khawlī. Beirut: Dār Iḥyāʾ al-Turāth al-ʿArabī, 1960.

———. *Tawḍīḥ al-Afkār li-Maʿānī Tanqīḥ al-Anẓār.* 2 vols. Ed. Muḥammad Muḥyī al-Dīn ʿAbd al-Ḥamīd. Madīna: al-Maktabat al-Salafiyya, n.d.

Al-Shāṭibī. *Al-Iʿtiṣām bil-Kitābi wal-Sunna.* Ed. Aḥmad ʿAbd al-Shāfī. Beirut: Dār al-Kutub al-ʿIlmiyya, 1988.

———. *Al-Iʿtiṣām bil-Kitābi wal-Sunna.* 4 vols. Ed. Mashhūr Ḥasan Salmān. Manāma: Maktabat al-Tawḥīd, 2000.

Al-Shawkānī. *Al-Fawāʾid al-Majmūʿa fīl-Aḥādīth al-Mawḍūʿa.* Ed. Muḥammad ʿAbd al-Raḥmān ʿAwaḍ. Beirut: Dār al-Kitāb al-ʿArabī, 1986.

———. *Al-Fawāʾid al-Majmūʿa fīl-Aḥādīth al-Mawḍūʿa.* Ed. ʿAbd al-Raḥmān al-Muʿallimī al-Yamānī. Cairo: Maktabat al-Sunnat al-Muḥammadiyya, 1960. 3rd ed. Beirut: al-Maktab al-Islāmī, 1987.

———. *Irshād al-Fuḥūl ilā Taḥqīq al-Ḥaqqi min ʿIlmi al-Uṣūl*. 2 vols. Ed. Abū Ḥafṣ Sāmī ibn al-ʿArabī al-Atharī. Ryadh and Beirut: Dār al-Faḍīla & Muʾassasat al-Rayyān, 2000.

———. *Ibid*. Beirut: Dār al-Maʿrifa, 1979 and Beirut: Dār al-Fikr, 1992.

———. *Nayl al-Awṭār*. 9 vols. Beirut: Dār al-Jīl, 1973.

———. *Al-Qawl al-Mufīd fī Adillat al-Ijtihād wal-Taqlīd*. In *al-Rasāʾil al-Salafiyya*. Beirut: Dār al-Kutub al-ʿIlmiyya, n.d. Repr. of the 1930 ed.

Al-Sibāʿī, *Al-Sunna wa-Makānatuhā fīl-Tashrīʿ al-Islāmī*. Beirut: al-Maktab al-Islāmī, 1985.

Al-Simʿānī [=Ibn al-Simʿānī]. *Adab al-Imlāʾ wal-Istimlāʾ*. Ed. Max Weisweiler, *Die Methode des Diktatkollegs*. Leiden: Brill, 1952. Repr. Beirut: Dār al-Kutub al-ʿIlmiyya, 1981.

Al-Subkī. *Shifāʾ al-Siqām bi-Ziyārati Khayri al-Anām*. Beirut: Lajnat al-Turāth al-ʿArabī, 1971.

Al-Sulamī. *Ṭabaqāt al-Ṣūfiyya*. Ed. Nūr al-Dīn Shurayba. Aleppo: Dār al-Kitāb al-Nafīs, 1986. Reprint of the 1953 edition.

Al-Suyūṭī, Jalāl al-Dīn. *Al-Ashbāh wal-Naẓāʾir*. 3rd ed. Beirut: Dār al-Kitāb al-ʿArabī, 1996.

———. *Al-Durr al-Manthūr fīl-Tafsīr al-Maʾthūr*. 8 vols. Beirut: Dār al-Fikr, 1994.

———. *Al-Fānīd fī Ḥalāwat al-Asānīd*. Ed. Ramzī Dimashqiyya. Beirut: Dār al-Bashāʾir al-Islāmiyya, 1999.

———. *Al-Ḥāwī lil-Fatāwī*. 2 vols. 3rd ed. Ed. Muḥammad Muḥyī al-Dīn ʿAbd al-Ḥamīd. Cairo: al-Maktabat al-Tijāriyyat al-Kubrā, 1959.

———. *Al-Jāmiʿ al-Ṣaghīr min Ḥadīth al-Bashīr al-Nadhīr* p. 2 vols. Ed. Muḥammad Muḥyī al-Dīn ʿAbd al-Ḥamīd. Damascus: Maktabat al-Ḥalbūnī, 1983.

———. *Al-Khaṣāʾiṣ al-Kubrā aw Kifāyat al-Ṭālib al-Labīb fī Khaṣāʾiṣ al-Ḥabīb* ﷺ. 2 vols. Hyderabad al-Dakn: Dāʾirat al-Maʿārif al-Niẓāmiyya, 1901-1903. Beirut: Dār al-Kutub al-ʿIlmiyya, 1985. See also below, *Tahdhīb al-Khaṣāʾiṣ*.

———. *Al-Laʾālīʾ al-Maṣnūʿa fīl-Aḥādīth al-Mawḍūʿa*. 2 vols. Beirut: Dār al-Maʿrifa, 1983.

———. *Manāhil al-Ṣafā fī Takhrīj Aḥādīth al-Shifā*. Beirut, 1988.

———. *Al-Maṣābīḥ fī Ṣalāt al-Tarāwīḥ*. Ed. ʿAbd al-Raḥīm Aḥmad Qamḥiyya. Ḥimṣ: Dār al-Nābigha, 1992.

———. *Miftāḥ al-Janna fil-I'tiṣām bil-Sunna*. Ed. Badr ibn 'Abd Allāh al-Badr. Beirut and Kuwait: Mu'assasat al-Rayyān and Dār al-Nafā'is, 1993.

———. *Tabyīḍ al-Ṣaḥīfa bi-Manāqib al-Imām Abī Ḥanīfa*. Ed. 'Abd al-Raḥīm al-Kaḥḥāla. Damascus: s.n., 1992.

———. *Tahdhīb al-Khaṣā'iṣ al-Nabawiyya al-Kubrā*. 2nd ed. By 'Abd Allāh al-Talīdī. Beirut: Dār al-Bashā'ir al-Islāmiyya, 1990.

———. *Tanwīr al-Ḥawālik bi-Sharḥ Muwaṭṭa' Mālik*. 2 vols. Cairo: al-Maktabat al-Tijāriyya al-Kubrā, 1969.

———. *Tārīkh al-Khulafā'*. Ed. Raḥāb Khiḍr 'Akkāwī. Beirut: Mu'assasat 'Izz al-Dīn, 1992.

Al-Ṭabarānī. *Al-Du'ā'*. Ed. Muṣṭafā 'Abd al-Qādir 'Aṭā'. Beirut: Dār al-Kutub al-'Ilmiyya, 1993.

———. *Al-Mu'jam al-Awsaṭ*. 10 vols. Eds. Ṭāriq ibn 'Awaḍ Allāh and 'Abd al-Muḥsin ibn Ibrāhīm al-Ḥusaynī. Cairo: Dār al-Ḥaramayn, 1995.

———. *Al-Mu'jam al-Kabīr*. 20 vols. Ed. Ḥamdī ibn 'Abd al-Majīd al-Salafī. Mosul: Maktabat al-'Ulūm wal-Ḥikam, 1983.

———. *Al-Mu'jam al-Ṣaghīr*. 2 vols. Ed. Muḥammad Shakūr Maḥmūd. Beirut and Amman: Al-Maktab al-Islāmī, Dār 'Ammār, 1985.

———. *Musnad al-Shāmiyyīn*. 2 vols. Ed. Ḥamdī ibn 'Abd al-Majīd al-Salafī. Beirut: Mu'assasat al-Risāla, 1984.

Al-Ṭabarī, Muḥammad ibn Jarīr. *Jāmi' al-Bayān fī Tafsīr al-Qur'ān*. 30 vols. Beirut: Dār al-Ma'ārif, 1980; Dār al-Fikr, 1985.

Al-Ṭabarī, Muḥibb al-Dīn. *Al-Riyāḍ al-Naḍira fī Manāqib al-'Ashara*. 2 vols. Ed. 'Īsā al-Ḥimayrī. Beirut: Dār al-Gharb al-Islāmī, 1996.

Al-Tahānawī. *I'lā' al-Sunan*. 21 vols. Ed. Muḥammad Taqī 'Uthmānī. Karachi: Idārat al-Qur'ān wal-'Ulūm al-Islamiyya, 1995. First two introductory volumes contain [1] al-Tahānawī's *Qawā'id fī 'Ulūm al-Ḥadīth*, ed. 'Abd al-Fattāḥ Abū Ghudda; [2] al-Kirānawī's *Fawā'id fī 'Ulūm al-Fiqh* and al-Tahānawī's *Abū Ḥanīfa wa-Aṣḥābuhu al-Muḥaddithūn*.

Al-Ṭaḥāwī. *Mushkil al-Āthār*. 4 vols. Hyderabad: Dā'irat al-Ma'ārif al-'Uthmāniyya, 1915. Repr. Beirut: Dār Sadir, n.d.

———. *Sharḥ Ma'ānī al-Āthār*. 4 vols. Ed. Muḥammad Zuhrī al-Najjār. Beirut: Dār al-Kutub al-'Ilmiyya, 1979.

———. *Sharḥ Mushkil al-Āthār*. 16 vols. Ed. Shuʿayb al-Arnaʾūṭ. Beirut: Muʾassasat al-Risāla, 1994.

Al-Talīdī, ʿAbd Allāh. *Tahdhīb al-Khaṣāʾiṣ*. See al-Suyūṭī.

Al-Ṭanṭāwī, ʿAlī and Nājī. *Akhbār ʿUmar*. 8th ed. Beirut: al-Maktab al-Islāmī, 1983.

Al-Ṭayālisī, Abū Dāwūd. *Musnad*. Beirut: Dār al-Kitāb al-Lubnānī; Dār al-Maʿrifa; Dār al-Tawfīq, n.d. All three are offset reprints of the 1321/1903 edition of Dāʾirat al-Maʿārif al-ʿUthmāniyya in Hyderabad.

Tayyim, Asʿad Salīm. *Bayān Awhām al-Albānī fī Taḥqīqihi li-Kitāb Faḍl al-Ṣalāt ʿalā al-Nabī ﷺ līl-Qāḍī Ismāʿīl ibn Isḥāq al-Azdī wa-Yalīhi Takhrīj Ḥadīth Aws al-Thaqafī fī Faḍl al-Jumuʿa*. Amman: Dār al-Rāzī, 1999.

Al-Tirmidhī. *Al-ʿIlal*. See Ibn Rajab's *Sharḥ ʿIlal al-Tirmidhī*.

———. *Sunan*. 5 vols. Ed. Aḥmad Shākir and Muḥammad Fuʾād ʿAbd al-Bāqī. Beirut: Dār Iḥyāʾ al-Turāth al-ʿArabī, n.d.

Al-Ṭurṭūshī. *Al-Ḥawādith wal-Bidaʿ*. Ed. ʿAbd al-Majīd al-Turkī. Beirut: Dār al-Gharb al-Islāmī, 1990.

Al-ʿUqaylī, *al-Ḍuʿafāʾ min al-Ruwāt*. 4 vols. Ed. ʿAbd al-Muʿṭī Amīn Qalʿajī. Beirut: Dār al-Kutub al-ʿIlmiyya, 1984.

Al-Yāfiʿī. *Mirʾāt al-Janān wa-ʿIbrat al-Yaqẓān fī Maʿrifati Mā Yuʿtabaru min Ḥawādith al-Zamān*. 4 vols. Ed Khalīl al-Manṣūr. Beirut: Dār al-Kutub al-ʿIlmiyya, 1997.

Al-Zabīdī. *Itḥāf al-Sādat al-Muttaqīn bi-Sharḥ Asrār Iḥyāʾ ʿUlūm al-Dīn*. With the text of the *Iḥyāʾ* in the margins, ʿAbd al-Qādir ibn ʿAbd Allāh al-ʿAydarūs Bā ʿAlawī's *Taʿrif al-Aḥyāʾ bi-Faḍāʾil al-Iḥyāʾ*, and al-Ghazzālī's *al-Imlā ʿan Ishkālāt al-Iḥyāʾ*. 10 vols. Cairo: al-Maṭbaʿat al-Maymuniyya, 1311/1893.

Al-Zamakhsharī. *Al-Fāʾiq fī Gharīb al-Ḥadīth*. Eds. ʿAlī Muḥammad al-Bijāwī and Muḥammad Abū al-Faḍl Ibrāhīm. 2nd ed. 4 vols. Cairo: ʿĪsā Bābī al-Ḥalabī, 1969. Repr. Beirut: Dār al-Maʿrifa.

Al-Zarkashī. *Al-Tadhkira fīl-Aḥādīth al-Mushtahara*. Ed. Muṣṭafā ʿAbd al-Qādir ʿAṭā. Beirut: Dār al-Kutub al-ʿIlmiyya, 1986.

Al-Zarqānī. *Sharḥ al-Muwaṭṭaʾ*. 4 vols. Beirut: Dār al-Kutub al-ʿIlmiyya, 1981.

Al-Zaylaʿī. *Naṣb al-Rāya li-Aḥādīth al-Hidāya*. 4 vols. Ed. Muḥammad Yūsuf al-Binūrī. Cairo: Dār al-Ḥadīth, 1357/1938.

www.ingramcontent.com/pod-product-compliance
Lightning Source LLC
Chambersburg PA
CBHW030514080526
44586CB00011B/181
* 9 7 8 1 9 3 8 0 5 8 7 9 0 *